繁荣与共享
东亚国际旅游合作研究

PROSPERITY & SHARING:
East Asia International Tourism Cooperation Research

中国旅游研究院
China Tourism Academy

陕西省旅游局 ◎ 著
Tourism Administration of Shaanxi Province

北京·旅游教育出版社

特约编辑：李　薇
责任编辑：郭珍宏

封面地图来源于国家测绘地理信息局网站，审图号：GS（2016）1561号。

图书在版编目（CIP）数据

繁荣与共享：东亚国际旅游合作研究：汉英对照 / 中国旅游研究院，陕西省旅游局著．-- 北京：旅游教育出版社，2017.11

ISBN 978-7-5637-3667-6

Ⅰ．①繁… Ⅱ．①中… ②陕… Ⅲ．①旅游业－国际合作－经济合作－研究－中国、东亚－汉、英 Ⅳ．① F592.3 ② F593.103

中国版本图书馆CIP数据核字（2017）第289404号

繁荣与共享：东亚国际旅游合作研究
中国旅游研究院　陕西省旅游局　著

出版单位	旅游教育出版社
地　　址	北京市朝阳区定福庄南里1号
邮　　编	100024
发行电话	（010）65778403　65728372　65767462（传真）
本社网址	www.tepcb.com
E - mail	tepfx@163.com
排版单位	北京旅教文化传播有限公司
印刷单位	北京中科印刷有限公司
经销单位	新华书店
开　　本	787毫米×1092毫米　1/16
印　　张	15.75
字　　数	172千字
版　　次	2017年11月第1版
印　　次	2017年11月第1次印刷
定　　价	220.00元（海外发行USD 160）

（图书如有装订差错请与发行部联系）

《繁荣与共享：东亚国际旅游合作研究》编辑委员会

主 任 委 员 戴　斌　中国旅游研究院院长、教授、博士
　　　　　　 杨忠武　陕西省旅游局党组书记、局长

副主任委员 陈梦榆　陕西省旅游局副局长
　　　　　　 蒋依依　中国旅游研究院国际旅游研究所所长、博士

编　　　委 戴　斌　杨忠武　陈梦榆　蒋依依　李仲广
　　　　　　 宋子千　唐晓云　马晓龙　马仪亮　夏少颜

《繁荣与共享：东亚国际旅游合作研究》编写组

主　　　编 蒋依依　中国旅游研究院国际旅游研究所所长、博士
　　　　　　 戴卫红　陕西省旅游局国际旅游促进处处长

执行主编 李创新　中国旅游研究院国际旅游研究所博士
　　　　　　 孙　岩　陕西省旅游局国际旅游促进处副处长

成　　　员 杨劲松　杨丽琼　肖　勇　李仲广　何琼峰　拓　倩
　　　　　　 蔡　凤　刘宇峰　王永明　魏　颖　吕洋洋　童时萍
　　　　　　 蔡文婧　陈小姣　晏　梅　宋丽娜　王雅倩　余　力
　　　　　　 邓　宇　周　敏

Editorial Board of *Prosperity & Sharing: East Asia International Tourism Cooperation Research*

Executive Members:
DAI Bin, Professor, PhD, President of China Tourism Academy
YANG Zhongwu, Party Secretary and Director-General of Tourism Administration of Shaanxi Province

Vice Executive Members:
CHEN Mengyu, Deputy Director-General of Tourism Administration of Shaanxi Province
JIANG Yiyi, PhD, Director of Institute of International Tourism Development, China Tourism Academy

Editorial Board:
DAI Bin, YANG Zhongwu, CHEN Mengyu, JIANG Yiyi, LI Zhongguang, SONG Ziqian, TANG Xiaoyun, MA Xialong, Ma Yiliang, XIA Shaoyan

Editorial Team of *Prosperity & Sharing: East Asia International Tourism Cooperation Research*

Editor-in-Chief:
JIANG Yiyi, PhD, Director of Institute of International Tourism Development, China Tourism Academy
DAI Weihong, Director of International Tourism Promotion Division of Tourism Administration of Shaanxi Province

Executive Editors-in-Chief:
LI Chuangxin, PhD, Institute of International Tourism Development, China Tourism Academy
SUN Yan, Deputy Director of International Tourism Promotion Division of Tourism Administration of Shaanxi Province

Members:
YANG Jinsong, YANG Liqiong, XIAO Yong, LI Zhongguang, HE Qiongfeng,
TUO Qian, CAI Feng, LIU Yufeng, WANG Yongming, WEI Ying, LYU Yangyang;
TONG Shiping, CAI Wenjing, CHEN Xiaojiao, YAN Mei, SONG Lina,
WANG Yaqian, YU Li, DENG Yu, ZHOU Min.

目 录
CONTENTS

第一章　繁荣的东亚国际旅游市场 ·················· 1

第一节　东北亚国际旅游市场 ·················· 2

第二节　东南亚国际旅游市场 ·················· 6

第二章　东亚代表性国家的国际旅游市场状况 ·················· 11

第一节　中国 ·················· 12

第二节　日本 ·················· 17

第三节　韩国 ·················· 20

第四节　越南 ·················· 22

第五节　马来西亚 ·················· 22

第六节　菲律宾 ·················· 25

第七节　印度尼西亚 ·················· 26

第三章　共享中国出境旅游市场的发展红利 ·················· 31

第一节　中国出境旅游市场行为调查 ·················· 32

第二节　中国出境游客对东亚各国的满意度评价 ·················· 41

第四章 东亚在中国入境旅游市场中的基础地位与行为特征 …… 49

第一节 东亚各国来华旅游的市场总量 …… 50

第二节 东亚各国来华旅游的市场结构 …… 54

第三节 中国入境旅游市场行为调查 …… 63

第五章 共建东亚国际旅游合作的美好明天 …… 73

第一节 东亚国际旅游合作的前景展望 …… 74

第二节 东亚国际旅游合作的政策建议 …… 76

附录1 东亚地区旅游合作状况 …… 79

附录2 历届东亚地方政府会议状况 …… 82

附录3 东亚国际旅游合作的进程回顾 …… 91

Chapter 1 Prosperous East Asian International Tourism Market …… 105

Section 1 Northeast Asian International Tourism Market …… 106

Section 2 Southeast Asian International Tourism Market …… 112

Chapter 2 International Tourism Market Conditions in Typical Countries of East Asia …… 119

Section 1 China …… 120

Section 2 Japan …… 126

Section 3 South Korea …… 129

Section 4 Vietnam …… 131

Section 5 Malaysia …… 132

Section 6 Philippines …… 135

Section 7 Indonesia …… 137

Chapter 3 Sharing of Development Bonus from Chinese Outbound Tourism Market ·············· 143

Section 1 Chinese Outbound Tourism Market Behavior Survey ············· 144
Section 2 Evaluation for Chinese Outbound Tourists' Satisfaction Degrees of East Asian Countries ·············· 157

Chapter 4 Basic Status and Behavioral Characteristics of East Asia on Chinese Inbound Tourism Market ·············· 165

Section 1 Aggregate Market Size of East Asian Inbound Tourism to China ········ 166
Section 2 Market Structure of East Asia Inbound Tourism to China ············· 172
Section 3 Investigation on Market Behavior of East Asian Inbound Tourism to China ·············· 182

Chapter 5 Ushering in Bright Future for International Tourism Cooperation in East Asia ·············· 195

Section 1 Prospects for International Tourism Cooperation in East Asia ············ 196
Section 2 Policy Recommendations for International Tourism Cooperation in East Asia ·············· 199

Appendix 1 East Asian Tourism Cooperation ················· 203
Appendix 2 East Asia Local and Regional Government Congress ·············· 207
Appendix 3 A Review of East Asia International Tourism Cooperation ············ 219

第一章
繁荣的东亚国际旅游市场

第一节　东北亚国际旅游市场

东北亚各国都有着悠久的历史、灿烂的文化、绚丽的风光和巨大的旅游市场需求，经过近几十年的发展，东北亚已经成为国际旅游市场格局中的重要组成部分，越来越受到来自世界各地游客的青睐，东北亚国际旅游市场正呈现出一片欣欣向荣的繁荣景象。

一、东北亚入境旅游的发展现状

（一）入境旅游保持增长态势

以 2015 年国际旅游组织发布的数据为例，到东北亚的国际游客到访量实现 7% 的增长，东北亚主要目的地日本增长 29%、韩国增长 17%。而作为东北亚第一大目的地的中国，游客到访量超过 5 600 万人次。

（二）东北亚区域合作基础良好

由于东北亚区域在经济上联系密切，文化上不断交融互补，东北亚正成为全球最具活力的地区之一，也成为旅游业最具潜力的地区之一。各国山水相依，交往密切，文化多元，底蕴深厚，资源组合良好，有着众多标志性的世界性资源，彼此互为客源市场。20 个世纪 90 年代初，中国、日本、韩国等国政府代表就发起成立了东北亚地区地方政府联合会及一些相关的旅游组织，都在致力于扩大成员国之间的政策对话，进一步促进地区间国际旅游交流。这些组织的建立和有效工作，有力地促进了东北亚区域旅游的政府间协作、信息共享、人员交往和旅游经济的发展。

当前经济全球化和区域一体化的进程也深刻地影响着世界旅游业的发展轨迹。亚太经济的崛起，特别是中国跃升为世界第二经济体，世界旅游的热点正逐步向亚太转移。东北亚旅游市场潜力巨大、前景广阔，旅游合作趋势日益明显。在不久的将来，东北亚将是亚太地区最重要的旅游区域。

（三）东北亚区域内各国互为主要的客源地与目的地

近年来，中日韩三方游客人数不断攀升，互为重要的客源国。日本和韩国一直是中国最大的两个客源国家，而同时日本和中国也是韩国最主要的两个客源国家。三方互相依存，这是三方开展旅游合作的坚实基础。2003 年，三国领导人签署的《中日韩推进三方合作共同宣言》，提出了联合开展旅游推广计划，以此来提升在全球中的旅游知名度。2014 年中日韩三国相互访问游客达到 2014 万人，其中，中韩两国间相互旅游到访人数达到 1 031 万人，中日两国间相互旅游到访人数达到 503 万人。

2015 年，中国接待入境游客 13 382.04 万人次，同比增长 4.14%。其中，接待韩国游客 444.44 万人次，占入境外国游客总量的 17.10%，排名第一。日本紧随其后，占旅华外国游客总量的 9.61%。日本在 2003 年提出"观光立国"战略之后，旅游发展相当迅猛，而在近几年，日本已经成为中国游客的主要目的地国家，购物也成了中国游客赴日旅游的重要目的之一。日本政府观光局发布的统计数据显示，2014 年访日外国游客达到了 1 341 万人次，同比增加 300 万人次以上，其中中国游客从 131 万人次增加至 241 万人次，排列第 3 位，到 2015 年全年突破 490 万人次大关，排名第一位。而韩国也把旅游业摆在经济发展战略中的关键地位，2015 年赴韩中国游客平均每人消费金额约 2 200 美元（约合人民币 14 283 元），高于赴韩游客平均消费额一倍以上。2015 年中国赴韩国旅游总人数达到 600 万人以上，占到赴韩外国游客总人数的四成多。中国游客在 2015 年为韩国贡献了 1.6% 的 GDP。

2015 年 4 月 12 日中日韩三国观光大会第七次会议在东京举行，在此次会议中，三国达成共同声明，争取到 2020 年，三国相互观光的游客达到 3 000 万人。并以 2018 年韩国平昌冬运会、2020 年日本奥运会为契机，吸引更多的旅游者来到东亚旅游。在此会议上还达成了将要放宽签证条件，使三国间的旅游变得更加便捷的共识。

二、东北亚入境旅游发展面临的问题

东北亚地区入境旅游当前虽然呈现出一片繁荣的景象,也取得了较为显著的成绩。但不能否认存在诸多问题,影响着各国旅游业的合作发展。

(一)政治因素问题

东北亚地区政治环境复杂多变。如何协调好各地区的关系、建立政治互信、营造良好的政治环境成为东北亚各国共同面对的课题。

(二)突发事件的问题

东北亚地处活跃地带,自然灾害频发,特别是 2011 年 3 月 11 日日本发生 9.0 级地震而引发的海啸,以及次生灾害核泄漏事故,影响了当时的东北亚旅游市场。

(三)经济的问题

东北亚地区是一个经济发展水平不平衡的地区,这里既有发达国家,也有发展中国家。经济体制、市场机制、经济发展战略等都存在较大差异。

(四)制度因素的问题

目前,东北亚地区的合作已经形成多形式、多渠道、多层次、多领域的新格局,但是双边合作以及多边合作都停留在松散的对话阶段,约束力相当有限。各种合作的机构和会议很多,但是解决实际问题的能力不足,通过的协议保障不够,也没有制度立法的保护。与欧盟相比,缺乏一个稳定的统一的组织机构从地区的整体利益出发制订长远的合作规划,制约着合作的质量和效力。

三、东北亚入境旅游发展潜力

在《2020 年全球旅游展望》的报告中,估计在未来几年内,东北亚地区的旅游业会将以 7.2% 的速度增长,这将成为全球旅游业发展最快的地区。因此,全球旅游业不再只是欧洲和美洲的蛋糕,亚太旅游市场必将取得很大一块份额。据世界旅游组织统计,2012 年世界旅游人数达 10 亿,亚太地区的旅游人数增长了8%，东北亚地区的旅游总需求比上年增长8.6%，居世界第二位。世界旅游组织预测，到2020年全球国际游客数量将达到16.23亿人次，东北亚为2.23亿人次，占全球规模总量的15%，旅游业必将成为该地区的新兴产业。

近年来，以新型国家崛起为代表的新型旅游客源地和目的地出现，国际旅游区域的重心正向东方转移，东北亚正是这一趋势的代表，旅游市场前景非常乐观，旅游发展空间不断拓展，为本就繁荣的东北亚国际旅游市场提供了很好的机遇。

（一）东北亚特殊的地理布局拉动邮轮游产品的发展

目前，国际旅游消费需求的基本态势是：从人们出游的组织方式来看，在追求个性化的浪潮下，散客旅游特别是家庭旅游成为全球流行趋势；从旅游动机和目的来看，生态旅游、文化旅游、奖励旅游、探险旅游、科考旅游、潜海旅游以及其他各种形式的主题旅游，构成了人们外出旅游的主旋律。

东北亚地区拉动了全球邮轮行业的发展。该区域的邮轮更大，主要邮轮商在中国的营销预算也最高。在中国，厦门延长了其邮轮季，天津增设了邮轮码头，青岛计划开设通往迪拜的航线，上海计划成立自己的邮轮公司，南京计划建设邮轮码头。中国的旅行社也在寻求多元化的邮轮旅游：携程购买了邮轮，春秋航空也签约近15艘邮轮。2015年中国乘坐邮轮出境的游客人次达到190万人次，市场交易规模达45亿元；其中在线邮轮市场规模13.3亿元，同比增长60.1%，邮轮出游正在以高性价比、舒适轻松的跨境旅游和休闲免税购物等特色吸引着游客的极大兴趣。伴随着休闲游与出境游的持续走高，中国邮轮旅游已进入爆发增长期。在众多邮轮线路中，83%以上的中国游客出海偏向选择日韩航线，其次为东南亚（越南）航线等。2015年日本港口大放异彩，加上日本对邮轮新实施的免签政策，赴日邮轮产品呈现出空前的高丰富度。最受游客青睐的邮轮目的地为鹿儿岛、福冈和长崎。邮轮产品的开发和高速发展，为东北亚入境旅游带来了更丰富的体验。

（二）亚太经济崛起，为东北亚开展入境旅游区域合作提供了更为坚实的基础

由于中日韩三国地理位置相近，彼此之间联系紧密，并且各个地区的旅游资源非常丰富，随着亚太经济在全球的崛起，三国建立更加紧密的区域合作顺应世界旅游业发展的客观要求，已成为必然趋势。

第二节　东南亚国际旅游市场

一、东南亚入境旅游的发展现状

（一）入境旅游保持持续稳定增长

从20世纪80年代以来，除了1997年受亚洲金融影响、2003年受非典影响、2004年受海啸影响外，东南亚地区的入境旅游以高于世界平均增长率的速度发展。目前，东盟国家接待的年入境游客量已超过6 500万人次。

（二）区域内游客仍是东南亚入境市场的主要部分

从入境客源的地区构成来看，东南亚地区接待的入境旅游者主要来自东盟内部国家。东盟国家间实际上已形成互为主要旅游客源国的关系。2005年，东南亚地区共接待5 128.76万入境旅游者，其中东盟内部的游客就占了45.3%，达到2 325.43万人次。2006年、2007年这一比重稍有下降，但2008年、2009年，东盟内部游客占东南亚入境旅游接待总人数的比重已增加到46.3%和47.1%。2010年以来，伴随东南亚各国旅游的进一步发展，这一趋势得到巩固和强化。

（三）各国之间入境旅游发展水平有一定差距

东南亚各国经济发展水平悬殊，旅游起步时间各异，目前旅游业的发展水平有一定差距。新加坡、泰国、马来西亚三国为旅游业发展较为成熟的国家，其接待的入境旅游人数也最多。2005年马来西亚接待的外国游客在东盟国家中最多，达到1 643.1万人次，占东盟总接待入境游客的32%，泰国和新加坡

接待的外国游客分别为 1 151.7 万人和 894.2 万人，占的比例分别为 22.46% 和 17.43%，再加上印尼、菲律宾和文莱在内的东南亚六国在当年接待的入境旅游者占整个地区入境游客总人数的 87%，其他东南亚 4 国（越南、缅甸、老挝和柬埔寨）所占的比例为 13%。2009 年，马来西亚仍排名为接待入境游客最多的国家，接待人数创下历史新高，为 2 364.6 万人，占地区总接待外国游客的 36.14%，东南亚六国接待外国游客人数的比例为 85.87%。时至今日，这一格局也未发生太大的改变。这说明，东南亚六国的旅游开发较早，文化观光旅游产品特突出，滨海休闲度假旅游、城市商务会展旅游比较完善，已成为亚太地区的著名国际旅游目的地。同时也应该看到，越南、柬埔寨、缅甸和老挝等国，虽然旅游开发起步较晚，但拥有丰富、富有特色的旅游资源，近年来旅游业发展较快，追赶的势头很大。

（四）各国的旅游发展存在一定的竞争

东南亚各国在地理概况、地缘文化、历史经历等方面都比较接近。除了老挝（内陆国）和新加坡外，各国的自然旅游资源主要以海岛、海滩和热带风光为主，人文资源主要是历史古迹、宗教建筑和民俗风情。因此，各国的旅游产品结构在一定程度上趋同。

二、东南亚入境旅游发展的优势条件

（一）丰富的旅游资源

东南亚地区旅游资源构成复杂多样，丰富多彩，自然景观和人文景观都十分丰富。

从自然旅游资源方面看，东南亚充满热带气息的自然风光、美丽的海滩岛屿对旅游者具有很大的吸引力。在那里，绝大部分地区气候湿润，植被繁茂，生长着茂盛的热带原始森林和珍禽异兽。许多热带森林人迹罕至，保持着原始生态面貌，为开展森林探险、科学考察和度假观光提供取之不尽的旅游资源。而且，在马来群岛和中南半岛分布着许许多多风光秀丽、景色迷人、风采各异的海滩和岛屿。这些美丽优质的海滩和星罗棋布的海岛，以温暖的阳光、碧青的海水、松软的沙滩以及热带雨林景观吸引了大量的旅游者前来休闲、度假，如泰国的帕塔亚海滨、普吉岛，印尼的巴厘岛，新加坡的圣淘沙岛，菲律宾的宿务海滨，越南的下龙湾等都已成为世界著名的旅游胜地。此外，东南亚地区的火山、岩溶景观也为旅游业的发展提供了宝贵的资源。

从人文旅游资源方面看，东南亚有众多的历史文物古迹和多彩的民族风情。东南亚地区具有悠久的历史，是人类的发祥地之一。当地人民在漫长的历史发展过程中，创造了灿烂的文化，留下了众多的历史古迹。其中帝王宫殿和各种宗教建筑都是东南亚地区最富特色的历史文化遗产。如泰国的大王宫，印尼的日惹苏丹王宫，菲律宾的马拉卡南宫，柬埔寨的吴哥窟，泰国的卧佛寺、玉佛寺，印尼的婆罗浮屠，马来西亚的清真寺等都成了各国的著名旅游景点。而且，东南亚地区民族众多，宗教信仰复杂，各民族都形成了自己独特的民族文化、民俗风情，呈现出浓郁的神秘色彩，深深地吸引着旅游者。

除此之外，东南亚地区在现代化发展过程中创建的各类会展、会议、购物中心以及现代娱乐设施也成为重要的旅游吸引物。

（二）政府对旅游业的高度重视和积极支持

在东南亚地区，各国政府充分认识到旅游业对社会经济的重要地位和贡献，纷纷把旅游业作为支柱产业或新兴产业来发展。为了发展入境旅游，各国纷纷从加强旅游立法和管理、完善基础设施建设、开发更新旅游项目、增强旅游宣传、简化入境手续、给予政策优惠等方面入手，制定了相关发展战略，实施了一系列措施。

马来西亚政府在 2006 年就推出落地签证措施，让 23 个国家的游客可以在抵达马来西亚入境关卡时，才申请单次入境落地签证，以促进入境旅游的发展。同样，为了促进入境旅游发展，旅游业不发达的缅甸在 2010 年也积极推进落地签证政策。

泰国在 2009 年实施了刺激旅游的系列措施，要求酒店和航空公司下调旺季价格，通过优惠价格吸引游客，并把旅游宣传口号从"神奇泰国"变为"神奇泰国，神奇价格"；泰国政府还专门在中国广州市举行了"泰国旅游重启"的新闻发布会。

（三）区域合作的良好平台

在经济全球化和区域经济一体化的大趋势下，区域合作、共同发展已成为必然。尤其是对东南亚各国来说，日益加深的区域内外合作为其入境旅游的发展创造了难得的机遇。

从区域内部来看，东南亚国家在20世纪70年代就开始了区域内旅游合作，至今东南亚区域旅游合作已形成多层次多渠道的合作机制，东南亚旅游的国际形象逐渐形成，旅游合作也凸显成效，包括定期举行旅游论坛、旅游部长会议、对部分国家客人给予免签证、落地签证待遇，减收签证费等。目前，东南亚各国正在努力推进区域内的旅游市场，利用当地的自然、文化、遗产等各方面资源，把东南亚地区整合成世界最大的旅游市场；同时，为入境旅游的发展创造更好的条件和平台，区域内的各国之间也在共同开发旅游资源、建设旅游基础设施等方面积极开展合作。

从区域外部来看，东南亚及东南亚各国与其周边国家的合作正在不断加深。中国—东盟自由贸易区已建成，东盟同日韩及澳大利亚、印度、新西兰的经贸合作正在深化，交往日益频繁，而且这些国家也是东南亚入境旅游的主要客源市场，东南亚可以利用区域合作的平台加强对这一旅游市场的重点开拓。

（四）稳定的客源市场

东南亚地区的主体客源市场是本区域的国家，尤其是旅游业较为发达的马来西亚、泰国、新加坡、印尼和菲律宾。东南亚地区是一个拥有5.6亿人口的巨大市场。各国之间民族、文化相同或相近，地理距离较近，旅游心理也接近；而且，各国经济运行情况较好，经济发展一直较快，整个地区的经济发展潜力巨大。随着当地经济的持续发展，人民收入的逐渐提高，居民的旅游需求也会有所增加。再加上近年来，东南亚移民政策明显放宽，东盟国家间居民互访的扩大，区域内旅游也就成为最佳选择。

除此之外，入境东南亚的主要客源国中，中国、日本、澳大利亚、韩国及欧美国家的经济已逐渐复苏或快速发展，出境旅游需求有所增加，这将有利于东南亚入境旅游的开拓。尤其是与东南亚渊源颇深的中国，由于经济的快速发展和人民生活的显著提高，居民出国旅游的需求日益上升，是东盟区域内旅游大国发展入境旅游的主要客源国之一。预计到 2020 年，中国将成为东南亚国家入境旅游的最大客源国。

第二章
东亚代表性国家的国际旅游市场状况

第一节 中国

2015年中国共接待国内外游客超过41亿人次，旅游总收入达4.13万亿元。其中，国内旅游人数达40亿人次，国内旅游收入达3.42万亿元，同比分别增长10.5%和13.1%，居民人均出游率达到2.98次。全年接待入境旅游人数1.33亿人次，实现国际旅游收入1 136.5亿美元，同比分别增长4.0%和7.8%。2015年中国公民出境旅游人数达到1.2亿人次，旅游花费1 045亿美元，同比分别增长12.0%和16.7%。

2016年上半年，中国旅游市场规模稳步扩大。其中，国内旅游接待22.36亿人次，比上年同期增长10.47%；实现旅游总收入2.25万亿元，增长12.4%；入境旅游人数和国际旅游收入分别达到6 787万人次和570亿美元，比上年同期分别增长3.8%和5.3%；中国公民出境旅游人数5 903万人次，比上年同期增长4.3%。

一、中国入境旅游市场状况

1. 入境旅游的市场总量

2006—2015年，旅华游客的规模总量持续波动，旅华游客数量的增长率随之反复波动变化。2006年接待入境游客12 494.2万人次，同比增长3.87%；2007年接待入境游客13 187.33万人次，同比增长5.55%；2008年接待入境游客减少至13 002.7万人次，同比降低1.40%；2009年接待入境游客减少至12 647.59万人次，同比降低2.73%；2010年接待入境游客回升至13 376.22万人次，同比增长5.76%；2011年接待入境游客进一步升至13 542.36万人次，同比增长1.24%；2012年接待入境游客降至13 240.53万人次，同比降低2.23%；2013年接待入境游客进一步降至12 907.78万人次，同比降低2.51%；2014年接待入境游客降至12 849.83万人次，同比下降0.45%；2015年接待入境游客回升至13 382.04万人次，同比增长4.14%。2015年入境旅游市场在三年持续下滑后首次呈现回升迹象。就当前的发展趋势来看，预计未来入境旅游的人次规模有望逐步回升。

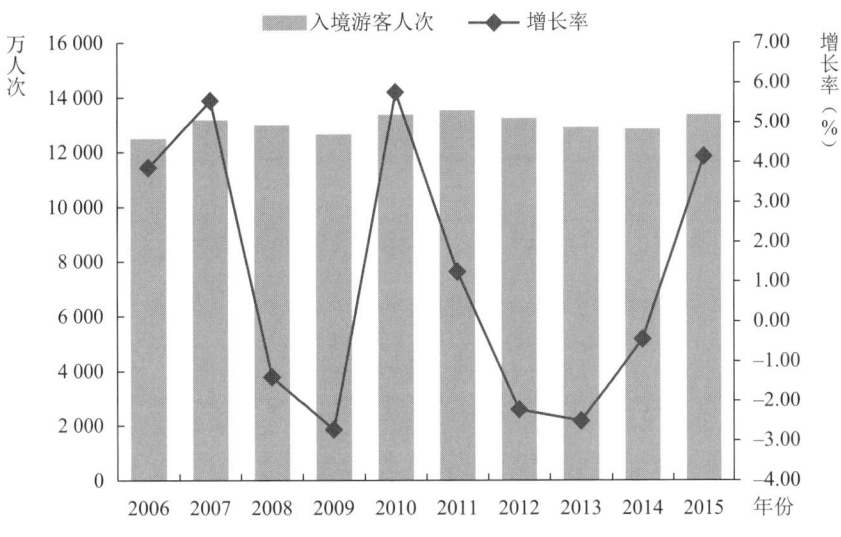

图 2-1　2006—2015 年中国入境旅游市场规模与增长情况

2. 入境过夜游客数量世界第四，仅次于法国、美国、西班牙

联合国世界旅游组织（UNWTO）公布的数据显示：2015年，在入境过夜游客接待人次排名中，中国以5 688.57万人次位列第四。法国以8 446万人次再度排名榜首，美国以7 751万人次位列第二名，西班牙以6 822万人次位列第三名。

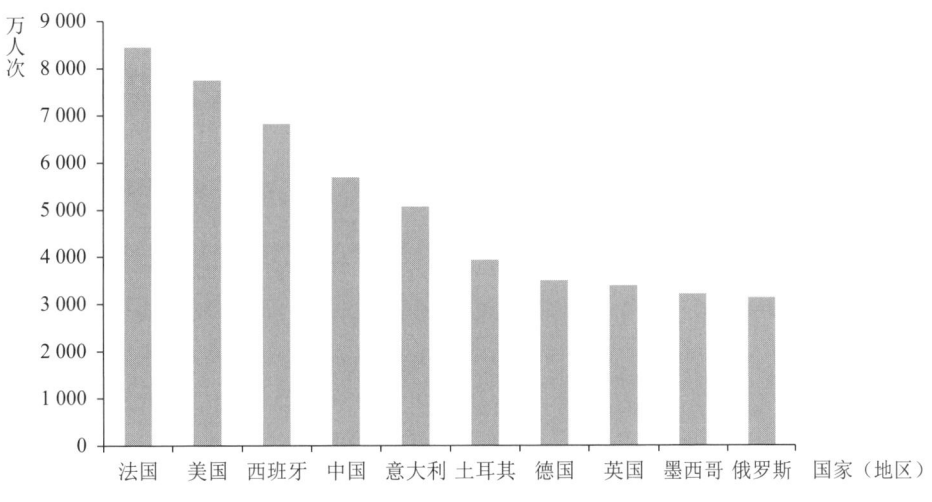

图 2-2　2015 年全球入境过夜旅游人次十强排名图

3. 亚洲客源的主导地位十分稳固

据2011—2015年数据统计，中国的主要客源为亚洲周边国家（62%），其

他客源目的地较之所占百分比较小,欧洲和美洲共占33%。

由图2-3可知,主要客源市场——亚洲入境游客数量所占比例年均高于50%,近年来数量维持在一个较为平稳的区间内,且绝对数远远高于其他各洲。

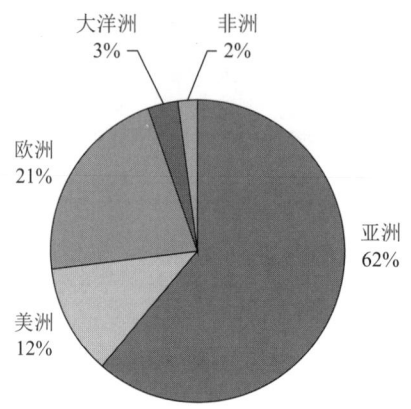

图2-3　2011—2015年中国入境旅游各大客源市场平均份额

4.近程客源市场对中国入境旅游具有战略意义

从旅华外国游客的客源构成来看,2015年接待韩国游客444.44万人次,占入境外国游客总量的17.10%,排名第一;接待日本游客249.77万人次,占入境外国游客总量的9.61%,排名第二;接待越南游客216.08万人次,占入境外国游客总量的8.32%,排名从第五上升到第三;接待美国游客208.58万人次,占入境外国游客总量的8.03%,排名从第三下降到第四;接待俄罗斯游客158.23万人次,占入境外国游客总量的6.09%,排名从第四下降到第五。韩国、日本、越南、美国、俄罗斯合计向中国输送游客1 277.10万人次,占中国接待入境外国游客总量的49.15%。接近五成的入境客源市场主要集中在这五大客源国。

2015年,紧随五大客源国之后的其他客源市场状况如下:接待马来西亚游客107.55万人次,占入境外国游客总量的4.14%,排名第六;接待蒙古游客101.41万人次,占入境外国游客总量的3.90%,排名第七;接待菲律宾游客100.40万人次,占入境外国游客总量的3.86%,排名从第九回升至第八;接待新加坡游客90.53万人次,占入境外国游客总量的3.48%,排名从第八回落至第九;接待印度游客73.05万人次,占入境外国游客总量的2.81%,排名保持第十;接待加拿大游客 67.98 万人次，占入境外国游客总量的 2.62%，排名从第十二上升至第十一；接待泰国游客 64.15 万人次，占入境外国游客总量的 2.47%，排名从第十四上升至第十二；接待澳大利亚游客 63.73 万人次，占入境外国游客总量的 2.45%，排名从第十一下降至第十三；接待德国游客 62.34 万人次，占入境外国游客总量的 2.40%，排名保持第十四；接待英国游客 57.96 万人次，占入境外国游客总量的 2.23%，排名保持第十五；接待印度尼西亚游客 54.48 万人次，占入境外国游客总量的 2.10%，排名保持第十六；接待法国游客 48.69 万人次，占入境外国游客总量的 1.87%，排名保持第十七；接待意大利游客 24.61 万人次，占入境外国游客总量的 0.95%，排名上升至第十八。

韩国、日本、越南、美国、俄罗斯、马来西亚、蒙古、菲律宾、新加坡、印度合计向中国输送游客 1 750.04 万人次，占中国接待入境外国游客总量的 67.35%，接近七成的入境客源市场主要集中在前十大客源国。

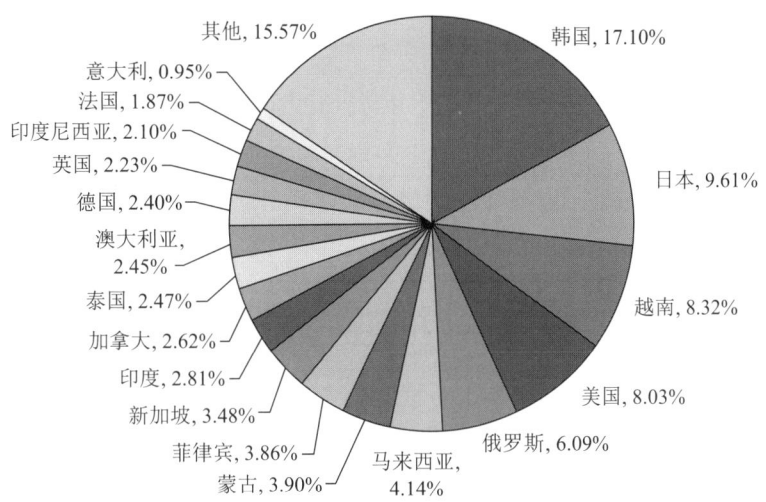

图 2-4　2015 年中国入境旅游主要客源国的结构状况

二、中国出境旅游市场状况

1. 出境旅游的市场总量

2015 年中国出境旅游市场保持增长势头，全年出境旅游人数达到 1.17 亿人次，比2014年增长8.96%。

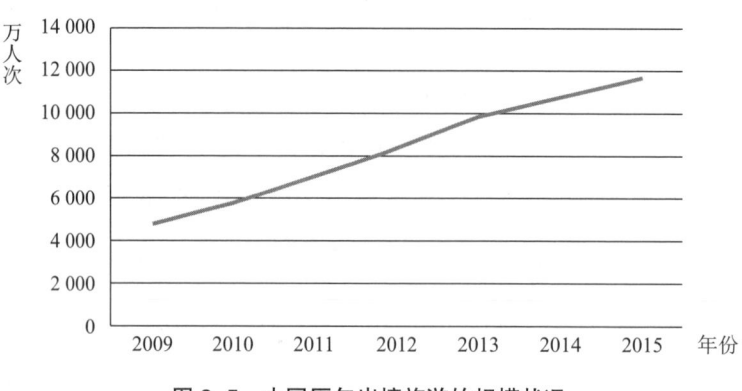

图2-5 中国历年出境旅游的规模状况

2. 出境旅游以近程目的地占据绝对主导地位

2015年中国出境旅游目的地依然以近程目的地为主。中国赴亚洲地区的游客所占比例为73.3%，之后依次为欧洲（11.5%）、美洲（8.2%）、大洋洲（3.6%）、非洲（2.7%）和其他地区（0.7%）。赴欧洲游客增长迅猛，同比增长23.8%。2015年赴非洲游客人次大幅减少，同比减少61.8%。赴大洋洲游客增长速度略有下降，同比增长速度由2014年的13.8%降至2015年的12.4%。

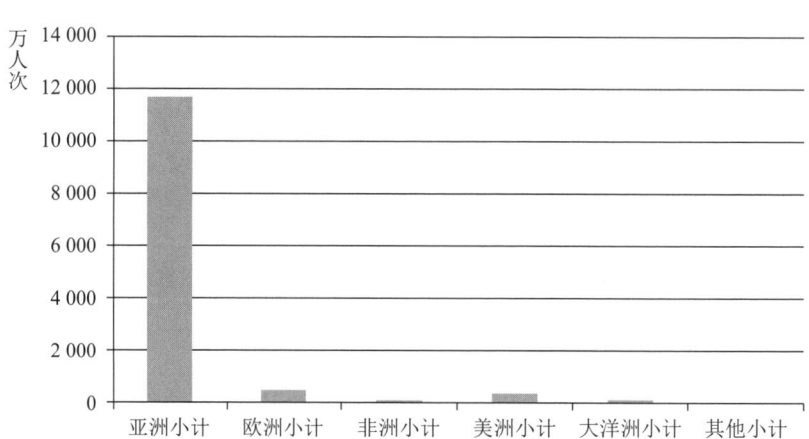

图2-6 2015年中国出境旅游目的地的洲际市场数量对比图

2015年中国游客出国旅游目的地中，泰国、韩国、日本、越南、美国、新加坡、俄罗斯、澳大利亚、印度尼西亚、马来西亚排名前十位。

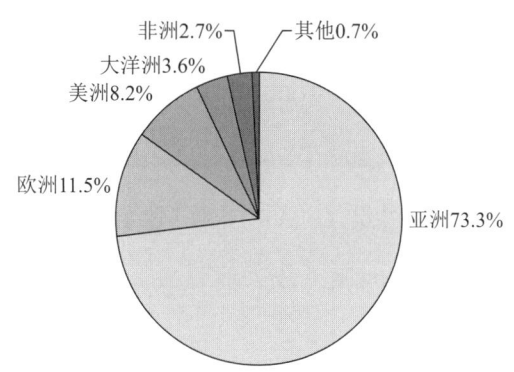

图 2-7　2015 年中国出境旅游目的地的洲际市场份额

第二节　日本

一、日本入境旅游市场状况

由于近年来日本政府一直积极贯彻实施"观光立国"战略,日本的入境游总体上发展较好。

1. 市场构成相对稳定,亚洲市场地位突出

各大洲近年来所占日本入境游客源市场的份额大致稳定,其变化幅度都比较微小。其中亚洲所占比例基本维持在 70% 以上,即使是在发生新型流感的 2009 年和发生 3·11 大地震的 2011 年,亚洲赴日游客的比例也不曾出现太大浮动。北美洲维持在 11% 上下,欧洲比北美洲略低,基本维持在 10% 左右,还有不到 10% 的游客来自其他地区。

目前中国已经取代韩国,成为日本的第一大客源国。据日本观光厅统计,2015 年到访日本的中国游客达 499 万人次,较上年同期增长 107%,中国已成为日本最大客源国。

形成这种格局的主要原因有两方面。首先,地理位置邻近、文化习俗相近。日本与中国、韩国都是一衣带水的邻邦,文化传统与风俗习惯在很多方面都极为相似,游客容易产生亲近感,因此同为汉字文化圈的游客们更愿意选择日本作为出境游目的地。其次，政府推出相应的入境旅游配套政策。日本政府逐步放宽对亚洲各国游客的入境限制，2009年7月，日本开始对中国赴日游客发放自由行个人签证，2010年7月起，日本政府又大幅放宽中国赴日自由行个人签证，2011年7月起，对于从冲绳入境的中国游客给予三年内多次往返签证，这些相对优惠的签证政策在一定程度上较大地刺激了中国游客的赴日游。

2. 受突发事件影响较大

在2009年与2011年日本入境旅游人数出现了负增长，这都是由于受突发事件影响。2009年，日本国内出现了新型流感，2011年发生了3·11东日本大地震，使得这两年的入境人数出现下降。

3. 入境旅游收入在旅游经济总量中比重较小

根据日本观光厅的统计数据，2011年全年的旅游消费收入为23.8万亿日元，而外国游客在日本境内消费为1.3万亿日元，只占所有旅游消费5.5%。2010年全年旅游消费收入为25.5万亿日元，外国人在日本境内消费1.2万亿日元，所占比例为4.7%。

4. 国际旅游景点相对集中

根据JNTO的调查，外国游客访日的地点多集中在少数大城市，到访率最高的是东京，2010年的到访率为60.3%，2009年的东京到访率为58.8%，其次为大阪、京都、神奈川、北海道等地区。

二、日本出境旅游市场状况

1. 市场总量相对稳定

日本经济发达、人口众多，是世界上较大的旅游输出国之一。自1987年日本推出"海外旅游倍增计划"以来，出境旅游人数大幅度提高，在1990年首次突破1 000万人次，达到一个前所未有的高度，从此成为出境旅游大国，出境旅游开始高速增长。2000年以后，日本出境旅游在波动中缓慢增长。2000年日本出境游客数量为1 782万人次，2014年该数字为1 690万人次，总体而言，日本出境旅游市场基本保持相对稳定的状态。近年来，日本出境旅游游客数正持续下滑，由2012年1 849.07万人次下降至2015年的1 621.38万人次，平均每年减少4.5%。

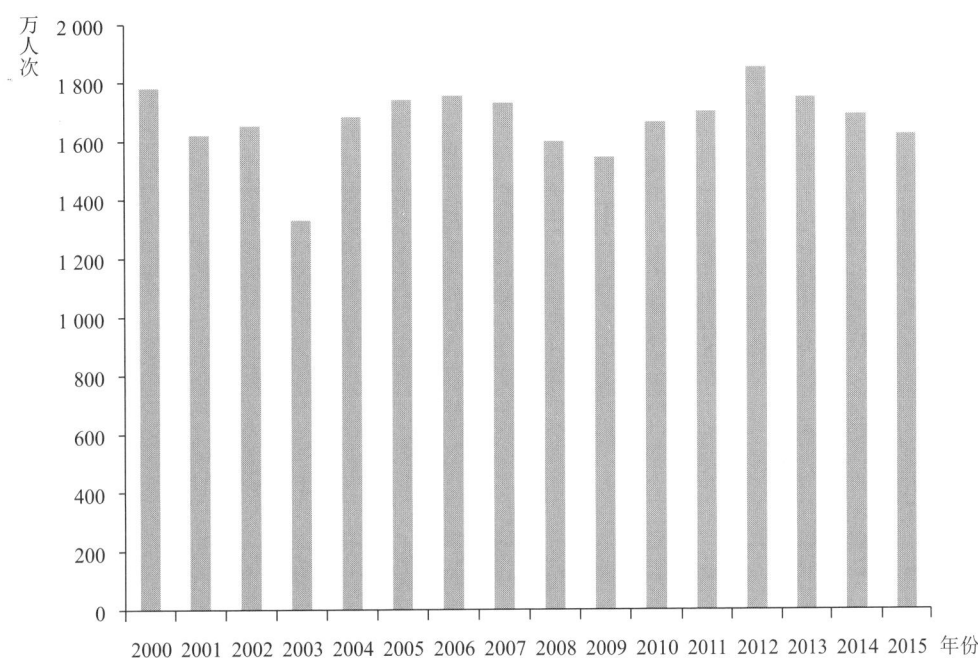

图2-8　2000—2015年日本出境旅游市场规模序列图

2. 市场结构相对稳定

2014年日本出境人次达1 690.34万人次，比2013年减少3.3%。其中，赴美国旅游的游客总数为357.94万人次，占出境旅游总数的21.18%；赴中国的出境旅游人数为271.77万人，占日本出境旅游总数的16.08%。

表2-1　2008—2014年日本游客出境旅游前两名国家及数量规模

单位：万人次

年份	总数	国家	数量	国家	数量
2008	1 598.73	中国	344.60	美国	325.00
2009	1 544.57	中国	331.70	韩国	305.30
2010	1 663.72	中国	373.10	美国	338.60

续表

年份	总数	国家	数量	国家	数量
2011	1 699.42	中国	365.82	韩国	328.91
2012	1 848.97	韩国	351.87	中国	351.82
2013	1 747.27	中国	287.75	韩国	274.78
2014	1 690.34	美国	357.94	中国	271.77

第三节　韩国

一、韩国入境旅游市场状况

1. 中国是韩国第一大入境旅游市场

2015年中国赴韩旅游总数量达611万人次，占赴韩外国游客四成之多。按韩国观光公社的预计，2015年全年，中国游客在住宿、交通、购物等方面，给韩国带来的综合经济效益为220亿美元，约占韩国GDP的1.6%。韩国观光公社和韩亚大投证券公司2014年发布消息说，访韩中国游客数量将以年平均19.8%的速度增加，到2020年将达1 490万人次，即目前的3.5倍左右。届时，中国游客在韩消费规模将超30万亿韩元（约1 800亿元人民币），支撑起韩国约8%的零售市场。

2. 韩国旅游成功吸引回头客

2015年赴韩旅游的海外游客中，有46.1%的游客访韩次数为两次以上，多数游客赴韩主要目的为购物。

在访韩次数方面，访问次数为一次的游客占53.9%，两次为16.3%，三次为7.9%，四次以上为21.9%。访韩次数为两次以上的入境游客人数占比高达46.1%。特别是日本游客该比重相对较高，属于第二次以上来访的游客占比高达78.7%。其后依次是新加坡、中国香港、俄罗斯和中国。被问及将韩国选为旅游目的地时考虑最多的因素是什么时，回答"购物"的人占67.8%，占比最大。回答美食（42.8%）、历史和文化遗址（27.6%）、服装和时尚（23.6%）的海外游客比重较持续增加。就"最喜欢的韩国旅游景点"问题，回答"明洞"的游客最多，其后依次为东大门市场、古代宫阙、南山N首尔塔和新村弘大入口等。

3. 中国游客在韩消费相对较高

外国游客在韩国的人均旅游成本为2 127.4美元，中国游客人均成本最高，为2 204.5美元。

从消费领域来看，外国游客在购物方面的消费最多，达到983美元，其后依次是住宿费（417.7美元）、餐饮费（291.1美元）、向本国旅行社支付的费用（120.0美元）、在韩国的交通费（109.4美元）。

从游客来源国来看，中国游客的人均消费额位居榜首，达2 204.5美元。欧美地区游客的人均旅游成本排第二位，为2 066.9美元，来自东南亚地区的游客消费为1 852.2美元。

按年龄看，年龄越小，旅游成本越高。15~20岁年龄段的游客成本最高，达到2 527.1美元，其后依次是20~29岁（2 092.5美元）、30~39岁（2 074.1美元）、41岁以上（1 075.5美元）。

二、韩国出境旅游市场状况

2005年韩国出国旅游的人数首次超过1 000万，达1 008万人次，2006年和2007年分别增加到1 161万和1 332.5万人次。2008、2009年受金融危机和甲型H1N1流感疫情的影响，出国游客大幅缩水，年增长率分别为-10%和-20.9%，自2010年起才开始反弹，出国游客人数逐年攀升，2010年的年增长率更是达到了31.5%。

近年来，虽然韩国经济陷入长期不景气状态，2015年GDP更是创三年来新低，但韩国的出境游热度不减，出境旅游人数较往年有大幅度增加。2015年韩国出国旅游人数接近2 000万人次，达到了1 931.43万，创下了历史新高，比2014年的1 608.07万人次增加20.1%。

第四节 越南

一、入境旅游市场近期增长迅速

越南早在20世纪60年代已成立国家旅游局，但在80年代以前，因受多种因素的影响，旅游业发展较为缓慢，主要接待一些苏联和东欧国家的旅游者。1981年越南正式加入世界旅游组织。越南旅游业虽然起步较晚，但经过多年的努力，旅游业有了长足的进步。进入90年代，更有了突飞猛进的发展，近年来，国际游客赴越南旅游的人数明显增长。

2016年1—9月，越南接待的国际总入境人数达到7 265 380人，比去年同期增长25.7%。

按客源国来分，来自不同国家的游客在越南旅游的时间有所不同。远程市场游客在越南停留的时间更长，而近程市场游客在越南停留时间相对较短一些。

二、入境游客的消费水平还有较大的提升空间

越南的旅游资源非常丰富，分布在全国各地，旅游资源适合发展多种旅游产品，满足市场的不同需求。但是，因为国际旅游人才还不能满足需求，旅游资源还有待进一步开发等原因，越南旅游业接待的国际游客人次和旅游外汇收入，还存在较大的提升空间。

第五节 马来西亚

一、旅游资源品质较高

马来西亚是一个位于赤道附近的热带岛国，宜人的气候、优越的地理位置赋予了马来西亚得天独厚的自然旅游资源。在马来西亚，既有明媚的阳光，美

丽的沙滩，风景秀丽的海岛，繁茂的原始森林，也有千姿百态的洞穴，高大的山川，热带风光特色尤为显著。同时，悠久的历史、各具特色的多元种族及其多姿多彩的民族文化为马来西亚创造了无数独具魅力的人文景观。

马来西亚近几年来旅游业发展很迅速，在国际旅游市场上的地位、声誉提高很快。吉隆坡、马六甲、槟城、云顶度假城、沙巴、兰卡威、热浪岛等都已成为世界著名的旅游胜地，马来西亚也先后获得"世界最佳旅游目的地""最佳生态旅游目的地"、亚洲"最佳品牌推广和最佳生态游目的地""最佳旅游组织"等多个奖项，并被世界经济论坛评为"最值得消费的旅游目的地之一"。众多奖项的获取为马来西亚增添了无穷的吸引力。马来西亚购物（Shopping Malaysia）最终变成一个与顶级购物相关的知名品牌。国家和国际层面的旅游代表团、对话和会议都在不断宣传推广着马来西亚购物。这是《2020马来西亚旅游转型计划迈向36∶168》战略的重要部分，它将文化旅游部置于鼓励革新和创造力的最前沿，期望到2020年游客人数达到3 600万，旅游收入达到1 680亿马币。

二、入境旅游市场十分可观

除丰富的旅游资源、良好的商业环境及基础设施外，旅游政策的正确制定和实施是马来西亚旅游业快速发展的另一个重要原因。其旅游政策的内容主要包括在国家经济纲领中提出发展旅游业的目标和主要措施，围绕这一政策目标制定国家旅游发展政策和各专项旅游政策等。政府制定和实施的专项旅游政策包括：乡村旅游总体规划、国家生态旅游计划、学生旅游项目、第二家园项目等。

为了促进入境旅游的发展，马来西亚政府于1992年成立了旅游促进局，致力于把马来西亚发展成为著名的国际旅游观光国。除了推出"旅游观光年"，旅游促进局一直注重旅游业的海外市场推广，在一些主要客源国设立办事处，进行旅游宣传、推广活动，让更多的人了解马来西亚。据悉，马来西亚政府早在2000年时，就在美国CNN电视台播放旅游广告，这在亚洲国家和地区还是首例。近年来，旅游业更是马来西亚政府倾力打造的一张世界名片。旅游部更是提出了"马来西亚,亚洲魅力所在"的旅游宣传口号。为了做好旅游推介,旅游促进局在全球聘用了13家公关公司和11家广告公司,针对不同国家的特点有针对性地进行公关推介活动。

马来西亚的入境游客主要来自亚太地区,尤其是东南亚地区旅游业最为发达的国家更是其主体客源市场。东盟现在正努力推进区域旅游业的一体化,各国积极联手开发区域内的旅游市场,力争把东南亚地区整合成世界最大的旅游市场,这无疑为马来西亚的入境旅游市场的开拓提供了很好的机会。

马来西亚在亚太地区的主要客源国——中国、日本、澳大利亚、韩国及欧美国家的经济已逐渐复苏或快速发展,出境旅游需求有所增加,这将有利于马来西亚入境旅游的开拓。尤其是与马来西亚渊源颇深的中国,由于经济的快速发展和人民生活的显著提高,居民出国旅游的兴趣日益强烈,现已和马来西亚形成了互为主要客源国的关系,是马来西亚接待入境游客的主要来源之一。2013年,有180万中国人赴马来西亚旅游,占该国入境旅游人数的30%以上。

马来西亚期望在2020年时能吸引3 600万游客到访,并创造最少1 680亿马币的收入。2016年2月17日马来西亚副总理阿末扎希出席第十九届马来西亚旅游奖颁奖礼时表示,政府希望借助中国赴马游客免签等政策,力争吸引800万中国游客访问马来西亚。

三、以旅游年为首的旅游文化品牌

马来西亚旅游年最早创建于1990年,主题为"魅力马来西亚,节庆之年",取得巨大成功,此后,马来西亚又陆续举办了1994年的"魅力马来西亚,自然至上"、2007年的"马来西亚50周年庆"等一系列活动。2014年,马来西亚政府对第四届马来西亚旅游年的举办提出了更高的要求和期待。

四、签证便利化稳步推进

为了更大程度地方便入境游客,马来西亚政府在入境制度方面也实行了新举措。政府在全国 44 个主要关卡实施了"无纸张入境制度",外国人入境时,不必填写白卡。同时,政府还启用了"电子签证"。即到马来西亚旅游的外国游客只需通过互联网申请入境签证,通过互联网提交游客个人资料,便可办理签证。

马来西亚电子签证启动仪式暨新闻发布会于 2016 年 3 月 1 日在京举行。马来西亚政府宣布对中国游客实施免签证和电子签证,方便中国游客到马来西亚旅游。

第六节　菲律宾

一、旅游资源丰富

菲律宾,一个拥有 7 107 个美丽岛屿、壮丽的自然景观、悠久的历史和热情人民的国度。一百多个民族部落,交织着异国风情,融合的文化和艺术……共同铸就了菲律宾独特的人文艺术和自然景观。

菲律宾可由马尼拉、老沃、苏比克、宿务和大堡五个国际关口入关。马尼拉是菲律宾的第一关口,是国家首都;老沃是吕宋极北北依罗戈省得一个国际关口;苏比克最近成立为国际港口,具备各类休憩、康乐及探险设施;宿务是南部第一大省会,有"南方帝后之都"的称谓;大堡充满浓厚的地方色彩、多元文化的风味和组合,标志着菲律宾及马来西亚的文化风情。其他受游客喜爱的特色旅游目的地还有八打雁市、海豚湾、黎家实比市、长滩岛、巴拉望等。其中长滩岛、宿雾和薄荷岛是国际游客最向往的菲律宾滨海旅游目的地。长滩岛因其 4 公里长的白沙滩闻名遐迩,美国著名旅游杂志《私家地理》将长滩岛评为"2012 世界最佳海滩度假胜地"。

菲律宾的主题旅游主要为户外探险、阳光海岸、水上活动、潜水游、文化体验、蜜月首选、奖励旅游和享乐生活。

二、入境旅游主要依赖近程客源市场

2015年菲律宾共接待外国游客536万人次,同比增长10.9%。旅游收入50亿美元,同比增长5.9%,约占GDP的8%。吸收就业500万人,占劳动力人口的12.7%。韩国、美国、日本是菲律宾前三大游客来源国,当年游客人数分别为134万、77.9万、49.6万人次;中国是菲律宾第四大外国游客来源国,达49.1万人次,同比增长24.3%,占比9.2%。

菲律宾国家旅游局2016年7月发布数据显示,1—5月,菲海外入境游客总计252万人次,同比增长13%,旅游业营收1066亿比索,同比增长14%。其中5月份单月入境游客44.5万人,同比增长8%;旅游业创收200亿比索,同比增长19%。2016年1—5月,韩国、美国、中国是海外赴菲游客前三大来源国,赴菲律宾旅游的中国游客同比增长81%,成为增速最大的来源国。

三、借助国际会议促进国际旅游发展

菲律宾旅游业的发展,与许多国际性会议在菲律宾召开也有关系。作为联合国的会员国及许多国际性组织的成员,菲律宾经常争取以东道国的身份接待各国代表到马尼拉来举行国际会议,例如国际货币基金会议、国际法律会议、东盟五国首脑会议与部长会议、世界医药会议、太平洋地区旅游会议以及联合国贸发会议等。

第七节 印度尼西亚

印度尼西亚旅游业起步较晚,但20世纪70年代中期以来发展迅速,外国游客和旅游外汇收入逐年递增。旅游业的快速发展,不仅为国民经济建设带来了大量的外汇收入,促进了相关产业的发展,尤其是为商业、酒店业以及旅游商品的生产带来了生机,而且解决了大批人员的就业问题。旅游业已成为印度尼西亚国民经济的一项支柱产业，而且是非油气行业中仅次于电子产品出口的第二大创汇行业。政府长期重视开发旅游景点，兴建饭店，培训人员和简化入境手续，以加速旅游业的发展。

一、旅游资源丰富多样

印度尼西亚由太平洋和印度洋之间17 508个大小岛屿组成，其中约6 000个有人居住。火山有400多座，其中活火山有77座。爪哇为印度尼西亚的中心，也是人口最多的一个岛，首都雅加达即位于此岛的西北岸。

印度尼西亚的动物资源也十分丰富，估计其动物种类有20多万种，其中受国家保护的属于珍稀动物的就有525种。印度尼西亚拥有广阔的海域和星罗棋布的河流湖泊，所以其水产资源相当丰富，盛产各种鱼、虾、蟹、螺、贝、海参、珍珠、食用海藻和燕窝等。

印度尼西亚拥有丰富的文化资源。中爪哇的千年古塔婆罗浮屠佛塔和普兰班南印度教陵庙群，均被联合国教科文组织列入世界文化遗产名录。此外，传统服装、烹饪、各地区的传统舞蹈和音乐表演都是闻名遐迩的旅游吸引物。

表2-2 印度尼西亚的世界遗产

名称	类型	所在地
婆罗浮屠寺庙群	文化遗产	中爪哇省
普兰班南寺庙群	文化遗产	日惹特区
桑吉兰早期人类化石遗址	文化遗产	亚齐特区
苏门答腊热带雨林	历史遗产	北苏门答腊省
乌戎库隆国家公园	历史遗产	西爪哇省
科莫多国家公园	历史遗产	东努沙登加拉省
洛伦茨国家公园	历史遗产	巴布亚省

这里还是世界上岛屿最多的一个国家，最令人神往的当首推巴厘岛。巴厘岛以典型的海滨自然风光和独特的风土人情而闻名。在这里所有与水有关的休闲活动都可以找得到。滑水、帆板、潜水、冲浪、水上摩托、快艇、漂流，还有一直

流行的矿物质温泉浴。由于海岸线漫长，岛上的旅游资源颇为丰富，以秀丽的热带风光最让人难忘。旅游景点有木雕、银器和蜡染纪念品出售。产于印度尼西亚的咖啡是购物的佳品，坎帕阿伈（KapalApi）是最受欢迎的咖啡品牌。

二、入境旅游市场具备较大的增长潜力空间

2000年，外国游客赴印度尼西亚的数量达到506万人次。此后外国游客赴印度尼西亚的数量有所波动，最高跌幅发生在2003年，其中外国游客来印度尼西亚的数额只有446万多人。2010年开始，印度尼西亚的入境旅游人次再次呈上升趋势。

虽然外国游客赴印度尼西亚的人数在2013年已经达到880万人次，但依然具备较大的增长空间，尤其是来自中国的游客市场极具潜力。2015年7月1日起印度尼西亚对中国公民实施免签，极大地促进了中国赴印尼旅游市场增长。

表2-3 2000—2013年印度尼西亚入境旅游人次

年份	入境游客人次	入境人次增长率（%）	外汇创收（百万美元）	外汇创收增长率（%）
2000	5 064 217		5 748.80	
2001	5 153 620	1.77	5 396.27	−6.13
2002	5 033 400	−2.33	4 305.56	−20.21
2003	4 467 021	−11.25	4 037.02	−6.04
2004	5 321 165	19.12	4 797.88	18.85
2005	5 002 101	−6.00	4 521.90	5.75
2006	4 871 351	−2.61	4 447.98	−1.63
2007	5 505 759	13.02	5 345.98	20.19
2008	6 234 497	13.24	7 347.60	37.44
2009	6 323 730	1.41	6 297.99	−14.29
2010	7 002 944	10.74	7 603.45	20.73
2011	7 649 731	9.24	8 554.39	12.51
2012	8 044 462	5.16	9 120.89	6.62
2013	8 802 129	9.42	——	——

三、积极与周边国家合作互动

印度尼西亚计划重点加强与东盟邻国的旅游业合作，吸引更多泰国、菲律宾、越南游客到印度尼西亚旅游。在具体国别方面，印度尼西亚已同新加坡和马来西亚达成协议，共同投资 5.7 亿美元，将三国沿海地区开发成国际旅游度假胜地，建成"东方加勒比旅游区"。印度尼西亚还与泰国和马来西亚的旅游机构协商，建立具有协调功能的常设旅游联盟机构，以加强三国旅游业之间的相互合作、联合促用和共同开发。历史上印度尼西亚与缅甸在政治、经济、社会、军事和安全方面曾经有过良好的合作，根据 1951 年签署的两国友好投资协议，印度尼西亚把缅甸定为自由友好国家。为了促进两国旅游业合作，两国于 2009 年 6 月底在缅甸仰光举行关于贸易和旅游业的研讨会，探讨进一步促进两国之间贸易商业联系，加强旅游业交流与合作的可能性。

四、选定重点国家，推进旅游复苏计划

作为振兴旅游业的计划之一，印度尼西亚政府尝试推动传统旅游市场的促销活动。营销市场的重点放在吸引中国、日本、东南亚国家、澳大利亚及中东的游客。这项旅游业复苏计划首先从临近的地区做起，转而发展到其他的市场。这些国家也是前几十年来印度尼西亚旅游业的主要客源。为实施复苏计划，旅游部成立了一个工作委员会，包括 5 个负责不同市场的小组，每个小组要组织一系列的诸如参与旅游展览会的活动。

第三章
共享中国出境旅游市场的发展红利

第一节　中国出境旅游市场行为调查

一、出境游游客消费决策影响因素

调查结果①显示首次出境旅游的中国游客居多，占46.3%；游览观光和休闲度假是中国游客出境旅游的主要目的，分别占56.2%和37.3%；61.7%的受访对象认为出境旅游是重大消费决策；对出游频率和决策重要程度的调查结果表明，出境旅游作为重大决策，仍然是中国人普遍难以决策的消费选择。

（一）首次出境的游客居多

首次出境旅游的中国游客居多，占总样本的46.3%，第二次出境的游客占26.0%，第三次出游者占12.25%，出境三次及三次以上者占15.4%，说明大部分中国游客的出境旅游频率并不高。

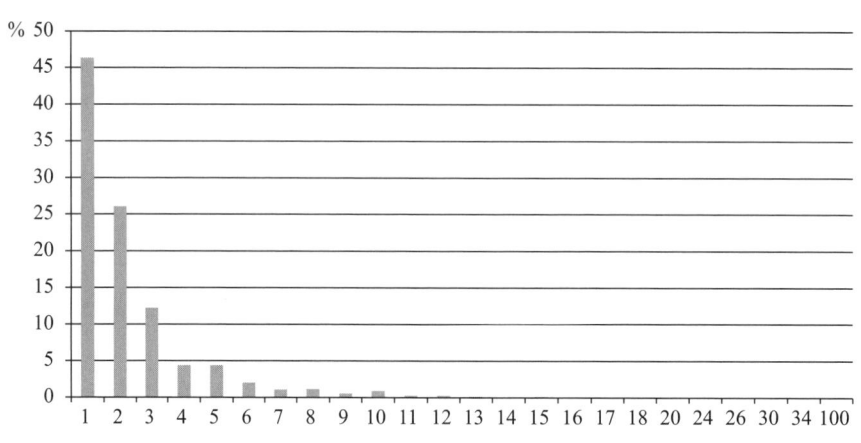

图3-1　2015年中国出境游客出境旅游的频次分布图

（二）出境旅游对于大多数消费来说仍属于重大消费

59.8%的受访者认为出境旅游是重大消费决策，这一比例比2014年的61.7%有所下降。

---

① 为2015年调查结果。

（三）出境旅游信息来源以网络、亲友介绍或旅行社咨询为主

中国游客在出境旅游前大都通过网站/BBS/论坛、亲朋好友介绍或到旅行社咨询来获得相关旅游信息，选择以上信息渠道的分别占总样本的60.5%、56.2%和49.7%，使用信息渠道的游客较少。

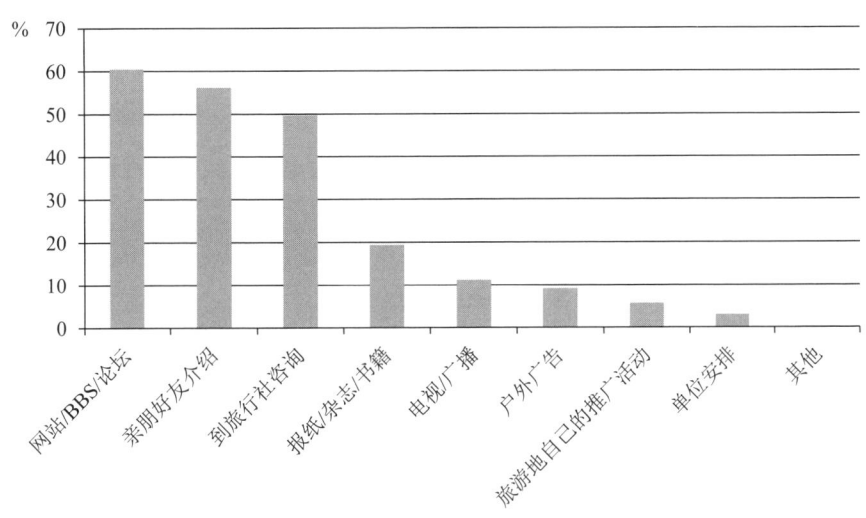

图3-2　2015年中国出境游客信息来源

（四）出游前主要查找景区、价格与民俗风情信息

中国游客在出游前主要了解的信息包括景区/景点信息（69.8%）、旅游价格信息（56.2%）、旅游地民俗风情信息（32.8%）以及交通信息（31.9%）。

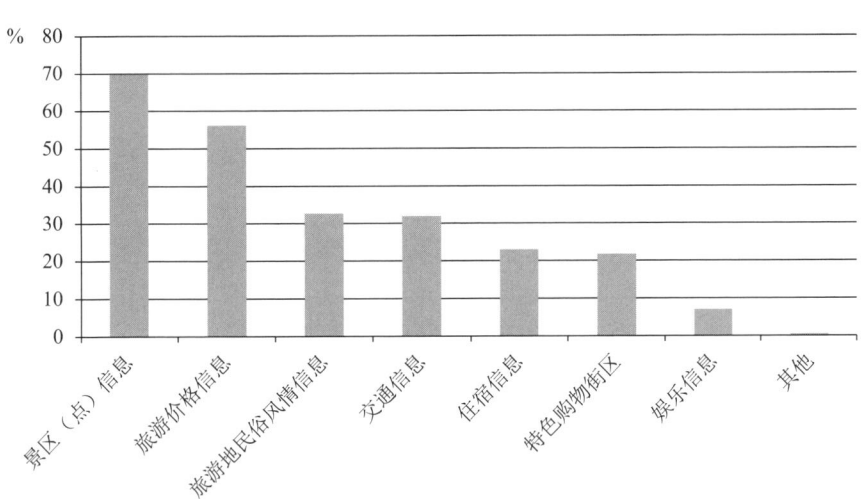

图3-3　2015年中国出境游客出游前了解的信息

二、未参团游客出境游游客消费决策特征

中国出境游客大都是和家人或朋友一起结伴而行；在选择境外旅游目的地时，更加注重景点/旅游地的吸引力；77.2%的受访者愿意通过旅行社安排境外旅游活动，在选择旅行社时游客更注重旅行社的知名度、朋友是否推荐和诚信度；中国游客在选择境外住宿酒店时青睐于中等价位酒店和经济型酒店；境外游览的景点数目较多，一般为3~9个，游览10个以上景点的游客也不在少数；大部分游客出游时间为两周以内，其中一周之内的最多，占比52.7%。

（一）出境游客偏好与家人、好友结伴出游

中国游客大多和家人一起赴境外旅游，占受访者总数的59.9%。和好友结伴进行境外旅游活动的游客也比较多，占26.8%，和这两类同伴出游的游客明显多于和其他类型同伴出游的游客。

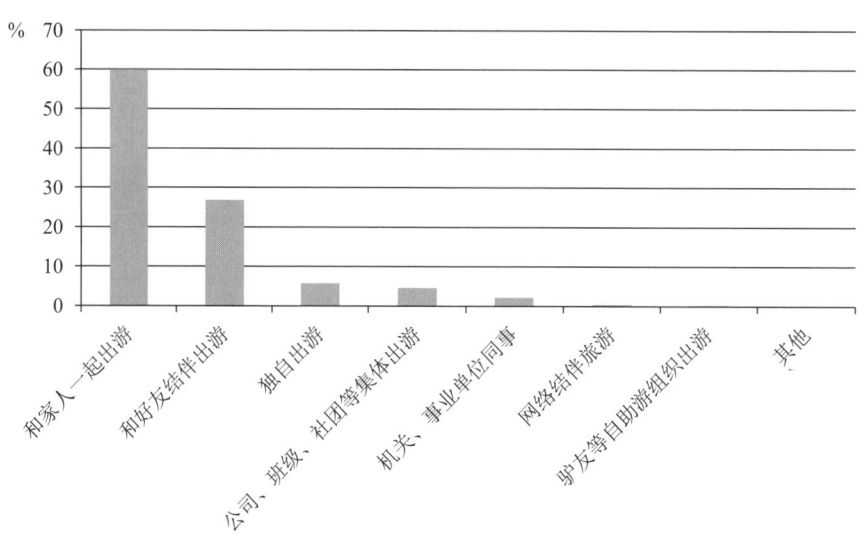

图3-4　2015年中国出境游客境外出游同伴

（二）出境游客目的地选择受景点/旅游地吸引力的影响最大

46.6%的中国游客在选择境外旅游目的地时，首先看重的是景点/旅游地的吸引力，其次是旅行费用因素（28.4%），选择其他影响因素的明显较少。

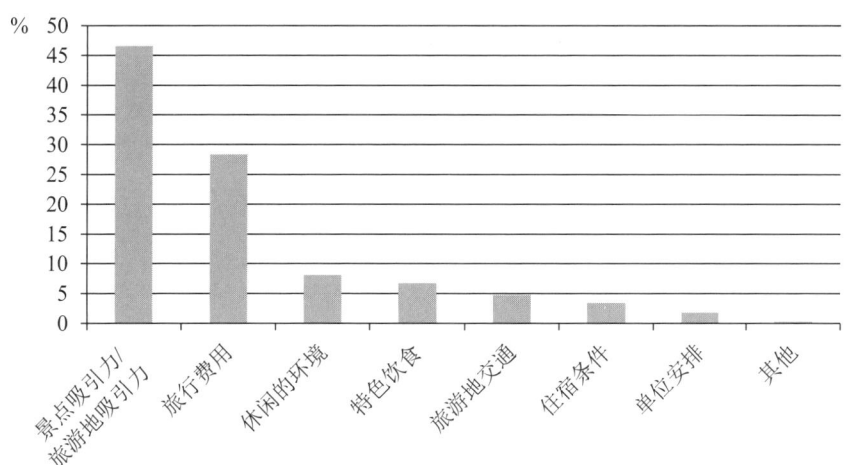

图 3-5　2015 年中国出境游客线路选择影响因素分布

（三）参加旅行社比例较高

境外旅游参加旅行社的中国游客比例高达 77.2%，高于 2014 年的 76.6%，说明大多数游客对于不太熟悉的境外旅游依然倾向于通过旅行社安排出游活动。

（四）品牌知名度的重要性提升

中国游客大多通过旅行社来组织境外旅游活动，影响游客旅行社选择的因素有旅行社的品牌知名度、朋友推荐、诚信度和旅行社的收费标准，其中 49.1% 的受访者选择品牌知名度，43.3% 选择朋友推荐，39.9% 选择诚信度，34.3% 选择收费标准。

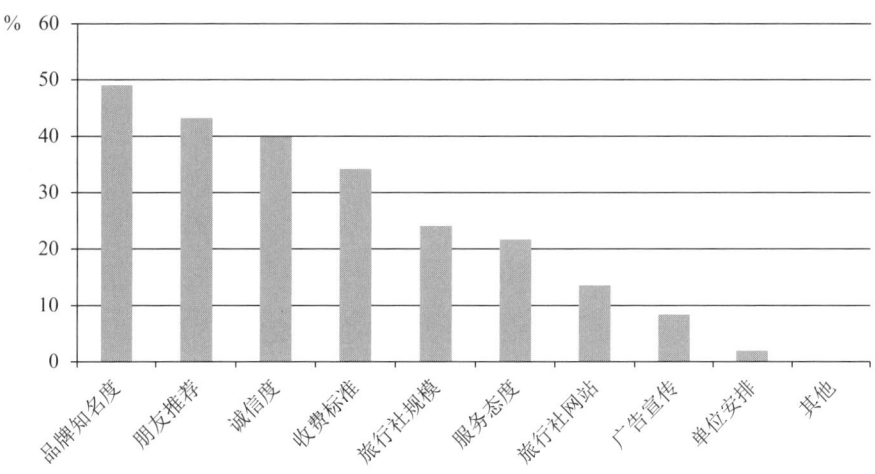

图 3-6　2015 年中国出境游客选择旅行社的影响因素

（五）中等价位酒店依然是出境游客的最重要选择

在住宿设施选择方面，中国游客偏向于选择中等价位酒店和经济型酒店，选择这两类住宿设施的游客分别占总样本的 45.4% 和 31.0%，与 2014 年相比基本持平。与此同时，选择入住豪华酒店的游客也不在少数，占 16.3%，选择其他类型住宿设施的游客相对较少。

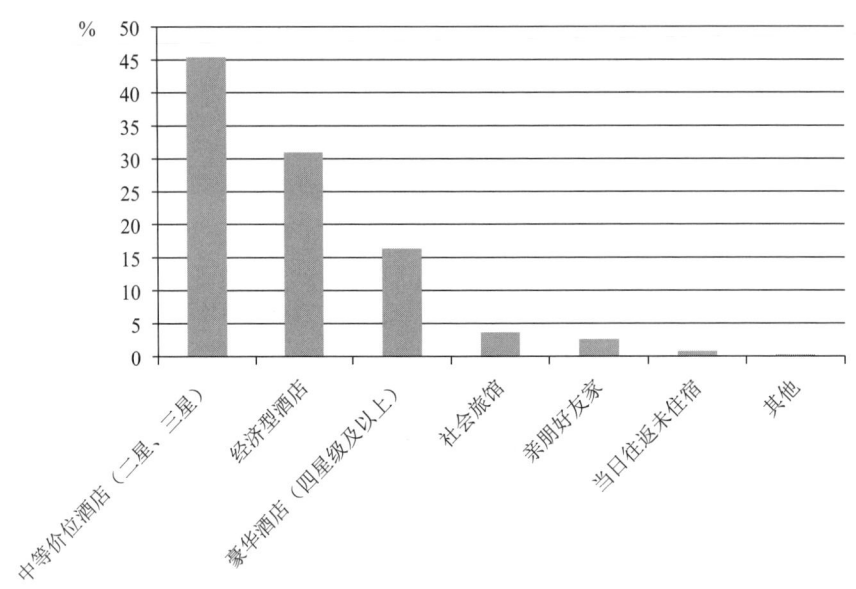

图 3-7　2015 年中国出境游客住宿选择分布

三、出境游游客消费结构特征

花费在 5 000~10 000 元的中国游客比例最高，占总样本的 31.5%。中国游客出境花费的项目主要包括购物、参团费用、餐饮和景点门票，其中，花费最高的项目是购物。

（一）中高端消费群体比例增长

中国出境游客表现出中高端消费特征，单次出境游花费在 10 001 元及以上的受访者占总样本的 60.5%，较 2014 年有明显增长。消费在 5 001~10 000 元的游客最多，占 31.5%。而花费在 5 000 元及以下的受访者仅占 8.0%。

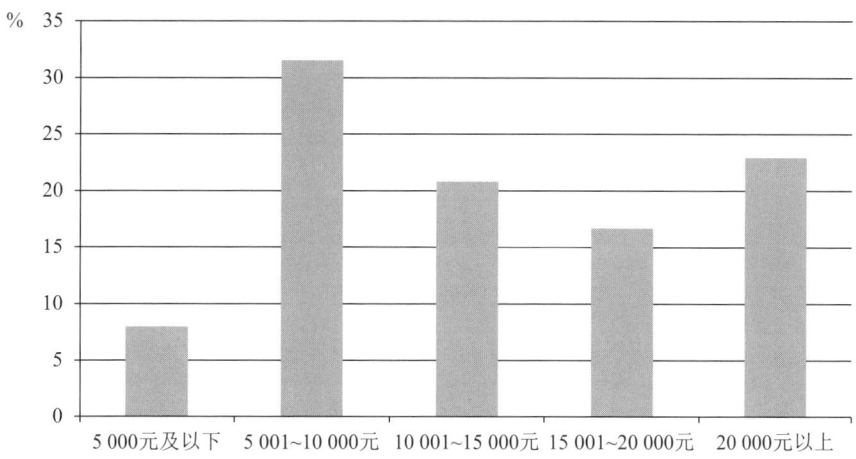

图 3-8 2015 年中国出境游客单次境外出游花费状况

（二）购物依然是境外旅游的最重要项目

选择购物项目的中国出境游客最多，占总样本的 85.9%；选择参团费用的游客占 61.8%；选择餐饮花费的游客占 58.7%。

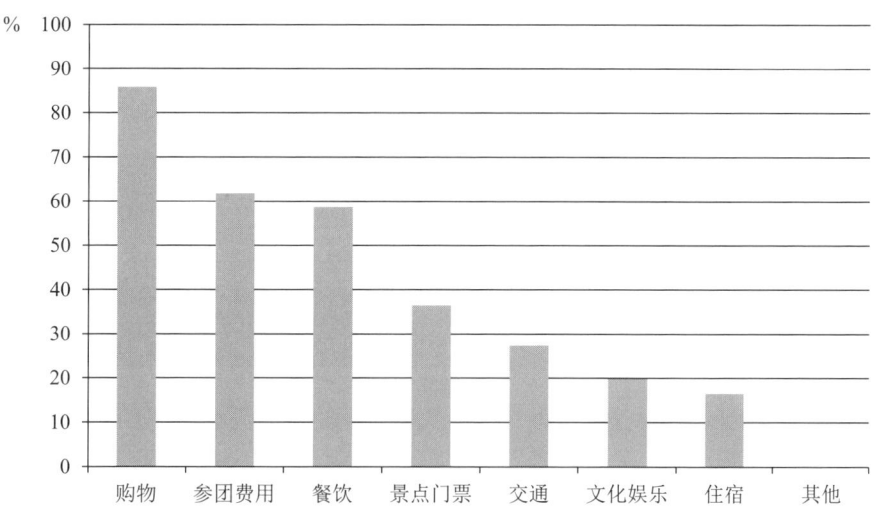

图 3-9 2015 年中国出境游客各消费项目的选择占比

（三）购物和参团费用是境外旅游花费最高的两项

有 42.5% 的中国出境游客认为购物花费最高，其中 40.33% 认为参团费用花费最高，认为其他项目平均花费较高的游客占比均不足 6%，这凸显出中国游客的境外主要花费和花费最多的项目是购物和参团费用。

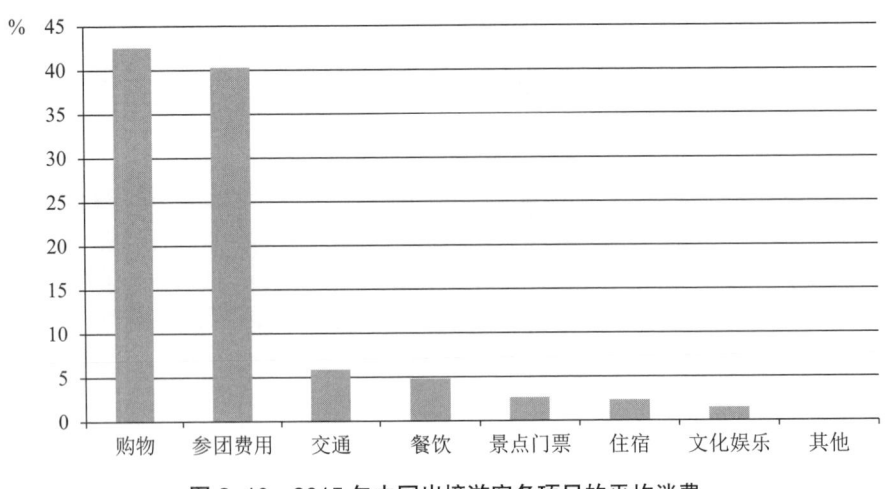

图 3-10 2015 年中国出境游客各项目的平均消费

四、未参团游客出境游游客消费预订渠道

数据统计发现，不论是在航班预订、酒店预订还是安排旅游线路，未参团的中国出境游客大都通过网络预订完成，网络在中国出境游客中的利用愈加频繁。

（一）境外航班预订渠道

在中国出境游客中，有 65.1% 的未参团游客通过网络完成机票的预订和购买，明显多于通过其他渠道购买的游客，如直接去售票点购买（11.4%）、电话预订（9.91%）或单位安排（7.8%）等。

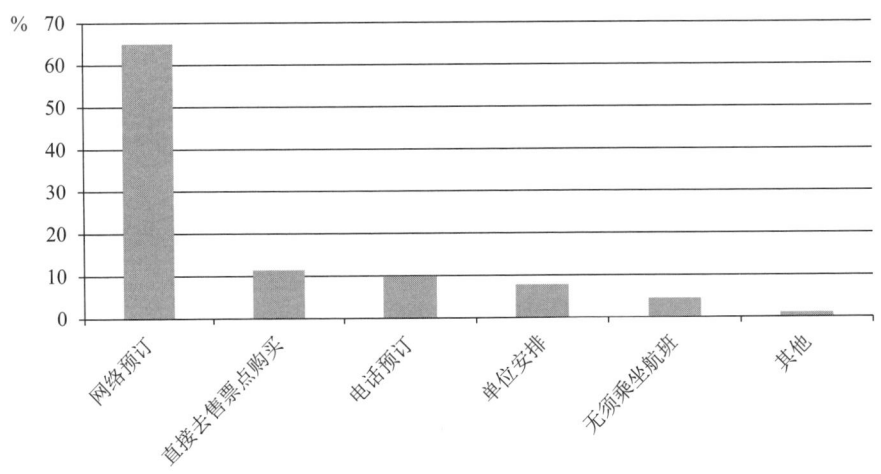

图 3-11 2015 年中国出境游客预订航班的渠道

(二)境外旅游预订酒店的渠道

在中国出境游客中,有56.5%的未参团游客通过网络完成酒店的预订和购买,其次是在当地直接入住(13.5%),而只有不到10%的游客通过其他预订和购买渠道选择住宿设施。

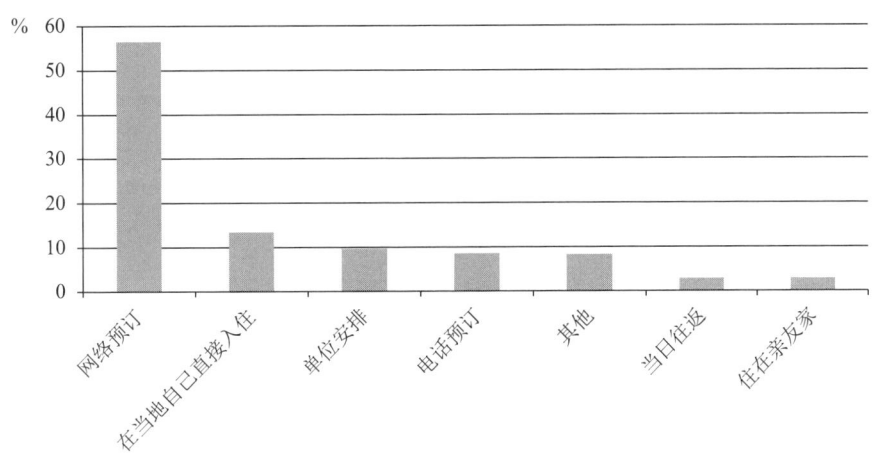

图3-12 2015年中国出境游客预订酒店的渠道

(三)旅游线路信息获取的渠道

在中国出境游客中,有57.7%的未参团游客通过网络查找相关信息完成旅游线路安排。此外,有18.0%的游客通过亲友介绍,15.4%的游客为临时安排,还有8.6%的游客通过单位安排。

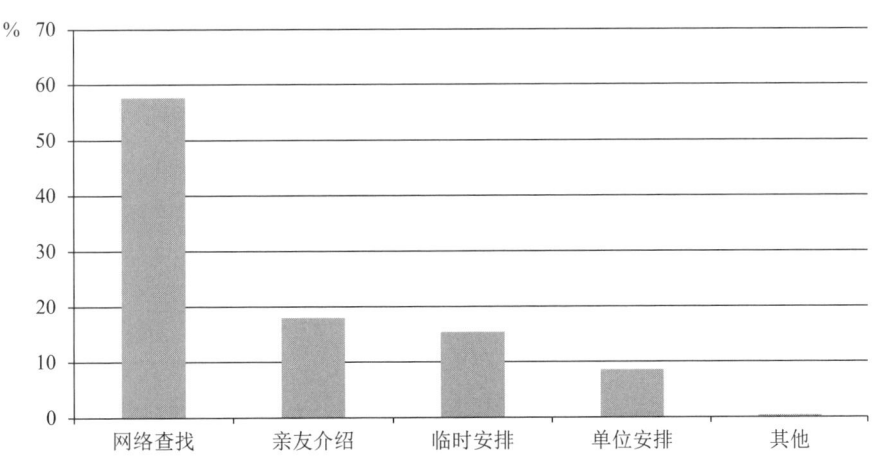

图3-13 2015年中国出境游客安排旅游路线的渠道

（四）境外旅游就餐地选择的渠道

在境外旅游时，未参团的中国游客大都通过"随意遇到"而选择就餐地，这种情况的受访者占总样本的40.4%，另外，通过网络查找选择就餐地的未参团游客占25.0%，通过当地人和亲友介绍就餐的未参团游客分别占20.9%及11.8%。说明对于就餐地的选择，未参团出境游客没有像选择航班、酒店和旅游线路那样依赖于网络查找和订购。

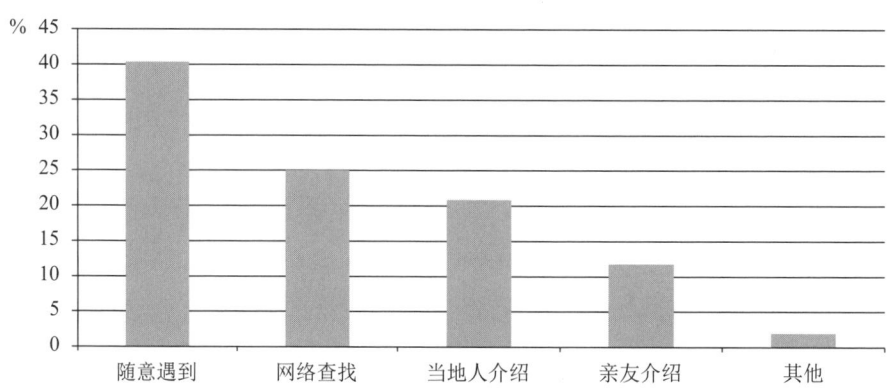

图3-14　2015年中国出境游客就餐地选择的渠道

五、出境游游客未来消费意向

（一）参加旅游团依然是出境旅游的重要选择

70.0%的中国出境游客表示愿意参加旅游团进行出境旅游活动，24.0%的受访者觉得无所谓，仅有6.0%表示不愿意参加出境旅游团。

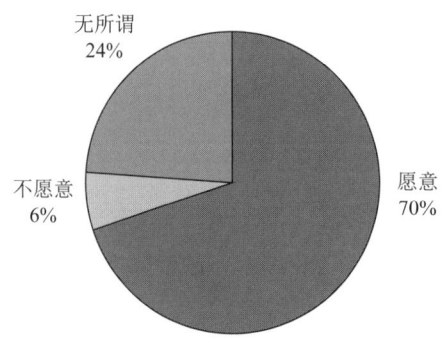

图3-15　2015年中国出境游客对参加旅游团出境旅游的态度

（二）出境游客未来出境主要意向保持稳定，集中在观光游览

从问卷统计结果来看，中国出境游客未来出境主要意向以观光游览为主，选择该选项的受访者占66.0%，意在参与性娱乐活动、探险活动和了解当地居民情况的游客分别占10%左右。

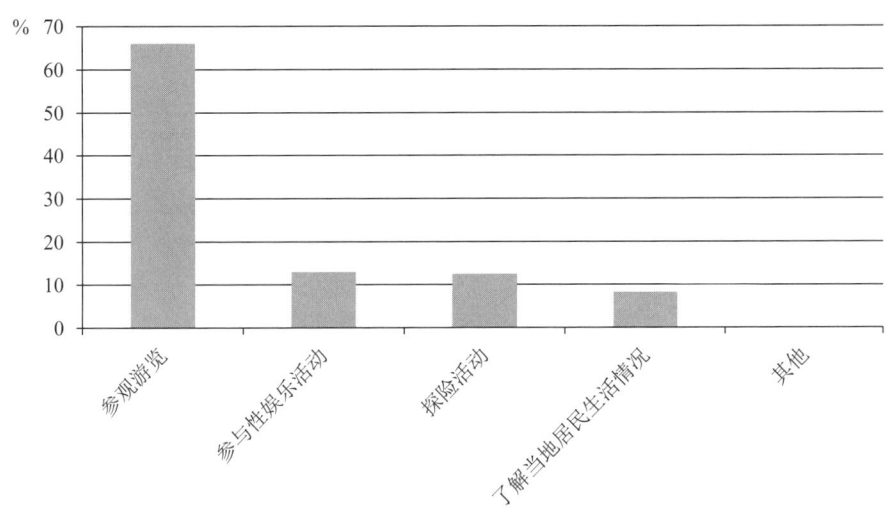

图3-16　2015年中国游客未来出境旅游消费项目意向分布

第二节　中国出境游客对东亚各国的满意度评价

一、日本

（一）游客满意度得分及排名

全年到访日本的中国出境游客的满意度为78.07，在24个抽样国家中排名第9。

（二）问卷调查分析

中国出境游客的问卷满意度平均得分为8.12分，比总体平均分7.94分高0.18分，在被调查的24个国家中排第7名；得分最高的三项是美丽程度、卫生设施和信息化程度，得分分别为8.49、8.45和8.43；得分最低的三项是外方导游、

中文标识、信息和服务和旅游价格,得分分别为7.77、7.72和7.70。

(三)网络评论分析

2015年日本评论调查的中国出境游客满意度指数为80.86,较境外游总体满意度平均值高1.07。各单项满意度皆高于73分,其中,当地居民态度得分最高,为88.99分;满意度最低的是旅游行业管理,为73.13分。

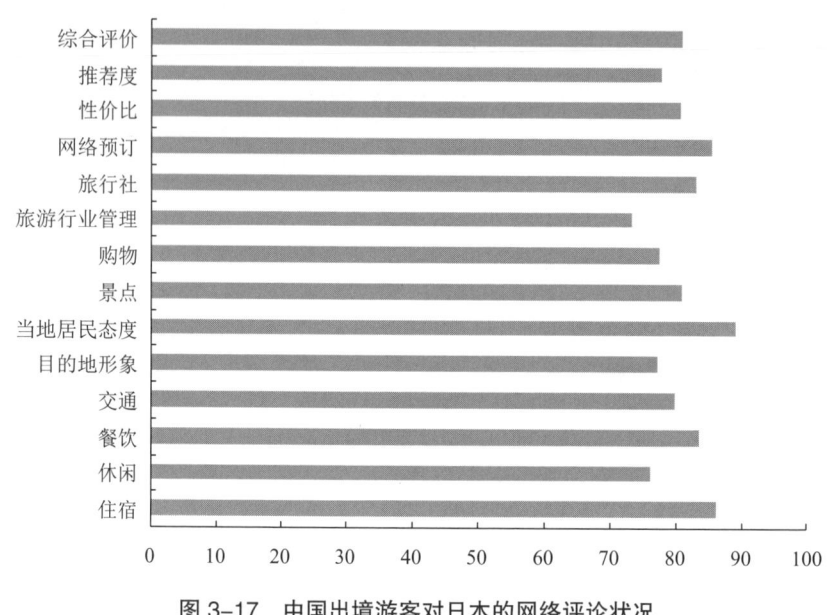

图3-17 中国出境游客对日本的网络评论状况

二、韩国

(一)游客满意度得分及排名

全年到访韩国的中国出境游客的满意度为77.58,在24个抽样国家中排名第11。

(二)问卷调查分析

中国出境游客的问卷满意度平均得分为7.94分,与总体平均分7.94分相同,在被调查的24个国家中排第12名;得分最高的三项是美丽程度、知名度和银行刷卡便利性,得分分别为8.32、8.28和8.21;得分最低的三项是中文标识、信息和服务、农业现代化和工业旅游,得分分别为7.59、7.58和7.56。

（三）网络评论分析

2015年韩国评论调查的中国出境游客满意度指数为81.21，较境外游总体满意度平均值高1.42。各单项满意度皆高于75分，其中，当地居民态度得分最高，为89.39分；满意度最低的是旅游行业管理，为75.90分。

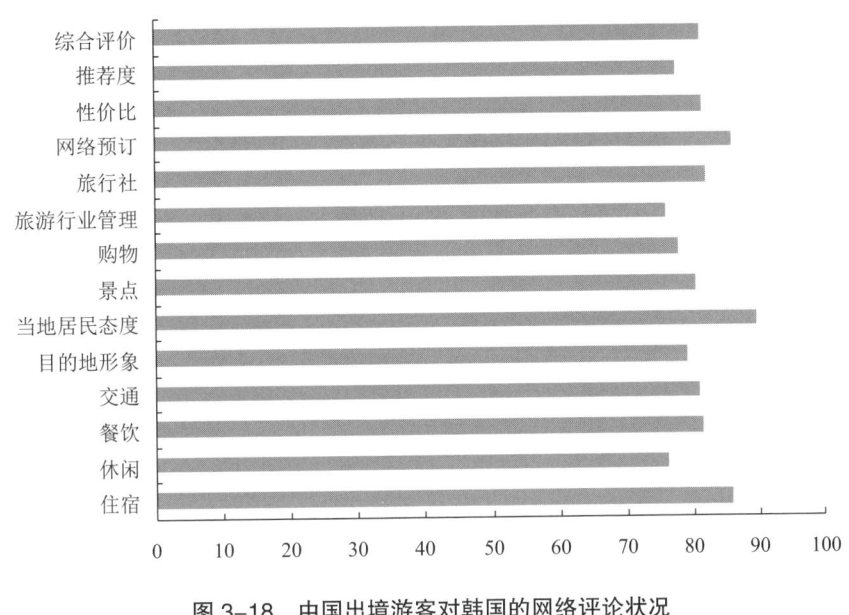

图3-18 中国出境游客对韩国的网络评论状况

三、马来西亚

（一）游客满意度得分及排名

全年到访马来西亚的中国出境游客的满意度为77.01，在24个抽样国家中排名第15。

（二）问卷调查分析

中国出境游客的问卷满意度平均得分为7.94分，与总体平均分7.94分持平，在被调查的24个国家中排第12名；得分最高的三项是自然生态、美丽程度和空气质量，得分分别为8.30、8.29和8.26；得分最低的三项是长途客运、中文标识、信息和服务和工业旅游，得分分别为7.69、7.57和7.55。

（三）网络评论分析

2015年马来西亚评论调查的中国出境游客满意度指数为78.86，较境外游总体满意度平均值低0.93。各单项满意度皆高于73分，其中，当地居民态度得分最高，为89.24分；满意度最低的是旅游行业管理，为73.69分。

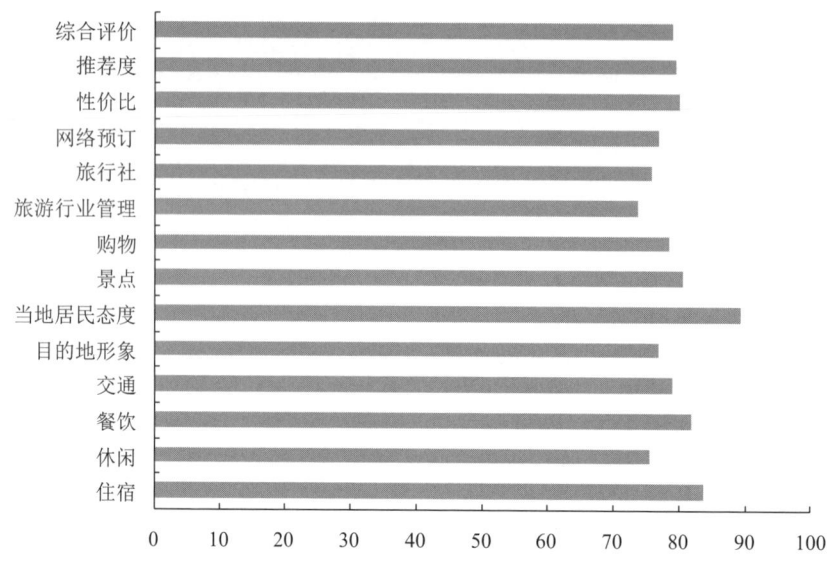

图3-19　中国出境游客对马来西亚的网络评论状况

四、越南

（一）游客满意度得分及排名

全年到访越南的中国出境游客的满意度为74.70，在24个抽样国家中排名第22。

（二）问卷调查分析

中国出境游客的问卷满意度平均得分为7.62分，比总体平均分7.94分低0.32分，在被调查的24个国家中排第22名；得分最高的三项是自然生态、空气质量和园林绿化，得分分别为7.96、7.96和7.93；得分最低的三项是无障碍设施、卫生设施和中文标识、信息和服务，得分分别为7.37、7.34和7.25。

（三）网络评论分析

2015年越南评论调查的中国出境游客满意度指数为80.26，较境外游总体满意度平均值高0.47。各单项满意度皆高于75分，其中，当地居民态度得分最高，为88.70分；满意度最低的是购物和旅游行业管理，分别为75.91、75.01分。

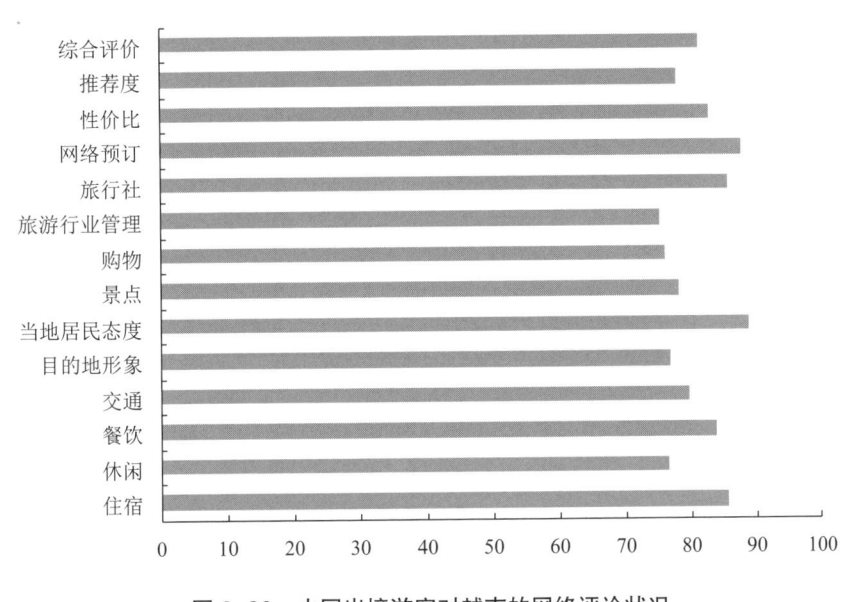

图3-20 中国出境游客对越南的网络评论状况

五、菲律宾

（一）游客满意度得分及排名

全年到访菲律宾的中国出境游客的满意度为75.24，在24个抽样国家中排名第19。

（二）问卷调查分析

中国出境游客的问卷满意度平均得分为7.73分，比总体平均分7.94分低0.21分，在被调查的24个国家中排第18名；得分最高的三项是自然生态、美丽程度和空气质量，得分分别为8.04、8.04和8.03；得分最低的三项是安全感、工业旅游和中文标识、信息和服务，得分分别为7.52、7.50和7.40。

（三）网络评论分析

2015年菲律宾评论调查的中国出境游客满意度指数为79.09，较境外游总体满意度平均值低0.70。各单项满意度皆高于71分，其中，当地居民态度得分最高，为88.33分；满意度最低的是旅游行业管理，为71.57分。

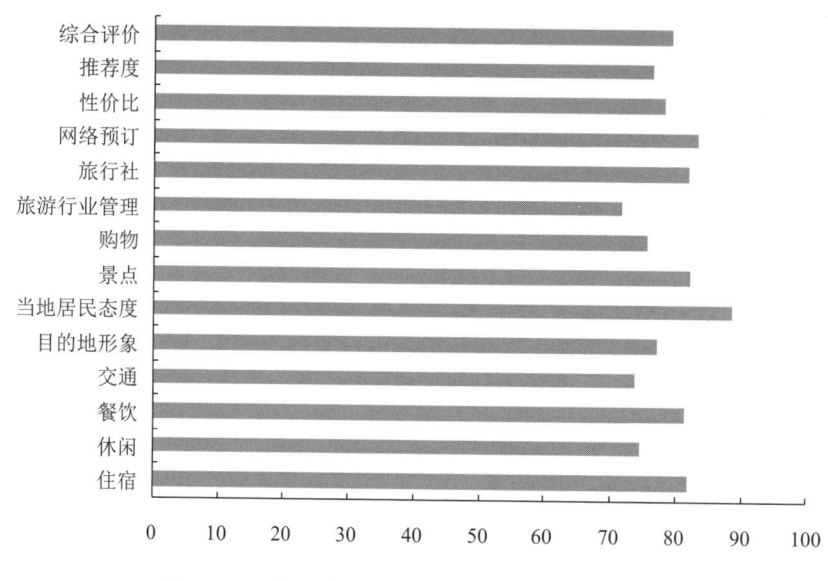

图3-21 中国出境游客对菲律宾的网络评论状况

六、印度尼西亚

（一）游客满意度得分及排名

全年到访印度尼西亚的中国出境游客的满意度为76.80，在24个抽样国家中排名第16。

（二）问卷调查分析

中国出境游客的问卷满意度平均得分为7.71分，比总体平均分7.94分低0.23分，在被调查的24个国家中排第19名；得分最高的三项是空气质量、美丽程度和自然生态，得分分别为8.16、8.10和8.07；得分最低的三项是施工管理、长途客运和中文标识、信息和服务，得分分别为7.44、7.42和7.32。

（三）网络评论分析

2015年印度尼西亚评论调查的中国出境游客满意度指数为80.34，较境外游总体满意度平均值高0.55。各单项满意度皆高于71分，其中，当地居民态度得分最高，为88.77分；满意度最低的是旅行社旅游行业管理，为71.31分。

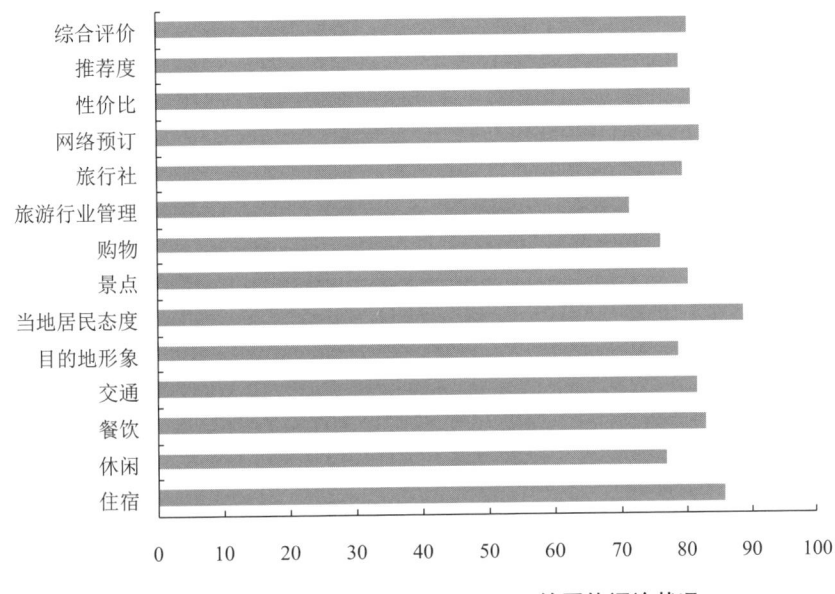

图3-22 中国出境游客对印度尼西亚的网络评论状况

第四章
东亚在中国入境旅游市场中的基础地位与行为特征

第一节 东亚各国来华旅游的市场总量

一、日本

2011—2015年中国接待的入境日本游客数量持续下降，旅华日本游客数量的增长率在2013年大幅下降，2014年增长率开始回升，2015年继续呈下降趋势。2011年接待入境日本游客365.82万人次，同比下降1.96%；2012年接待入境日本游客351.82万人次，同比下降3.83%；2013年接待入境日本游客287.75万人次，同比下降18.21%；2014年接待入境日本游客271.76万人次，同比下降5.60%；2015年接待入境日本游客249.77万人次，同比下降8.10%。就当前的发展趋势来看，预计未来旅华日本市场将继续呈现小幅下降趋势。

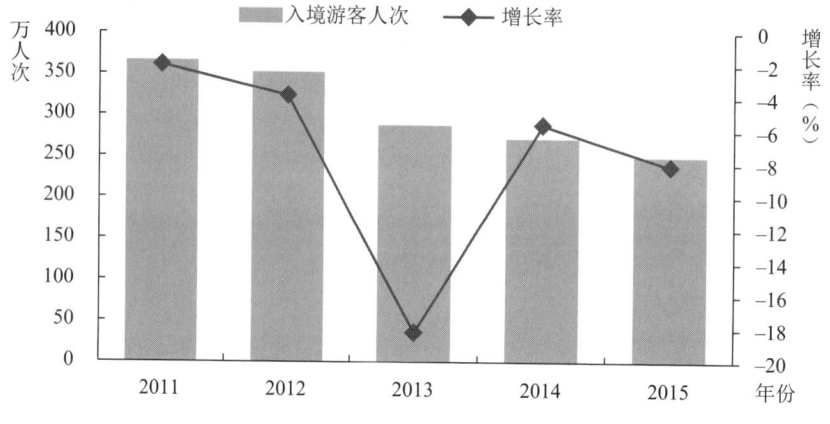

图4-1 2011—2015年日本来华旅游市场总量与增长情况

二、韩国

2011—2015年中国接待的入境韩国游客总量持续波动，旅华韩国游客数量的增长率也随之波动。2011年接待入境韩国游客418.54万人次，同比增长2.67%；2012年接待入境韩国游客406.99万人次，同比下降2.76%；2013年接待入境韩国游客396.90万人次，同比下降2.48%；2014年接待入境韩国游客418.17万人次，同比增长5.36%；2015年接待入境韩国游客444.44万人次，同比增长6.30%。总体上看，旅华韩国游客的数量呈增长趋势，其中2014年有大幅增长，预计未来旅华韩国游客的规模将稳定增长。

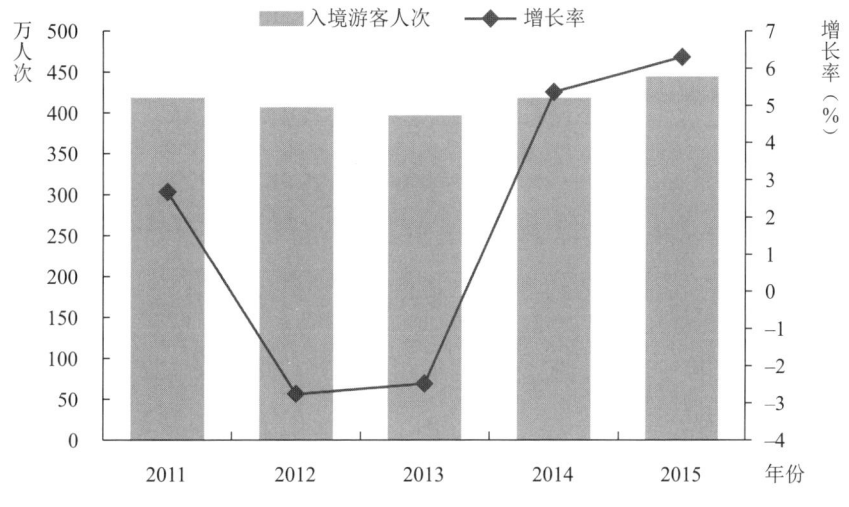

图4-2　2011—2015年韩国来华旅游市场总量与增长情况

三、越南

2011—2015年中国接待的入境越南游客总量不断攀升，旅华越南游客数量的增长率也呈持续增长趋势。2011年接待入境越南游客100.65万人次，同比增长9.40%；2012年接待入境越南游客113.72万人次，同比增长12.99%；2013年接待入境越南游客136.54万人次，同比增长20.07%；2014年接待入境越南游客170.94万人次，同比增长25.19%；2015年接待入境越南游客216.08万人次，同比增长26.41%。就当前的发展趋势来看，预计未来旅华越南市场将继续稳步增长。

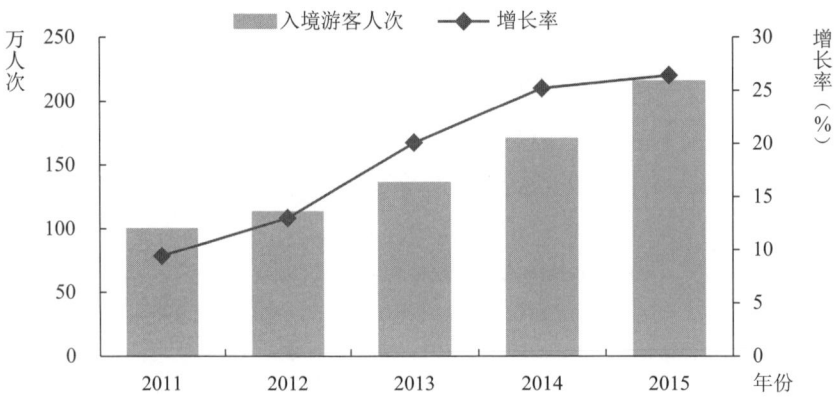

图 4-3　2011—2015 越南来华旅游市场规模与增长情况

四、马来西亚

2011—2015 年中国接待的入境马来西亚游客总量不断下降，旅华马来西亚游客数量的增长率在 2015 年呈增长趋势。2011 年接待入境马来西亚游客 124.51 万人次，同比下降 0.01%；2012 年接待入境马来西亚游客 123.55 万人次，同比下降 0.77%；2013 年接待入境马来西亚游客 120.65 万人次，同比下降 2.35%；2014 年接待入境马来西亚游客 112.96 万人次，同比下降 6.37%；2015 年接待入境马来西亚游客 107.55 万人次，同比下降 4.79%。预计未来旅华越南市场有望回升。

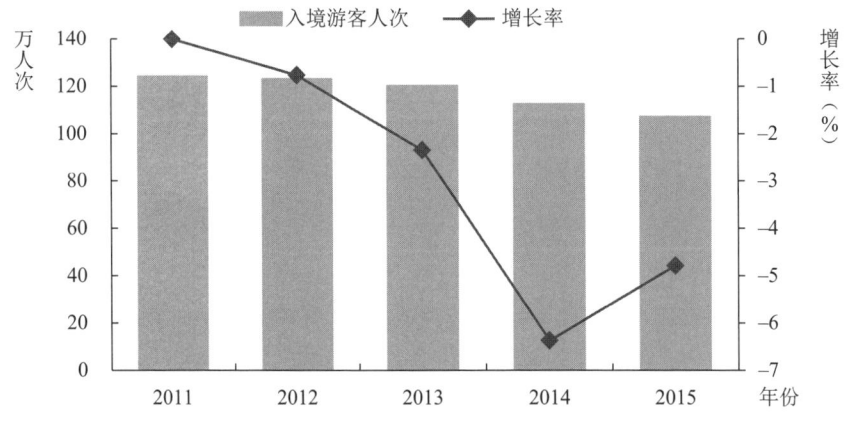

图 4-4　2011—2015 年马来西亚来华旅游市场规模与增长情况

五、菲律宾

2011—2015年中国接待的入境菲律宾游客总量不断波动，旅华菲律宾游客数量的增长率在2015年之前一直呈现下降趋势，2015年开始回升。2011年接待入境菲律宾游客89.34万人次，同比增长7.97%；2012年接待入境菲律宾游客96.2万人次，同比增长7.57%；2013年接待入境菲律宾游客99.67万人次，同比增长3.61%；2014年接待入境菲律宾游客96.79万人次，同比下降2.89%；2015年接待入境菲律宾游客100.4万人次，同比增长3.73%。就当前的发展趋势来看预计未来旅华菲律宾游客的人次规模有望增加。

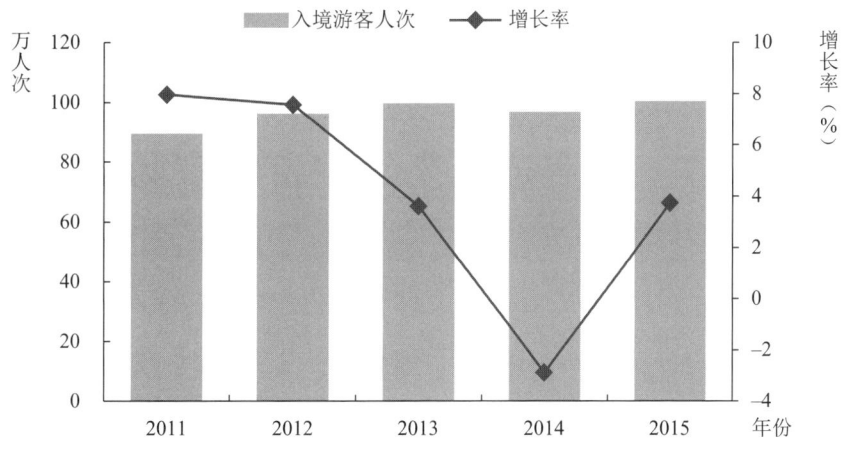

图4-5 2011—2015年菲律宾来华旅游市场规模与增长情况

六、印度尼西亚

2011—2015年中国接待的印度尼西亚游客总量在整体上呈下降趋势，旅华印度尼西亚游客数量的增长率在2015年之前持续下降，2015年开始有小幅回升。2011年接待入境印度尼西亚游客60.87万人次，同比增长6.15%；2012年接待入境印度尼西亚游客62.2万人次，同比增长2.18%；2013年接待入境印度尼西亚游客60.53万人次，同比下降2.68%；2014年接待入境印度尼西亚游客56.69万人次，同比下降6.34%；2015年接待入境印度尼西亚游客54.48万人次，同比下降 3.90%。预计未来旅华印度尼西亚游客的人次规模有望逐步回升。

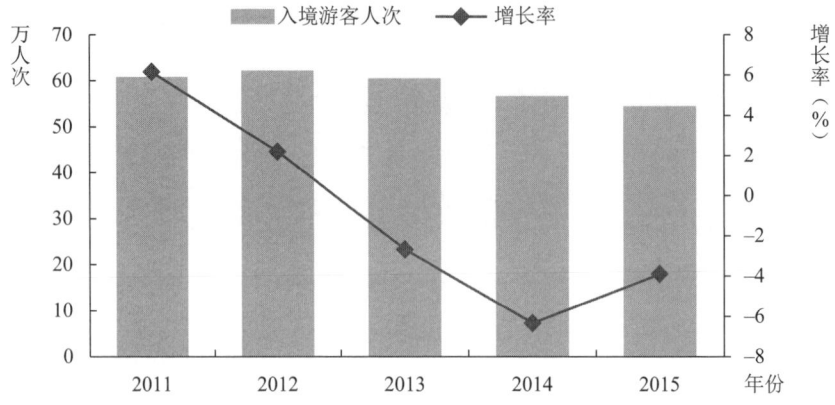

图 4-6　2011—2015 年印度尼西亚来华旅游市场规模与增长情况

第二节　东亚各国来华旅游的市场结构

一、日本

（一）旅华日本游客入境的交通方式分析

2015 年旅华日本游客中，59.92% 乘坐飞机入境，16.18% 徒步入境，12.50% 乘坐汽车入境，9.64% 乘坐船舶入境，1.75% 乘坐火车入境。

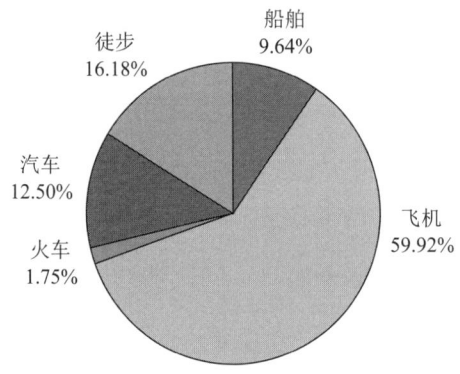

图 4-7　2015 年旅华日本游客进入中国的交通方式

(二)旅华日本游客的年龄结构分析

2015年旅华日本游客中,14岁以下占3.74%,15~24岁占2.98%,25~44岁占38.43%,45~64岁占46.31%,65岁以上占8.54%。

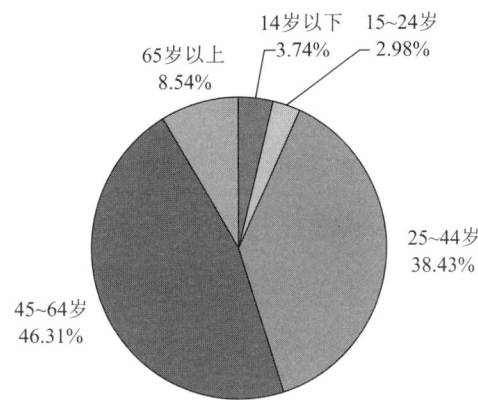

图4-8 2015年旅华日本游客的年龄结构状况

(三)旅华日本游客的性别结构分析

2015年旅华日本游客中,79.89%为男性,20.11%为女性。

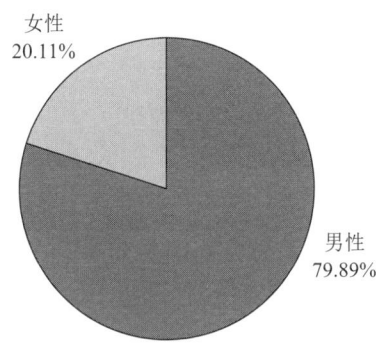

图4-9 2015年旅华日本游客的性别结构状况

(四)旅华日本游客的旅游目的结构分析

2015年,旅华日本游客中,15.73%持观光休闲目的,31.15%持会议/商务目的,4.69%为服务员工,2.14%持探亲访友目的,46.29%持其他目的。

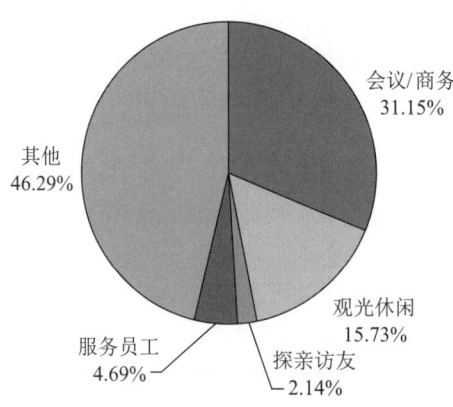

图 4-10　2015 年旅华日本游客的旅游目的结构状况

二、韩国

（一）旅华韩国游客入境的交通方式分析

2015 年旅华韩国游客中，84.96% 乘坐飞机入境，4.98% 徒步入境，7.43% 乘坐船舶入境，2.22% 乘坐汽车入境，0.41% 乘坐火车入境。

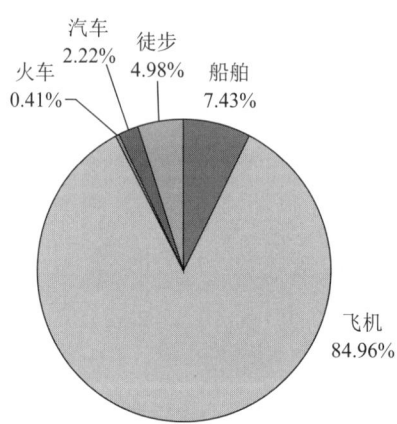

图 4-11　2015 年旅华韩国游客进入中国的交通方式

（二）旅华韩国游客的年龄结构分析

2015 年旅华韩国游客中，14 岁以下占 3.86%，15~24 岁占 6.75%，25~44 岁占 37.66%，45~64 岁占 43.35%，65 岁以上占 8.38%。

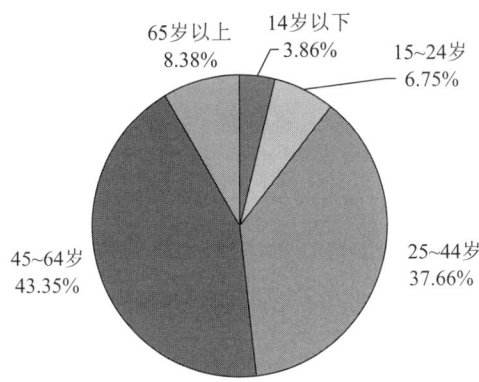

图 4-12　2015 年旅华韩国游客的年龄结构状况

（三）旅华韩国游客的性别结构分析

2015 年，旅华韩国游客中，61.42% 为男性，38.58% 为女性。

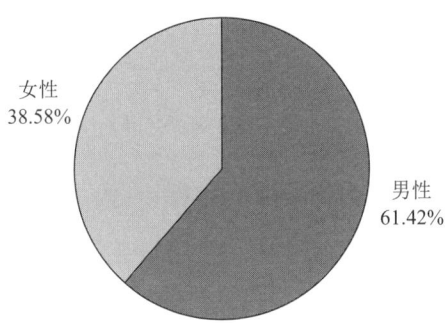

图 4-13　2015 年旅华韩国游客的性别结构状况

（四）旅华韩国游客的旅游目的结构分析

2015 年旅华韩国游客中，45.50% 持观光休闲目的，24.88% 持会议/商务目的，9.15% 为服务员工，0.77% 持探亲访友目的，19.70% 持其他目的。

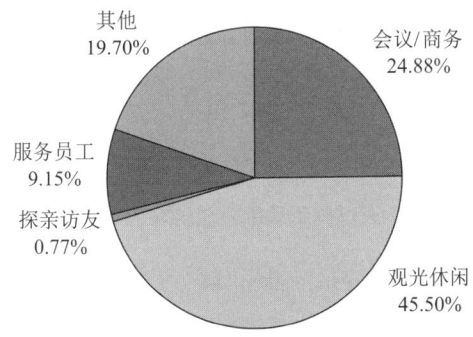

图 4-14　2015 年旅华韩国游客的旅游目的结构状况

三、马来西亚

（一）旅华马来西亚游客入境的交通方式分析

2015年旅华马来西亚游客中，74.16%乘坐飞机入境，15.50%徒步入境，3.69%乘坐船舶入境，5.71%乘坐汽车入境，0.94%乘坐火车入境。

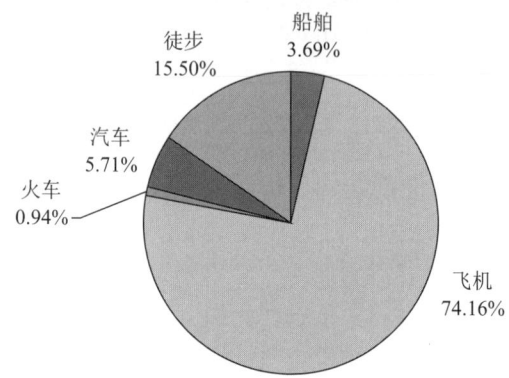

图4-15　2015年旅华马来西亚游客进入中国的交通方式

（二）旅华马来西亚游客的年龄结构分析

2015年旅华马来西亚游客中，14岁以下占3.90%，15~24岁占7.89%，25~44岁占45.57%，45~64岁占36.55%，65岁以上占6.08%。

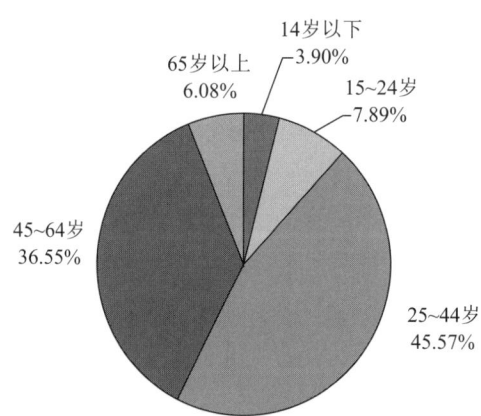

图4-16　2015年旅华马来西亚游客的年龄结构状况

（三）旅华马来西亚游客的性别结构分析

2015年旅华马来西亚游客中，61.65%为男性，38.35%为女性。

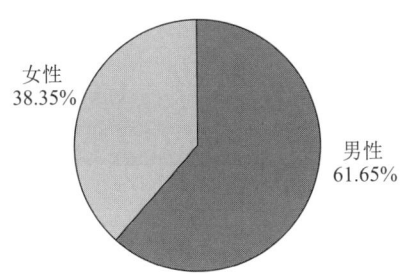

图 4-17　2015 年旅华马来西亚游客的性别结构状况

（四）旅华马来西亚游客的旅游目的结构分析

2015 年，旅华马来西亚游客中，59.69% 持观光休闲目的，14.71% 持会议/商务目的，8.90% 为服务员工，1.29% 持探亲访友目的，15.41% 持其他目的。

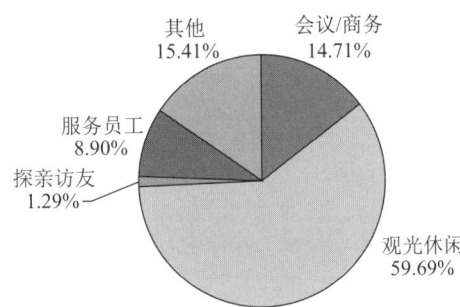

图 4-18　2015 年旅华马来西亚游客的旅游目的结构状况

四、菲律宾

（一）旅华菲律宾游客入境的交通方式分析

2015 年旅华菲律宾游客中，20.62% 乘坐飞机入境，10.04% 徒步入境，65.06% 乘坐船舶入境，3.63% 乘坐汽车入境，0.66% 乘坐火车入境。

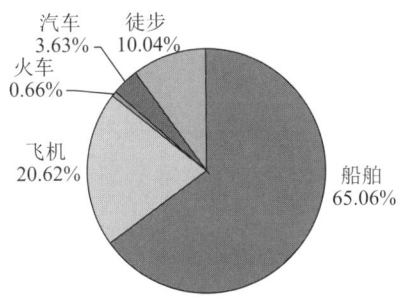

图 4-19　2015 年旅华菲律宾游客进入中国的交通方式

（二）旅华菲律宾游客的年龄结构分析

2015年旅华菲律宾游客中，14岁以下占1.34%，15~24岁占7.19%，25~44岁占64.10%，45~64岁占25.78%，65岁以上占1.58%。

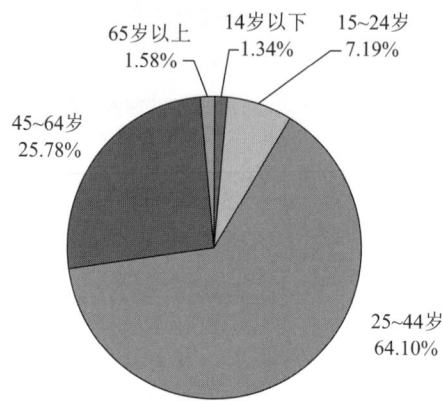

图4-20　2015年旅华菲律宾游客的年龄结构状况

（三）旅华菲律宾游客的性别结构分析

2015年旅华菲律宾游客中，79.17%为男性，20.83%为女性。

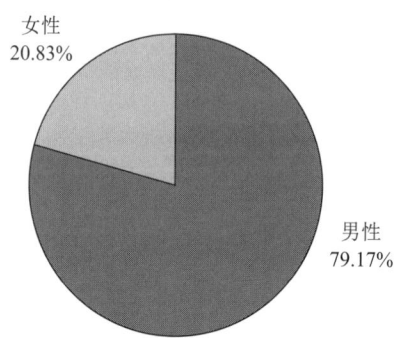

图4-21　2015年旅华菲律宾游客的性别结构状况

（四）旅华菲律宾游客的旅游目的结构分析

2015年旅华菲律宾游客中，19.26%持观光休闲目的，3.21%持会议/商务目的，67.41%为服务员工，0.27%持探亲访友目的，9.85%持其他目的。

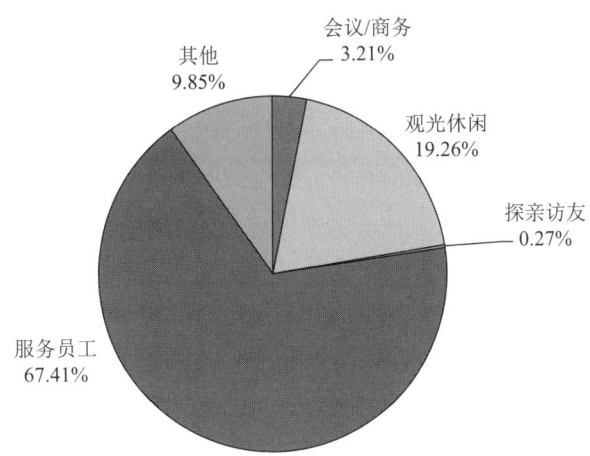

图 4-22　2015 年旅华菲律宾游客的旅游目的结构状况

五、印度尼西亚

（一）旅华印度尼西亚游客入境的交通方式分析

2015 年旅华印度尼西亚游客中，43.60% 乘坐飞机入境，19.31% 徒步入境，25.21% 乘坐船舶入境，10.04% 乘坐汽车入境，1.84% 乘坐火车入境。

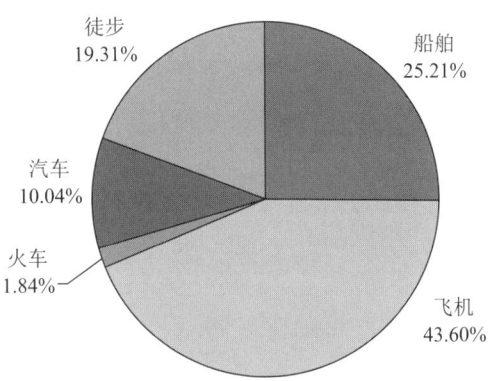

图 4-23　2015 年旅华印度尼西亚游客进入中国的交通方式

（二）旅华印度尼西亚游客的年龄结构分析

2015 年旅华印度尼西亚游客中，14 岁以下占 3.05%，15~24 岁占 10.87%，25~44 岁占 52.29%，45~64 岁占 27.46%，65 岁以上占 6.33%。

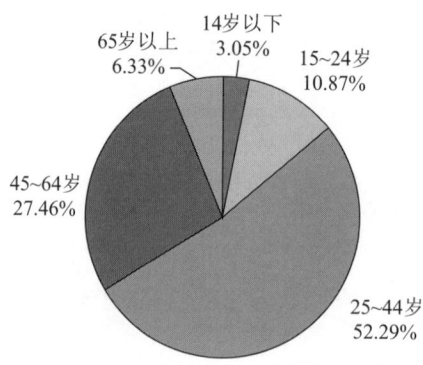

图 4-24　2015 年旅华印度尼西亚游客的年龄结构状况

（三）旅华印度尼西亚游客的性别结构分析

2015 年旅华印度尼西亚游客中，57.30% 为男性，42.70% 为女性。

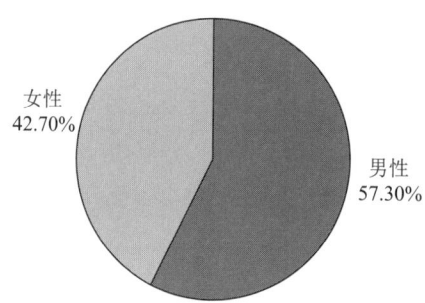

图 4-25　2015 年旅华印度尼西亚游客的性别结构状况

（四）旅华印度尼西亚游客的旅游目的结构分析

2015 年，旅华印度尼西亚游客中，57.42% 持观光休闲目的，5.34% 持会议/商务目的，26.69% 为服务员工，0.68% 持探亲访友目的，9.87% 持其他目的。

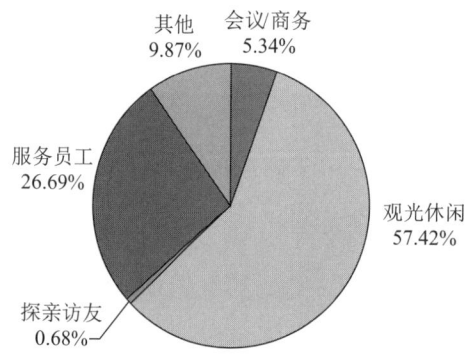

图 4-26　2015 年旅华印度尼西亚游客的旅游目的结构状况

第三节　中国入境旅游市场行为调查

一、入境游客的消费决策影响特征

调查结果[①]显示，入境游客中首次到访中国的游客明显多于多次到访中国的游客；从入境游客出游目的来看，了解中国特色文化以及游览观光仍是主要的旅华目的。

（一）超过半数的游客是第一次来中国

旅华游客中，58.19%的游客是第一次到中国旅游。

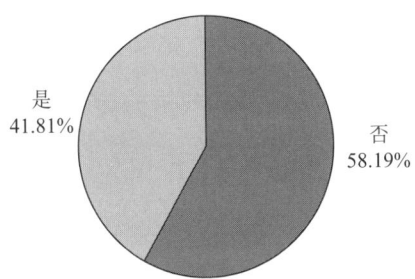

图4-27　2015年受访入境游客出游频率

（二）中国特色文化和游览观光最吸引游客

旅华游客中，主要的旅游目的是：了解中国特色文化（55.56%）、游览观光（28.24%）、休闲度假（5.09%）、商务（3.61%）。

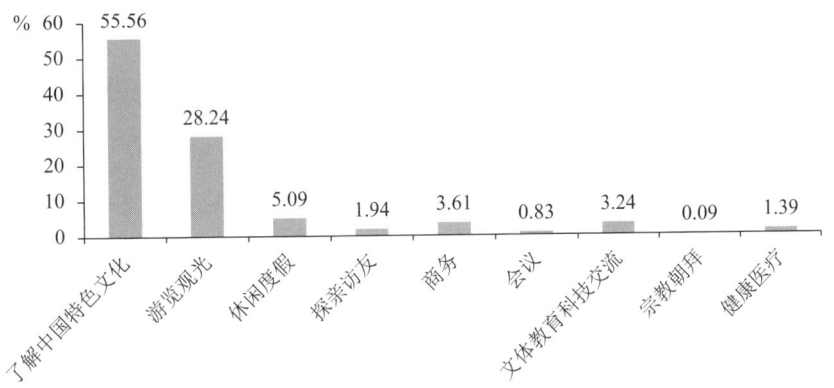

图4-28　2015年受访入境游客旅游目的

---

① 为2015年调查结果。

二、入境游客的消费决策特征

从调查结果来看,亲朋好友介绍是目前旅华入境游客最主要的信息获取渠道,有20.49%的游客出游前会受到亲朋好友介绍的影响;出游前入境游客多会了解特色文化娱乐活动、旅游购物环境情况、旅游交通及天气等生活信息;在选择目的地以及旅游景点时,旅行费用上升为游客最为关注的问题,其次是旅游地交通,旅行安全和休闲的环境也是影响入境游客目的地选择的因素;在出游伴侣的选择方面,约有34.58%的入境游客选择和好友结伴出游,其次有33.39%的入境游客选择和家人一起出游;入境游客主要的游览项目集中在山水风光、文化艺术、美食烹调,所占比例分别为16.75%、15.08%、13.88%;在景点数量的选择方面,27.32%的入境游客参观游览了3~5个旅游景点,具有最高的代表性;在华停留时长方面,30.26%的入境游客在华停留8~15天,最具代表性;在住宿选择方面经济型酒店超越中等价位酒店,成为入境游客的首选项。

(一)亲友介绍和到户外广告是最主要的信息来源

旅华游客中,主要的信息搜索渠道是:亲朋好友介绍(20.49%)、户外广告(15.75%)、网站/BBS/论坛(13.19%)、电视/广播(9.72%)等。

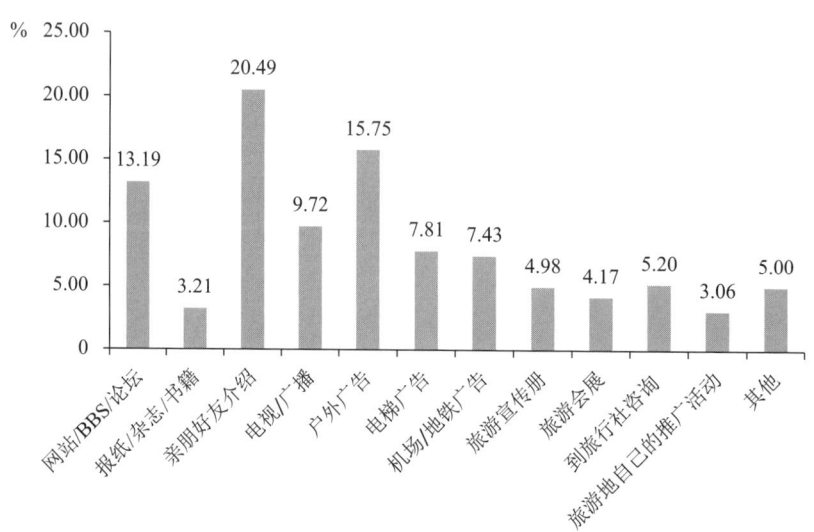

图4-29 2015年受访入境游客旅游信息获取渠道

（二）特色文化娱乐活动、旅游购物环境情况、旅游交通及天气等生活信息最受游客关注

旅华游客中，主要的信息搜索内容是：特色文化娱乐活动（19.30%）、旅游购物环境情况（15.71%）、旅游交通/天气等生活信息（14.46%）、旅游价格（13.73%）、旅游产品和服务介绍（12.42%）等。

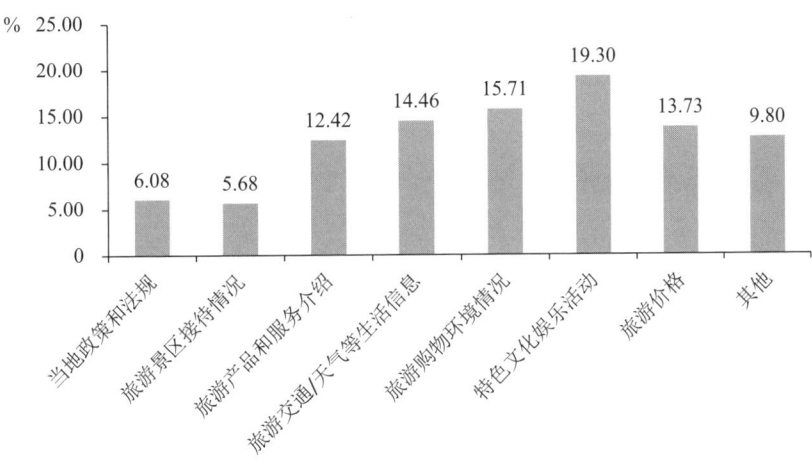

图 4-30　2015 年受访入境游客信息搜索内容

（三）旅行费用、旅游地交通对目的地选择最具影响

旅华游客中，目的地选择的主要影响因素是：旅行费用（15.44%）、旅游地交通（15.12%）、旅行安全（9.51%）、休闲的环境（7.93%）等。

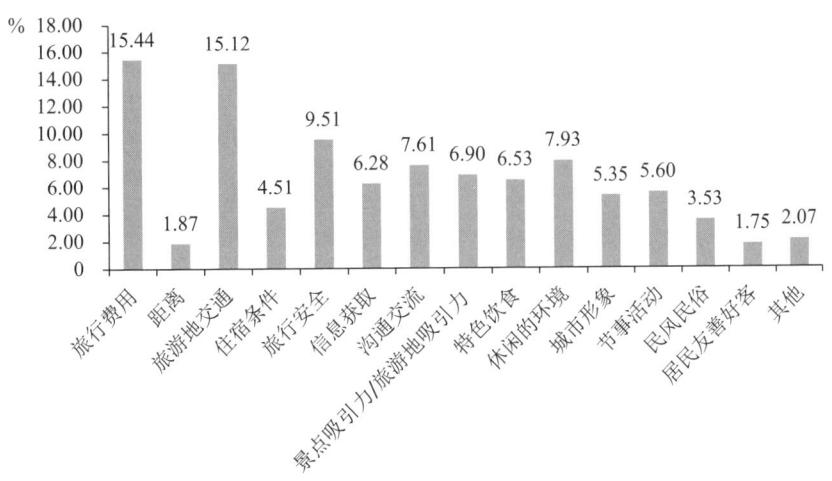

图 4-31　2015 年受访入境游客线路选择影响因素

（四）与好友、家人结伴出游最为常见

旅华游客中，旅游伴侣主要是：和好友结伴出游（34.58%）、和家人一起出游（33.39%）、独自出游（12.81%），公司、班级、社团等集体出游（10.10%），商务活动/会议培训旅游（3.81%）等。

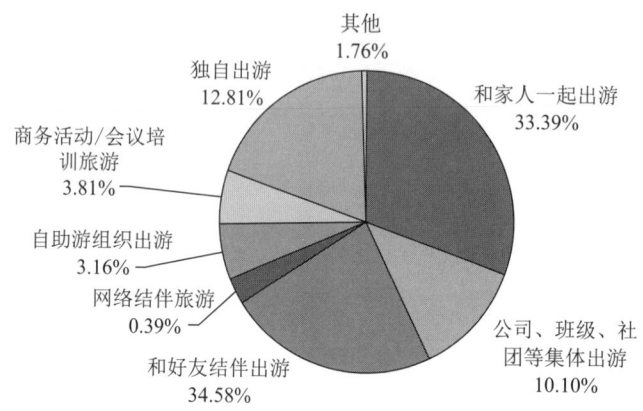

图 4-32　2015 年受访入境游客出游伴侣选择

（五）山水风光、文化艺术、美食烹调是游客最主要的游览项目

旅华游客中，主要的游览项目是：山水风光（16.75%）、文化艺术（15.08%）、美食烹调（13.88%）、医疗保健（13.59%）等。

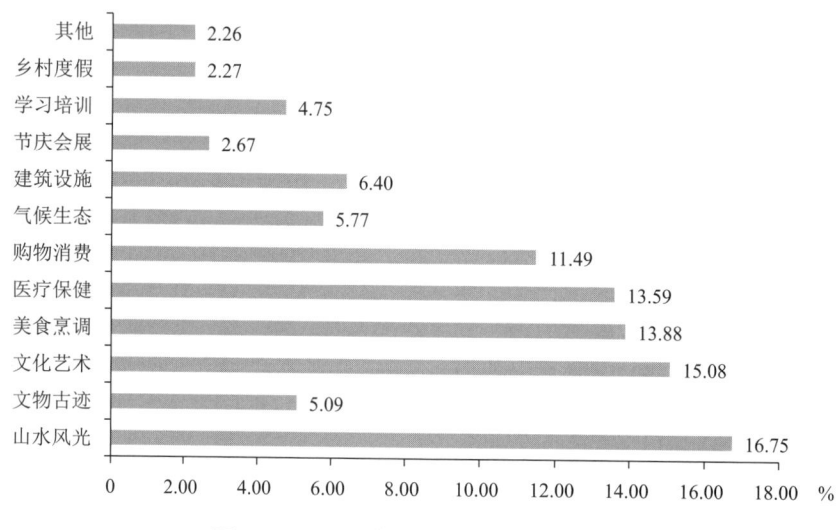

图 4-33　2015 年受访入境游客游览项目

（六）3~5 个景点的线路设计最受游客欢迎

旅华游客中，景点数量的选择集中在 3~9 个，其中以 3~5 个景点的线路设计（27.32%）居多，其次是 6~9 个景点的线路设计（25.79%）。

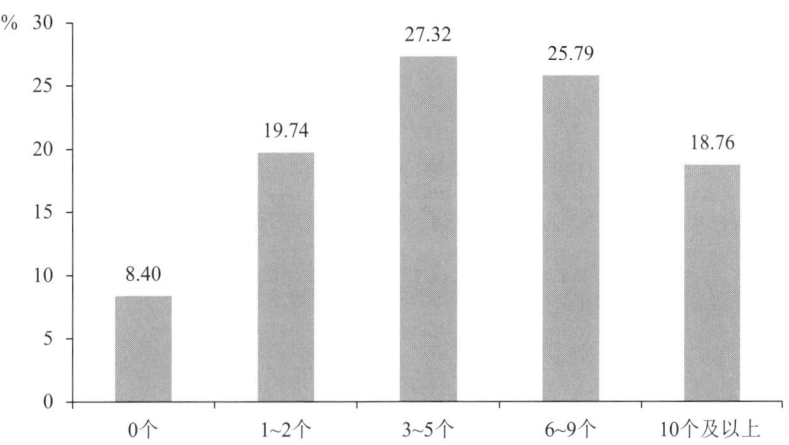

图 4-34　2015 年受访入境游客参观景点数

（七）8~15 天的停留时间最为普遍

旅华游客中，旅游时长的选择以 8~15 天（30.26%）、4~7 天（29.77%）居多。

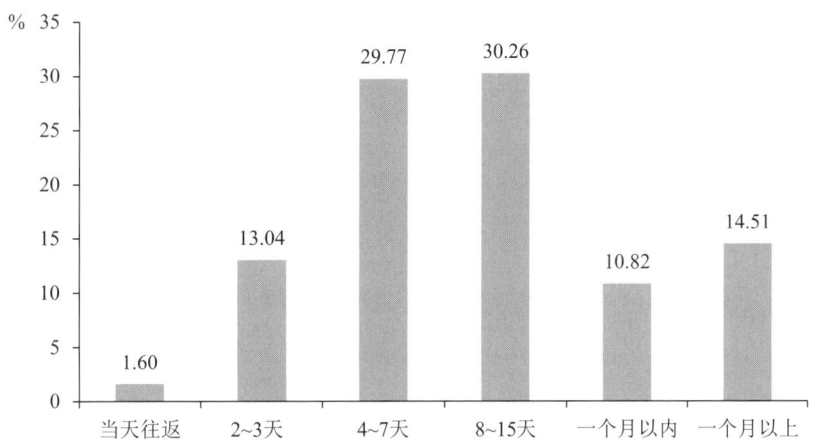

图 4-35　2015 年受访入境游客旅游停留时间

（八）经济型酒店最受游客青睐

旅华游客更倾向于选择经济型酒店（35.69%）、中等价位酒店（二星、三星酒店及同级酒店）（25.08%）、豪华酒店（22.88%）。

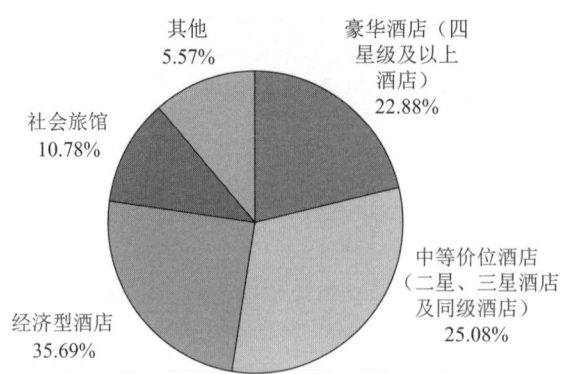

图 4-36 2015 年受访入境游客住宿选择

三、入境游客的消费结构特征

从调查结果来看，旅华游客人均消费呈现正态分布，中间大，两头小。超过 60% 的入境游客消费集中在 1 001 美元到 5 000 美元之间，另有 14.82% 的入境游客消费 501 美元到 1 000 美元，有 14.03% 的入境游客消费不足 500 美元，消费超过 5 000 美元的有 9.38%；从消费项目来看，22.88% 游客表示旅游交通是其最大的消费项目，其次是购物消费，占总消费支出的 20.94%。

（一）中等消费群体比例过半

旅华游客中，人均花费的主要分布区间是 1 001~2 000 美元（27.48%）、2 001~3 000 美元（18.81%）、3 001~5 000 美元（15.51%）。

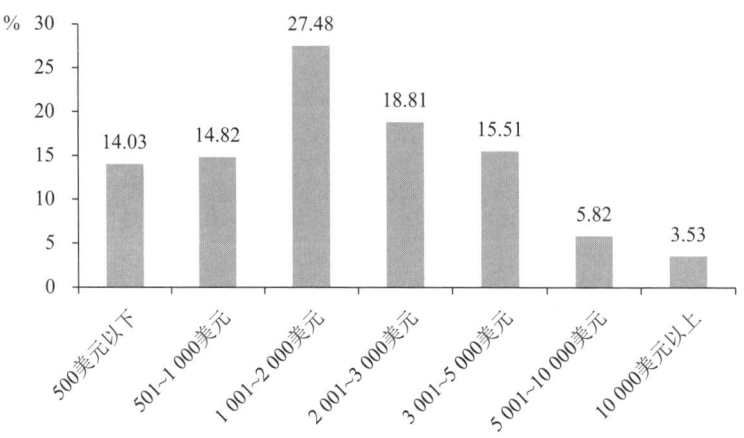

图 4-37 2015 年受访入境游客人均消费

（二）交通和购物支出占比最高

旅华游客中，花费最高的项目依次是交通（22.88%）、购物（20.94%）、餐饮（20.70%）、住宿（11.86%）。

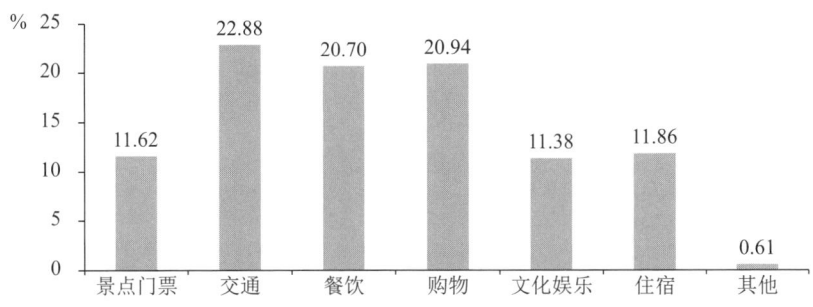

图 4-38　2015 年受访入境游客花费最高项目

四、入境游客的消费评价

调查结果显示，旅华游客对各方面的评价都较好。无论目的地总体形象、城市建设、城市管理、公共行业服务还是窗口服务，游客对其评价均值基本皆在 8 分以上。但各部分也有各自短板，如城市建设中的空气质量，公共行业服务中的手机信号覆盖、互联网覆盖，窗口服务中的交通、餐饮服务，其得分分别为 8.17、8.28、8.36、8.17、8.30，低于平均水平。

（一）信息化程度和开放度最受游客肯定

旅华游客对旅游目的地各项评价总体较高，其中信息化程度和开放度最受游客肯定，其得分分别为 8.90 和 8.87。

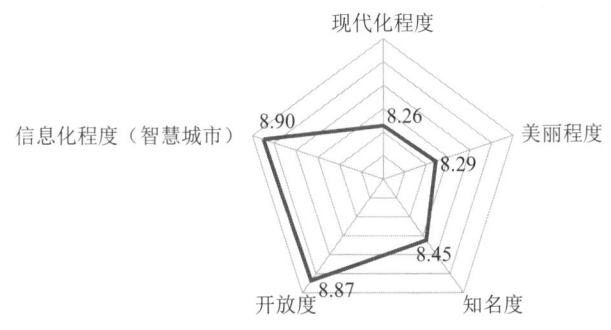

图 4-39　2015 年受访入境游客对我国旅游目的地的总体评价

（二）空气质量、卫生设施评价较低

旅华游客对旅游目的地的空气质量、卫生设施评价分别为 8.17 分和 8.21 分，低于平均水平。

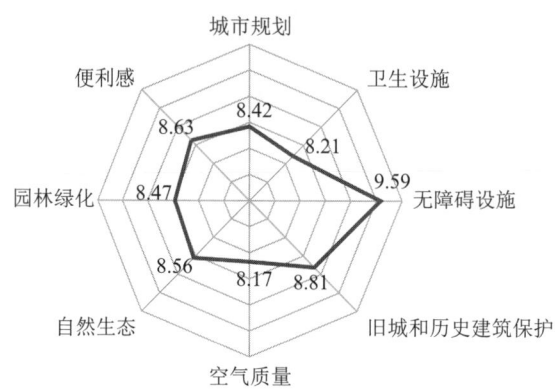

图 4-40　2015 年受访入境游客对我国旅游目的地城市建设评价

（三）应急救援系统获点赞，安全感评价较低

旅华游客对旅游目的地城市管理各项评价具有差异性，其中应急救援系统（卫生系统、天气预报）得分最高，为 9.59 分，安全感（安全及急救信息）得分最低，为 8.27 分。

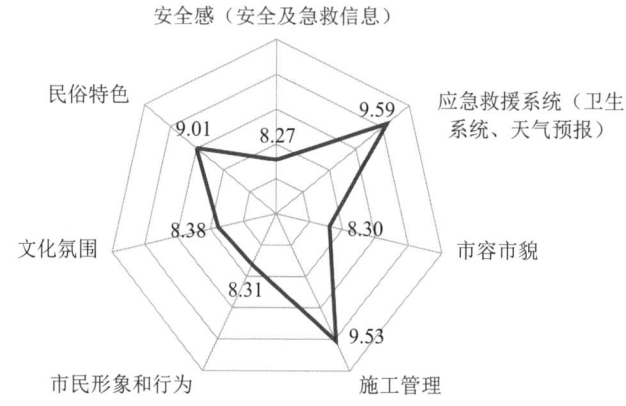

图 4-41　2015 年受访入境游客对我国旅游目的地城市管理评价

（四）手机信号覆盖、互联网覆盖的评价较低

旅华游客对手机信号覆盖、互联网覆盖的评价较低，分别为 8.28 分和 8.36 分。

第四章 东亚在中国入境旅游市场中的基础地位与行为特征
Chapter 4 Basic Status and Behavioral Characteristics of East Asia on Chinese Inbound Tourism Market

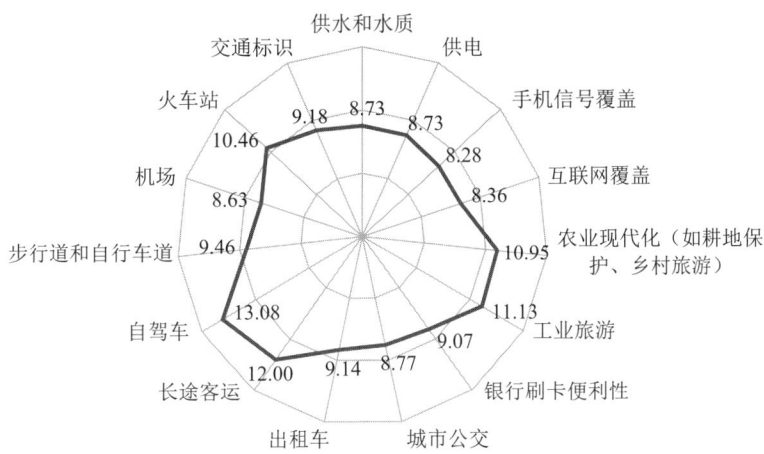

图 4-42 2015 年受访入境游客对我国旅游目的地公共行业服务的评价

（五）交通、餐饮服务的评价不乐观

旅华游客对交通、餐饮的服务评价较低，分别为 8.17 分和 8.30 分。

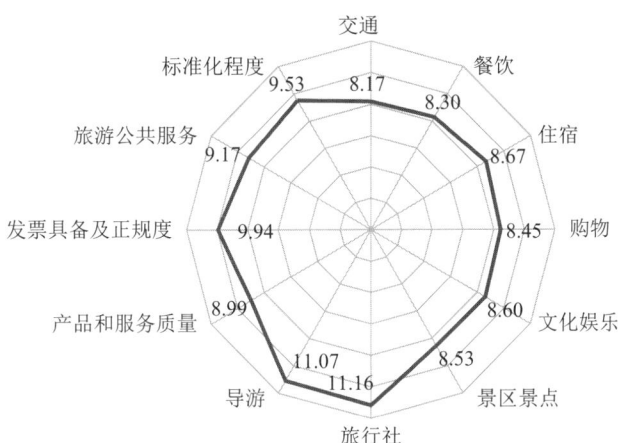

图 4-43 2015 年受访入境游客对我国旅游目的地窗口服务的评价

71

第五章
共建东亚国际旅游合作的美好明天

第一节　东亚国际旅游合作的前景展望

东亚旅游合作的发展走势，除受世界经济全球化、区域化的大环境的影响外，也与地缘关系上的相连性、相近性，东亚国家自然、人文等旅游资源的丰富性、互补性，以及东亚国家政府对旅游发展与合作的支持都有很大的关系。

一、东亚国家地缘和认知上的区域一体优势突出

东南亚十国中有 7 个属于半岛国家，中南半岛上的国家多相互接壤。除新加坡外，其他国家至少与两个国家接壤，泰国则更多，它分别与缅甸、老挝、柬埔寨和马来西亚为邻。而且半岛上国家的面积一般都不大。因而，从一个东南亚国家到另一个东南亚国家的空间距离相对较短。而东北亚地区的中国、韩国也是相互接壤，日本则是隔海相望，海、陆、空交通便捷。因此，地缘上相连或相近的特点，成为东亚国家开展旅行合作一个有利因素。

在认知上，国际旅游者对东亚有一体化的形象认知。西方人传统上习惯于把东亚看作一个整体。这是区域旅游形象树立和传播的先天条件，也是东亚旅游合作的重要基础。

二、东亚地区丰富的旅游资源具有典型的互补性优势

东亚地区各国的社会、经济发展存在着明显的差异，旅游发展程度不同，旅游市场差别很大，但该地区丰富的旅游资源却有着一些共同的互补性，构成东亚各国共同开展区域旅游合作的基础和依据。

东亚地区的自然旅游资源丰富，地域辽阔，自然景色丰富多彩，自然景观差异明显，是世界上山水风光最为壮美的旅游区之一。海洋景观、森林景观、草原湿地景观、火山熔岩景观、冰雪景观和寒带极地景观对比清晰，反差极大，带有粗犷的原始特性，因而有着与其他景观不可比拟的自然、真实、完美和

神秘。

东亚历史悠久，文化灿烂，有四大文明古国之一的中国，佛教文化之邦的泰国。东亚为多元文化的荟萃之地，世界上几大文化形态在该地区都可以找到代表：中南半岛成为佛教文化的聚焦地；新加坡则是东亚国家社会旅游资源的代表，因其居民中华人占大多数更多地反映出儒家文化的特征；日本为神道教文化的体现者。东亚地区各国文化上互相依存性和互补性，从而构成该地区开展文化交流特别是进行旅游活动的重要文化基础，这无疑是发展东亚区域旅游合作的非常有利的条件。东亚很多国家都有"礼仪之邦，微笑之国"之美称，富有人情味的东方式服务深受欧美游客的称道。东亚地区横跨亚寒带和亚热带，自然景观迥异多样。伴随其文化起源的同根性，形成了多彩而有序的旅游目的地景观。这是东亚旅游合作的物质条件。

三、政府支持为东亚国际旅游合作提供了有力保证

东亚各国政府高度重视发展旅游产业。素有发展旅游经济传统的新加坡，在1996年就制订了《21世纪旅游经济远景规划》。日本在2003年提出了观光立国的战略。韩国早在1961年就颁布了《旅游事业振兴法》，还制定了《21世纪旅游展望》。中国近年来出台了《旅游法》，将旅游业定位为战略性支柱产业与让人民群众更加满意的现代服务业。马来西亚加大了在旅游领域的基础设施投资。越南制定了2010年旅游发展战略。同时，东亚各国政府高度重视在双边、多边、次区域和区域等旅游领域的合作，就有关旅游合作问题举行各层次会议，进行探讨和研商，建立了有关区域旅游合作机制，签署了旅游合作协议，联合组织了一些旅游推广活动等。2002年在"10+3"框架下东盟与中、日、韩旅游合作机制的建立标志着全面发展东亚旅游合作进入了崭新的历史阶段。

第二节　东亚国际旅游合作的政策建议

东亚是目前全球国际旅游发展最快的地区之一，东亚各国之间的友好关系源远流长，友好交往由来已久。东亚地域广袤，旅游资源富集，经济发展迅速，有责任，也有使命在新的发展机遇中有更加积极的作为与合作。为此，建议东亚各国在以下几个方面加强磋商与协作：

一、重视地方政府在国际交流中的先导作用，务实推动多双边旅游话题交流

充分利用现有的东盟与中日韩领导人会议、东亚峰会、东盟与中日韩（10+3）旅游部长会议、中日韩三国旅游部长会议、东亚商务论坛、东亚国际旅游博览会等沟通交流机制，以"政府引导、企业参与、民众支持"的理念逐步完善和丰富东亚国际旅游合作机制。在重视东亚各国高层交流和往来的同时，更加重视东亚各国地方政府在东亚国际旅游合作中的先导作用，探索建立以地方和城市为合作单元的东亚各国国际旅游交流合作平台，并积极谋求常态化运转，务实推动多双边旅游话题交流和信息共享。在此基础上，充分结合地方和区域特色，可由地方政府牵头，探索建立区域一体化的合作开发机制，并积极谋求更加紧密的互联互通和更加深入的多双边政策性交流。

二、从增进便利性入手，探索实现市场开放和共享

东亚大部分国家既互为客源市场，也互为主要旅游目的地。从当前国际旅游发展的趋势来看，加大对本国旅游市场的开放力度既是旅游市场自身发展的基本规律，也是开展多双边旅游市场合作的基本前提。建议东亚各国从增进便利性入手，在签证、航权、免退税、快速通关、市场准入、自然人流动等方面积极作为并相向而行，进一步消减影响东亚各国游客流动的障碍因素。在相关

便利化措施实施的进程中，对外积极推动与相关国家的互联互通水平，对内勇于打破地方保护，将便利化政策落到实处，切实增进双向及多向的旅游市场开放和共享。

三、联合开发优质旅游产品和跨国精品旅游线路

结合当前的国际旅游市场需求特点，联合开发优质旅游产品，特别是跨国精品旅游线路。针对当前国际邮轮产业迅猛发展的战略机遇，在东北亚联合开发环黄海精品旅游线、环日本海精品旅游线，在东南亚联合开发精品海岛游旅游线。针对不同的旅游市场需求特征，联合设计跨国特色主题旅游线路，如商务会展旅游、文化旅游、宗教旅游、购物旅游等特种旅游产品。推动专项旅游产品合作，联合启动热点旅游产品开发，可在青少年修学旅游、高尔夫旅游、冰雪旅游、养老旅游等各国均有巨大潜力的领域加强合作，并借此扩大东亚各国在旅游领域的深度交流。

四、以更加开放的产业政策，引导和鼓励旅游产业合作

以自由贸易区和跨境旅游合作区的建设为契机和载体，在政策准许和不损害各自利益的前提下，积极探索出台并实施市场准入、税收、土地、资本、信息、特许经营等多种形式的产业开放政策，制定东亚地区旅游投资指导目录，努力推动东亚各国旅游领域开放程度的扩大，充分调动旅游企业参与东亚国际旅游合作的积极性。充分发挥旅游行业组织在国际旅游合作中的职能作用，使其成为能够代表旅游行业和政府沟通、服务企业的行业组织。

五、更加注重发挥教育、科技、人才的基础性支撑作用

加强东亚各国在旅游教育与科研方面的合作，进一步强化旅游人才培养、旅游科研投入、旅游专家智库研讨、旅游专项政策储备等方面的资源投入和组织保障。创新东亚地区国际旅游业人力资源开发机制，全面培养旅游从业人员

的语言能力，以提升接待能力；鼓励旅游从业人员到东亚各国或旅游发达城市交流，提高人才素质与能力；提升东亚各国旅游从业人员的整体素质，以高品质服务提升东亚旅游的品位和层次。建立更加广泛的人员交流和培养机制，重点围绕自然人流动、商业存在和紧急救护保障，争取除高级管理人员和高级技能人员外，自然人流动范围向导游、厨师、健康护理人员扩展。

附录1 东亚地区旅游合作状况

东亚旅游合作是整个东亚区域合作的一项重要内容。其发端可以追溯至2000年的"昆明会议"。在中国的倡议下,2000年8月21日中、泰、新、马四国旅游部长会议在昆明召开,签署了《四国联合治理区域旅游市场部长级会议纪要》,对零团费等出境旅游市场上的不规范行为进行了联合整顿,有效规范了旅游市场。覆盖最大范围的"10+3"区域旅游合作虽然起步较晚,但发展速度惊人。目前,东亚旅游合作主要包括东盟内部合作、东盟与中日韩合作、双边合作及次区域合作四个部分。

一、东盟内部的旅游合作

东盟的旅游合作始于1976年的东盟旅游工作委员会的成立。1979年,成立了"东盟旅游协会",接着成立了东盟饭店与餐馆协会、东盟旅游代理商联合会等行业组织。1998年9月26日,东盟成员国在马来西亚首都吉隆坡签署协议,成立东盟旅游信息中心,主要任务包括:介绍、公布东盟成员国的旅游资源和旅游投资机会;协调和实施促进出入东盟旅游的短期和长期市场项目等10项内容。

目前东盟内部的旅游合作已经走向机制化,自1998年以来,每年都定期召开东盟旅游部长会议,遇到特殊情况,还专门召开特别会议。东盟旅游部长会议自1998年首次举办以来已经成为一项制度,每年一月都会在"东盟旅游论坛"召开期间举行。近几年来,东盟在旅游合作方面加快了步伐,成果较为丰硕。东盟10个成员国计划于2020年前建立一个与欧盟相似的亚洲单一市场。

二、东南亚与中日韩的旅游合作

"10+3"框架下东盟与中日韩的旅游合作是东亚区域合作中东亚旅游合作的

一个组成部分，起步较晚。东盟与中、日、韩旅游部长会议是"10+3"合作框架下的七个部长级会议之一。从 2002 年起，每年在召开东盟旅游部长会议和东盟旅游论坛会议的同时，举行东盟与中、日、韩"10+3"旅游部长会议，加强东盟与中、日、韩旅游领域的合作。

三、东亚地区其他双边旅游合作

东亚地区国家间双边合作也发展很快。相对于多边合作而言，双边旅游合作往往可操作性更强，更具实质性意义。

近年来，围绕着提高旅游服务水平、简化出入境手续以及共同开发旅游资源等与区域旅游合作相关联的事项，东盟各国签署了一系列双边合作协议。比如越南和柬埔寨合作商定在简化过境手续、加强旅游宣传、开辟旅游线路等加强合作。为发展"黄金三角"旅游区，泰国与老挝签订《老泰旅游合作协议》，泰缅签署《缅泰旅游合作协定》。泰国还与越南、柬埔寨、印度尼西亚和马来西亚等国签订了旅游合作协定。日本在启动"观光立国"战略后，逐步重视与东亚其他国家开展双边旅游协作。2005 年 5 月跟越南在东京签署双边旅游合作协议，双方将制定互惠的旅游政策，2005 年 7 月跟中国签署旅游决定在已开放北京、上海、广东等八省市的基础上，全面开放中国公民赴日团体旅游，同时还签署了《关于进一步加强旅游合作与交流的磋商备忘录》，双方就进一步加强旅游交流与合作达成诸多共识，标志着两国旅游交流与合作迈入新的阶段。中国也与东盟十国陆续签署了有关推进双边旅游合作的协定、协议、谅解备忘录等，为中国与东盟国家开展旅游合作提供了框架和保障。此外中韩双方商定加强交流与合作，为促进中韩两国旅游业的发展共同努力。

四、东亚地区次区域的旅游合作

目前，东亚次区域旅游合作的主要是澜沧江—湄公河次区域旅游合作。20 世纪 90 年代以来，随着冷战的结束和国际关系的缓和，湄公河流域的合作开发受到了国际社会的广泛关注。澜沧江—湄公河次区域旅游合作于 1992 年由亚洲开发银行倡议发起并形成,湄公河流域相关国家在亚洲开发银行的支持下,参加了经济合作计划。

次区域国家提出了旅游产业为合作先导的设想,并提出了推进旅游合作的措施。澜沧江—湄公河次区域旅游合作是在次区域经济合作机制的基础上,由联合国亚太经社会、亚洲开发银行等国际组织主导和推动,旨在将次区域作为一个完整的旅游目的地进行合作开发,打造整体形象,统一推向世界旅游市场而建立起来的又一新的合作机制。

附录2 历届东亚地方政府会议状况

自 2010 年至今，东亚地方政府会议已成功举办了六届。2010 年，适逢平城京迁都 1300 周年，日本希望能与建成延续至今的国家基础框架的先驱们一样，来推动构建今后东亚发展的基础，使之成为一个确立这种渠道的契机。为此，作为平城迁都 1300 周年纪念活动的一个重要环节，开始举办以日本、中国、韩国地方政府为中心的"东亚地方政府会议"。会议的目的是通过地方政府的代表在这个会议上坦率真诚地相互报告本地区的实情与课题，并就共同的课题进行讨论，同时加深相互之间的了解。

一、东亚地方政府倡议者会议

2009 年 10 月 25 日至 28 日东亚地方政府倡议者会议在奈良召开，面向 2010 年成立东亚地方政府会议，进行商讨宪章（Charter）等筹备工作。来自中国、韩国和日本的共 19 个地方政府参加了本次会议。

参会地方政府：19 个地方政府

中国（6）：陕西省、河南省、江苏省、西安市、洛阳市、扬州市

韩国（6）：忠清南道、公州市、瑞山市、扶余郡、庆尚北道、庆州市

日本（7）：岐阜县、静冈县、奈良县、奈良市、天理市、橿原市、明日香村

在倡议会上，参会的所有地方政府相互汇报了"地方政府的实际情况和课题"。同时，还讨论了作为运作东亚地方政府会议的原则章程的《东亚地方政府会议奈良宪章（方案）》，通过了《关于成立东亚地方政府会议的奈良声明（方案）》。

2009 年 10 月 26 日在倡议会员上 19 个地方政府代表发表了各自所在地的现状和课题。奈良县知事荒井正吾表示奈良县拥有丰富的自然和文化遗产资源，

旅游观光在奈良占有重要地位。为了提高观光活动的宣传，奈良县制定了5A观光战略（Accommodation 住宿、Access 交通、Appetite 饮食、Attraction 有吸引力的设施、Amity 亲切）。奈良市市长仲川元庸也交代了奈良市文化遗产的保护，让自然可持续发展，推进城市建设。陕西省副秘书长周玉明陈述了陕西的概况，陕西无论在自然资源、历史还是交通方面都有自己的优势。"富士之乡"静冈县知事川胜平太介绍到静冈县旅游的外国人中，亚洲人占七层，其中中、韩游客居多，并提出迎接东亚新时代的到来。庆尚北道政务副知事孔元植介绍了韩国与中国、日本今后的发展方向，开展三方经济文化等方面的交流。其他地方政府就文化遗产、城市建设、生态保护、工农业发展等不同方面结合自己的政府的发展概况进行了介绍并提出战略目标。

在对话会议上，不仅参会政府之间进行了对话，10月27日上午经济贸易等领域的专家和地方政府对话也很活跃，对东亚的未来发展进行了探讨。社团法人、关西经济联合会副会长国际委员长松下正幸、奈良县知事荒井正吾、韩国扶余郡郡守金茂焕等分别回顾了中日韩在经济、历史等方面的交流，并分析了东亚及经济的现状和问题，纷纷表示建立紧密的中日韩关系。

为了更直接地解决东亚各地区人民的问题，为了在多领域加强东亚地区之间的多样化交流，通过东亚地方政府倡议者会议讨论的结果，决定成立"东亚地方政府会议"，并于2010年在奈良举行第一届会议。此外，在2010年的第一届会议上争取通过东亚地方政府会议奈良宪章（方案），这一事宜得到了确认。各地方政府也达成一致意见：呼吁与志同道合并有着各种关系的其他东亚地方政府参加"东亚地方政府会议"。

二、第一届东亚地方政府会议

2010年10月6日至8日第一届东亚地方政府会议在日本奈良举行，来自日本、中国、韩国、菲律宾、印度尼西亚和印度6个国家共34个地方政府的代表就深化地方政府间合作，推动实现东亚稳定发展等交换了意见。为纪念平城迁都 1300 周年召开"第一届东亚地方政府会议"。

参会地方政府：34 个地方政府

中国（5）：安徽省、河南省、陕西省、扬州市、敦煌市

印度（1）：瓦拉纳西市（鹿野苑）

印度尼西亚（1）：日惹特区

菲律宾（1）：奥罗拉省

韩国（8）：京畿道、忠清南道、公州市、瑞山市、扶余郡、全罗南道、庆尚北道、庆州市

日本（18）：青森县、山形县、福岛县、新潟县、富山县、福井县、岐阜县、静冈县、三重县、岛根县、高知县、熊本县、奈良县、新潟市、奈良市、天理市、橿原市、明日香村

本会议为构建未来我国与东亚间的和平与发展平台，确立地方间交流、长期合作机制，立足于上 2009 年度东亚地方政府会议倡议者会议成果，对东亚地方政府会议奈良宪章（草案）进行表决，成立东亚地方政府会议。

第一届东亚地方政府会议一致通过奈良宪章（草案）原文，并介绍了东亚地方政府会议的徽标。奈良宪章（草案）的协议说明了东亚地方会议的主要内容是互相报告各地区实情和相同课题，探讨课题解决方法。通过持续召开会议，增进地方政府之间的友好与信赖关系，进而为国家之间乃至东亚整体的稳定发展做出贡献。此外，协议对东亚地方政府会议的活动、会员和来宾组成、经费等也进行了说明。

第一届东亚地方政府会议也一致通过了共同声明（草案），共同声明（草案）中指出每年召开会议，共同解决面临的共同的问题，并决定将会议上的报告和讨论内容出版，此外，面向东亚以外的地方政府，广范围呼吁各方积极参会，共同构建地方政府间合作框架。共同声明（草案）宣布 2011 年的东亚地方政府会议在奈良举办。

在区域报告上，来自中、日、韩的各地方政府代表就"文化遗产的保护、

振兴观光"和"青少年交流"两个主题发言。其中在关于主题"文化遗产的保护、振兴观光"的发言中,各地方政府代表探讨了如何保护和维护各自的文化遗产的同时,也加入了节庆、艺术和科技等新的元素加以开发,努力吸引更多游客,促进经济发展。最后在第一届东亚地方政府会议成立纪念演讲会上,冈本 Associates 公司代表冈本行夫先生与韩国首任文化部长李御宁先生就东亚的现状和未来作了探讨。冈本行夫先生表示科技改变了世界的发展模式,只有将传统与新技术结合,各地方政府齐心协力,才能不断促进社会进步和社会和平。李御宁表示中日韩具有一定的历史渊源,各方应该抛弃偏见,相互扶持,扬长避短,形成具备持续性关系的东亚文化共同体。

三、第二届东亚地方政府会议

2011 年 10 月 18 日至 26 日,第二届东亚地方政府会议在日本奈良举行,来自中国、印度、菲律宾、韩国、越南和日本的 6 个国家的 44 个地方政府参加了会议,围绕"危机管理""区域振兴"等主题进行了广泛而深入的交流。

参会地方政府:44 个地方政府

中国(7):安徽省、山东省、河南省、陕西省、西安市、扬州市、黄山市

印度(1):瓦拉拿西市

菲律宾(2):本格特省、奥罗拉省

韩国(7):京畿道、忠清南道、公州市、扶余郡、全罗南道、庆尚北道、庆州市

越南(3):承天顺华省、顺华市、会安市

日本(24):青森县、山形县、福岛县、新潟县、富山县、福井县、岐阜县、静冈县、三重现、和歌山县、岛根县、香川县、高知县、熊本县、奈良县、多贺城市、新潟市、太宰府时、奈良市、天理市、橿原市、斑鸠町、明日香村、下市町

今年充实了地方政府领导间的讨论,并将行政具体负责人员研讨也纳入了

议程，取得了很大成果。希望通过持续召开这样的会议，能够在提高地方政府行政能力的同时，增进相互间的友好和信赖关系，愿更多地方政府参与进来，以实现本地方政府会议的宗旨。

第二届东亚地方政府会议，增加了 12 个新加盟的地方政府，其中中国 2 个：山东省、山东潍坊市。在会议上，各地方政府代表在地方政府网络框架下讨论了"政治制度及地方政府的作用"，分析了应对灾害之际"地方政府在危机管理中的应有做法和责任及职能"，另外在地方政府代表讨论之前，在专家的协助下，地方政府会议具体负责人员以"观光""城乡发展""文化财产保护"为题开展了课题研究。另外，还确立了开办东亚暑期学校。

四、第三届东亚地方政府会议

2012 年迎来第三届东亚地方政府会议，组织规模扩大，加盟会员数已达 7 个国家 64 个地方政府，中国 14 个省市为会议成员。

2012 年的第三届东亚地方政府会议针对在去年的会议上受到好评的各个主题进一步发展了小组讨论，分为 4 个主题作为地方政府的共同课题："思考人口少子老龄化时代的社会保障""为确保税收而采取的行动""地区振兴"及"人才培育"，并围绕这 4 个主题进行了小组讨论。各主题的讨论结果（概要）大致总结为以下两点：①地方政府的具体措施（最佳实践）；②为在今后实现进一步改善的具体措施（运用方面及制度方面）。其中在主题 3 地区振兴讨论组中，参会代表从为振兴旅游的交通、与非旅游行业人员合作、活用地区的特性及文化、产业融合和行政机构的职责分担等五个方面提出了具体措施和今后地区振兴的应有形态。

五、第四届东亚地方政府会议

2014 年 1 月 20 日至 22 日第四届东亚地方政府会议在日本奈良县举办，来自 5 个国家 39 个地方政府参加了本次会议。

参会地方政府：39 个地方政府

中国（1）：山东省

菲律宾（1）：巴莱尔市

韩国（7）：京畿道、忠清南道、瑞山市、扶余郡、全罗南道、庆尚北道、庆州市

越南（2）：富寿省、越池市

日本（28）：山形县、福岛县、新潟县、福井县、山梨县、长野县、岐阜县、静冈县、三重县、京都府、和歌山县、鸟取县、岛根县、德岛县、香川县、高知县、奈良县、多贺城市、新潟市、太宰府市、奈良市、天理市、橿原市、御所市、斑鸠町、明日香村、广陵町、下市町

※ 特别嘉宾：缅甸（仰光地区政府、曼德勒地区政府）

2014 年 1 月 21 日在全体会议上，二阶俊博（日本国众议院议员）发表了纪念演讲，各地方政府代表通过小组讨论，对两个主题分别提出了采取的措施和今后应有的形态，奈良县知事荒井正吾发表了议长报告。

2013 年度的第四届东亚地方政府会议，以小组讨论为中心，继续去年主题的"少子老龄化时代的社会保障"与新主题"地区经济的振兴与就业"，并围绕这两个主题进行了小组讨论。奈良市、香川县和巴莱尔市政府代表分享了各自了完善旅游资源，吸引游客方面的采取的措施。

其中在"地区经济的振兴与就业"这一主题上，奈良市认为以观光为主轴的产业振兴是一个课题，通过保存传统街道，设置"奈良町房屋银行"，将空置的房屋作为旅游资源进行重建，以及举办奈良灯花会等活动实现旅游资源的有效配置。另外香川县通过艺术带动旅游发展，巴莱尔市通过森林再生及完善登山道等的基础设施建设、培育登山导游及潜水导游等人才，打造生态旅游，使得游客不断增加。

六、第五届东亚地方政府会议

2014年10月27日至29日第五届东亚地方政府会议在日本奈良举办，来自6个国家40个地方政府参加了本次会议。会上东亚东盟经济研究中心学术咨询会议议长HANKLIM先生和联合国世界旅游组织（UNWTO）亚太中心事业与宣传部长詹妮弗·斯坦格女士分别做了主旨演讲，所有参会代表围绕"振兴旅游业""城乡建设""振兴地区经济"三个主题分组进行了广泛而深入的交流。

参会地方政府：40个地方政府

中国（4）：安徽省、山东省、潍坊市、东营市

印度尼西亚（1）：日惹特区

马来西亚（1）：马六甲州

韩国（5）：京畿道、忠清南道、公州市、瑞山市、庆尚北道

越南（3）：富寿省、承天顺化省、越池市

日本（26）：青森县、福岛县、新潟县、福井县、山梨县、长野县、静冈县、三重县、京都府、和歌山县、鸟取县、岛根县、德岛县、香川县、高知县、奈良县、多贺城市、新潟市、太宰府市、天理市、橿原市、御所市、斑鸠町、明日香村、广陵町、下市町

※ 特别嘉宾：缅甸（马圭地区政府、缅甸外交部）

在主题演讲报告中，联合国世界旅游组织（UNWTO）亚太中心事业与宣传部部长詹妮弗·斯坦格介绍了世界旅游组织（UNWTO）重点项目和伙伴关系，为参加东亚地方政府会议的地方政府发展旅游业指明了方向。

在2014年度的第五届东亚地方政府会议上，"旅游"被各地方政府代表多次提及。关于文化、旅游资源在城乡建设和地区振兴中的应用方面及发挥的作用，代表们根据各自地区的实际情况发表了各种事例，并针对如何让居民及当地企业成为主体，或者县与市政府应如何分工及开展协作，或者如何提高旅游目的地的管理水平等方面展开了讨论，各地方政府分别介绍了自己的经验。

通过讨论所有参会人员都达成了共识。那就是，旅游业不能只顾其作为地区商务获得收入的一面，还必须提高旅游质量，构建使地区社会富足和使地区居民幸福的机制。与会地方政府各位纷纷表示，通过具体事例的发表获得了众多有益信息，本次会议意义深远。

七、第六届东亚地方政府会议

2015年10月25日至27日第六届东亚地方政府会议在日本奈良县召开，来自6个国家42个地方政府出席了会议，会议围绕旅游振兴地区经济、城乡和地区建设、振兴农业及农村进行了专题讨论。

参会地方政府：42个地方政府

中国（6）：河南省、陕西省、成都市、黄山市、宿州市、东营市

印度尼西亚（2）：西爪哇省、日惹特区

马来西亚（1）：马六甲州

韩国（6）：京畿道、忠清南道、公州市、瑞山市、扶余郡、庆尚北道

越南（2）：富寿省、越池市

日本（25）：青森县、山形县、福岛县、新潟县、福井县、山梨县、长野县、静冈县、三重县、京都府、和歌山县、鸟取县、岛根县、德岛县、香川县、奈良县、荒川区、新潟市、奈良市、天理市、橿原市、御所市、斑鸠町、明日香村、广陵町

※ 特别嘉宾：奎松市（菲律宾）

奈良县知事荒井正吾在全体会议上作了议长报告，对中国四川省成都市、中国安徽省宿州市和日本东京都荒川区新加盟地方政府进行了介绍。事务局发表了关于召开第七届东亚地方政府会议报告。

在各地域分科会报告会上，三重县雇用经济部国际战略课课长辅佐太平和辉发表了"振兴旅游业'促进入境旅游'"的报告。太平和辉汇报了在分科会上促进入境旅游相关措施的事例与课题，例如从通过型观光向逗留观光转移、化

解外国游客集中在特定的访问地区、提升民间力量、与邻近县及市町村合作、完善接待环境。此外，还讨论了广域化的课题、完善当地接待环境、信息传播及处理穆斯林问题。

2015年度的第六届东亚地方政府会议，各地方政府从乡村旅游、体育旅游、文化旅游等不同的角度探讨了各自所在地旅游的发展措施。通过观光型旅游转向停留型旅游、开发旅游商品和应对淡季来提高旅游消费，以及自然保护在旅游观光中的灵活运用和提高当地居民的意识三个方面的举措，实现通过旅游业观光振兴地区经济的目标。

附录3 东亚国际旅游合作的进程回顾

一、东盟与中日韩（10+3）领导人会议

（一）背景资料

【背景】1995年，东盟曼谷首脑会议建议举行东盟与中日韩领导人会议。1997年，马来西亚作为东盟轮值主席国承办第二届东盟首脑非正式会议，积极促成了东盟与中日韩领导人非正式会议的召开。

【成员】东盟10个成员（文莱、柬埔寨、印度尼西亚、老挝、马来西亚、缅甸、菲律宾、新加坡、泰国、越南）与中国、日本和韩国。

【主要机制】东盟与中日韩合作已建立了65个对话与合作机制，形成了以领导人会议为核心，以部长会议、高官会、东盟常驻代表委员会与中日韩驻东盟大使会议（CPR+3）和工作组会议为支撑的合作体系。

领导人会议是最高层级机制，每年举行一次，主要对10+3发展做出战略规划和指导，迄今已举行19次。17个部长级会议机制负责相关领域政策规划和协调。高官会负责政策沟通。CPR+3负责就合作具体问题进行协调。此外，10+3框架下还建有官、产、学共同参与的东亚论坛（EAF）及二轨的东亚思想库网络（NEAT），为10+3合作提供智力支撑。

（二）相关成果

2014年11月，第17次东盟与中日韩领导人会议在缅甸内比都举行。李克强总理出席。李克强表示，东盟十国与中日韩三国地缘相近、经济互补、文化相通，10+3合作有力促进了东亚一体化进程。各方应坚定维护地区和平稳定，在此基础上继续加强协调，牢牢把握互利合作的大方向，开展相关领域务实合作，朝着东亚共同体的目标稳步迈进。李克强就加强10+3合作提出六点建议：第一，推动东亚经济一体化进程；第二，提升区域金融合作水平；第三，密切

地区互联互通；第四，深化民生领域合作；第五，扩大人文社会交流；第六，加强公共卫生合作。

在第 17 次东盟与中日韩（10+3）领导人会议上，李克强总理提出了加强 10+3 务实合作的六点建议，其中在"扩大人文交流渠道方面"提到成立中日韩三国分设的东盟中心的定期交流机制，进一步深化 10+3 文化、教育、旅游等领域的合作，并表示"希望各方尽快签署《10+3 旅游合作谅解备忘录》"。

2015 年 11 月，第 18 次东盟与中日韩领导人会议在马来西亚吉隆坡举行。李克强出席会议。李克强表示，当前东亚地区经济发展总体保持上升势头，仍然是全球最具活力和发展潜力的地区之一。为进一步深化合作，中方倡议本次会议发表"促进地区经济增长和金融稳定的联合声明"，各方制定"东亚经济共同体蓝图"，成立亚洲金融合作协会。李克强就 10+3 合作提出五点建议：一是加快推进东亚经济一体化；二是协力维护地区金融稳定；三是提升互联互通水平；四是开展国际产能合作；五是拓展人文交流。

李克强总理在第 18 次东盟与中日韩（10+3）领导人会议上再次表示中方支持加强"东亚文化之都"和"东盟文化城市"间交流互动，支持尽快签署《10+3 旅游合作谅解备忘录》。除此之外还提及了"一带一路"，建议促进在整个东亚范围的互通互联建设，为区域合作提供有力支撑。

2016 年 9 月，第 19 次东盟与中日韩领导人会议在老挝万象举行。李克强出席会议。李克强表示，明年将迎来 10+3 合作 20 周年，各方应以此为新起点，巩固 10+3 在区域经济一体化进程中的主渠道作用，谱写东亚合作新篇章。李克强就 10+3 合作提出六点建议：第一，加强金融安全合作；第二，深化贸易投资合作；第三，推动农业和减贫合作；第四，促进互联互通建设；第五，创新产能合作模式；第六，增进社会人文交流。

2016 年年初，东盟与中日韩（10+3）签署了《10+3 旅游合作谅解备忘录》。在第十八次东盟与中日韩（10+3）领导人会议上，为加强各方人文交流，加强"东亚文化之都"和"东盟文化城市"的交流，李克强总理宣布 2016 年中方将主办10+3"了解中国"和"亚洲主流媒体看中国"项目。

二、东亚峰会

2014年11月第九届东亚峰会在缅甸首都内比都举行,东盟10国及8个对话伙伴国的领导人围绕东亚一体化进程的相关战略性问题以及共同关心的地区和全球问题进行了讨论。李克强出席会议。李克强表示,东亚合作要政治和经济"两个轮子一起转";东亚快速发展归因于和平稳定的地区环境;推动东亚非传统安全领域合作;力争RCEP在2015年前结束谈判;尽快完成中国—东盟自贸区升级版谈判;中国坚定支持东盟明年建成政治安全、经济、社会文化共同体;提出东亚经济一体化六大重点合作领域;坚持"双轨思路"处理南海问题;中国主张朝鲜半岛无核化,维护半岛和东北亚长期和平稳定;中国将向埃博拉疫区增派医护人员增援物资;邻国低头不见抬头见,须秉持以诚相待、求同存异之心;中国正与东盟国家商签睦邻友好条约推动实现东亚持久和平。

2015年11月第十届东亚峰会在吉隆坡国际会议中心举行,李克强出席会议,就各国共同维护南海和平稳定提出五点倡议:一是各国承诺遵守《联合国宪章》的宗旨和原则,捍卫"二战"成果和战后秩序,珍惜来之不易的和平,共同维护国际和地区包括南海地区的和平与稳定。二是直接有关的主权国家承诺根据公认的国际法原则,包括1982年《联合国海洋法公约》,通过友好磋商和谈判,以和平方式解决领土和管辖权争议。三是中国和东盟国家承诺全面有效完整落实《南海各方行为宣言》,加快"南海行为准则"磋商,在协商一致的基础上尽早达成"准则",并采取措施不断完善地区互信合作机制建设。四是域外国家承诺尊重和支持地区国家维护南海和平稳定的努力,发挥积极和建设性的作用,不采取导致地区局势紧张的行动。五是各国承诺依据国际法行使和维护在南海享有的航行和飞行自由。

2016年9月第十一届东亚峰会在老挝万象举行。李克强出席会议。李克强指出,东亚地区和平稳定与繁荣既面临巨大机遇,也面临不少挑战,中方愿与各方齐心协力，化挑战为机遇，推动东亚合作稳步向前，为促进地区和平稳定与持久繁荣贡献力量，造福各国人民。李克强并阐述了中方在南海问题上的原则立场。

三、东盟与中日韩（10+3）旅游部长会议

表1 东盟与中日韩（10+3）旅游部长会议回顾

年份	届数	地点	会议主要内容
2002	第一届	印度尼西亚雅加达	成立一个高官会议以建立一个信息快速交流的机制，推进旅游便利化，促进以"10+3"国家为目的地旅游，加强私人部门的合作，在人力资源研究以及信息技术上开展合作等
2003	第二届	柬埔寨金边	决定成立东盟与中、日、韩旅游交流工作小组来进一步促进在旅游安全领域里信息的准确交流
2004	第三届	老挝万象	继续加强10+3旅游组织的合作，联合促进和开发旅游市场；增加旅游业投资，扩大人力资源开发；交流信息，建立早期预警机制，以有效地处理如政治动乱、恐怖活动、经济犯罪、自然灾害、非典型肺炎（SARS）和其他流行性疾病的蔓延，以确保地区旅游业的发展
2005	第四届	马来西亚兰卡威	鼓励东盟内和东盟外旅游，帮助东盟受灾国尽快恢复旅游业
2007	第六届	新加坡	支持在东盟与中日韩（10+3）合作中把重点放在旅游交往、人才交流、人力开发、旅游市场合作等领域
2012	第十一届	印度尼西亚万鸦	在10+3旅游航空便利性、邮轮旅游、10+3旅游合作备忘录、产品开发、人力资源培训等方面交换了意见
2013	第十二届	老挝万象	在10+3旅游航空便利性、邮轮旅游、10+3旅游合作备忘录、产品开发、人力资源培训及投资、危机应急处理等方面交换了意见，通过旨在推动本地区旅游业发展的联合声明
2014	第十三届	马来西亚古晋	就区域互联互通、联合线路开发、气候变化与灾害应对、人才培训、《东盟与中日韩2013—2017旅游合作工作计划》、商签《东盟10+3旅游合作备忘录》等议题交换了意见，并通过了联合媒体声明
2015	第十四届	缅甸内比都	研究了《东盟与中日韩旅游合作备忘录》文本草案，讨论并通过第25届和第26届东盟与中日韩旅游部门会议纪要，听取了菲律宾关于下一届东盟与中日韩旅游部长会议时间和地点等方面的情况介绍

续表

年份	届数	地点	会议主要内容
2016	第十五届	菲律宾马尼拉	就落实东盟与中日韩（10+3）领导人会议及东盟与中、日、韩（10+1）领导人会议成果涉旅内容进行了讨论，签署了《东盟与中日韩旅游合作备忘录》，通过了《联合媒体声明》和第27、28届东盟与中日韩旅游部门会议纪要，听取了新加坡关于下一届东盟与中日韩旅游部长会议时间和地点等方面的情况介绍

四、中日韩三国旅游部长会议

中日韩旅游部长会议是由三国旅游部门为落实三国领导人会议精神，在"东盟+中日韩"框架下建立起来的三国旅游部长定期会晤机制。中日韩旅游部长会议是世界上最成功的旅游合作机制之一，在增进人民了解、扩大部门合作、加强业界交流、互通市场信息、培养旅游人才、保障游客利益以及推动持续发展等方面做出了积极的、卓有成效的贡献，同时也是举办城市展示风采、打造品牌，扩大国际知名度，促进旅游业发展的极好机遇。

2006年第一届中日韩三国旅游部长会议在日本北海道札幌市举行《北海道宣言》会议还通过了"中日韩旅游交流"计划，目标是将三国间的旅游交流规模由2005年的1 200万人次扩大到2010年的1 700万人次。

2005年，中国接待入境过夜游客达4 680万人次，其中韩国游客354万人次、日本游客339万人次，在中国入境旅游客源国中分别居于前两位。2005年中国出境旅游人数达3 100万人次，成为亚洲第一大客源市场，比2004年增长8%。

2007年第二届中日韩三国旅游部长会议以"旅游、合作、和谐、共赢"为主题，以促进三国旅游交流与合作为主旨。会议在青岛开幕，大连闭幕，并签署了《青岛宣言》。

2008年第三届中日韩旅游部长会议在韩国釜山会展中心隆重开幕，加强合作，共同解决旅游业发展的障碍、实现旅游业可持续发展、共同开发具有吸引力的旅游产品、扩大三国旅游交流与合作为主要议题，三国旅游部长还签署了《釜山宣言》。会议在韩国釜山市开幕，在清州市闭幕。

2009年10月17日第四届中日韩旅游部长会议在日本名古屋市开幕。本次会议计划就三国旅游业界如何应对目前的危机、如何迎接亚洲旅游大交流时代的到来等议题展开深入讨论。会议在高山市闭幕。

第五届中日韩旅游部长会议2010年8月21日在杭州市举行，闭幕式于8月23日在湖州市举行。本次会议主题为"面向未来、全面合作、共同繁荣"。会议签署了《杭州联合声明》《中日韩共倡低碳旅游倡议书》。

2011年5月28日至31日，第六届中日韩三国旅游部长会议在韩国江原道平昌举行。本次会议旨在通过三国共同协作，推动三国旅游交流，共同制订旅游促进方案，巩固东北亚旅游合作的基础。会上三国旅游部长共同签署了《第六届中日韩旅游部长会议联合声明》和《中日韩诚信旅游倡议书》。会上讨论了"对于旅游紧急危机情况的发生共同建立应对体系""为扩大中日韩旅游交流规模，树立并推进2020旅游展望""促进签署中日韩诚信旅游倡议书"以及"为扩大中日韩旅游交流，开发共同项目"。

2015年4月12日，第七届中日韩旅游部长会议在日本东京举行，三国旅游部长会聚东京，共商旅游大计，就开启中日韩旅游交流新时代、推动游历东方活动、提高中日韩旅游交流品质等议题进行了深入探讨，达成了诸多共识。会议签署了《第七届中日韩旅游部长会议联合声明》。

表2 中日韩三国旅游部长会议回顾

年份	举办地	会议主要内容	达成共识
2006	日本北海道	中日韩三国齐心协力扩大三国之间的旅游交流合作，共同探讨制约旅游交流的因素，加强三国之间的人员交流，共同吸引区域外的游客到三国旅游	《北海道宣言》、"中日韩旅游交流计划"
2007	中国青岛、大连	以"旅游、合作、和谐、共赢"为主题，以促进三国旅游交流与合作为主旨	《青岛宣言》

附录 3 东亚国际旅游合作的进程回顾
Appendix 3 A Review of East Asia International Tourism Cooperation

续表

年份	举办地	会议主要内容	达成共识
2008	韩国釜山、清州	以加强合作,共同解决旅游业发展的障碍、实现旅游业可持续发展、共同开发具有吸引力的旅游产品、扩大三国旅游交流与合作为主要议题	《釜山宣言》
2009	日本名古屋、高山市	三国旅游业界如何应对当前国际金融危机、甲型H1N1流感等诸多困难,恢复国际旅游,迎接东亚地区旅游大交流时代的到来,应对全球变暖问题等	《第四届中日韩旅游部长会议联合声明》
2010	中国杭州市、湖州市	面向未来、全面合作、共同繁荣	《杭州联合声明》《中日韩共倡低碳旅游倡议书》
2011	韩国江原道平昌	通过三国共同协作,推动三国旅游交流,共同制订旅游促进方案,巩固东北亚旅游合作的基础	《第六届中日韩旅游部长会议联合声明》《中日韩诚信旅游倡议书》
2015	日本东京	开启中日韩旅游交流新时代、推动游历东方活动、提高中日韩旅游交流品质	《第七届中日韩旅游部长会议联合声明》

首次中日韩三国旅游部长会议于 2006 年 7 月 3 日在日本旅游胜地北海道举圆满闭幕。在为期三天的会议上,中日韩三国旅游部长围绕扩大三国旅游交流与合作、扩大与区域外的旅游合作,签署并发表了《北海道宣言》,制订了"中日韩旅游交流计划";三国旅游行业团体和业界代表在同期召开的民间旅游大会上,共同发表了促进三国旅游业的《北海道倡议》。此外,三国业界还进行了颇有成效的商务洽谈和旅游促销,举办了"友好城市旅游研讨会"。本次会议的召开,意义深远。作为东亚地区三个重要国家,中日韩三国的旅游部长聚首共商三国加强旅游交流与合作的大计,这在三国旅游界交往史上还是第一次。"三国旅游部长会议的成功举办,掀开了中日韩旅游合作与发展新的一页。"时任中国国家旅游局局长邵琪伟如是评价。

第二届中日韩旅游部长会议于 2007 年 6 月 26 日在青岛发表关于促进中日韩旅游交流与合作的青岛宣言,强调三国多边旅游国际事务是全球旅游国际事务的重要组成部分,对提升亚洲旅游形象、构建世界旅游新格局具有积极影响。三国旅游部长就反对任何形式的恐怖主义,全球气候变暖对旅游业发展的威胁,旅游业在消除贫困、缩小地区差距等方面的作用等问题达成共识，并强调将组织好"中日邦交正常化35周年中日双向旅游交流活动""2007年日韩朝鲜通信使者/400周年纪念交流活动""中韩建交15周年和中韩交流年'中韩旅游周'"等交流活动。青岛宣言强调，三国未来旅游合作重点包括扩大三国间青少年交流规模，加快完善旅游人才机制，加强民间组织往来，共同改善旅游统计等内容。三国旅游部长表示，三国将分享重大国际活动带来的机遇，鼓励本国公民到对方国家及区域外旅游，同时携手共塑区域形象、吸引区外客源到访三国。

第三届中日韩三国旅游部长会议于2008年6月22日至25日在韩国釜山和清州召开。23日在釜山举行三国旅游部长会议、中日韩旅游论坛，三国旅游部门和业界围绕本次会议的中心议题展开深入探讨。三国旅游部长表示，为扩大中日韩三国间旅游交流，三国将密切合作，努力消除制约旅游发展的不利因素，特别是为游客旅行提供安全保障，及时交换旅游危机管理及应急信息。三国部长特别强调，应在加强应对自然灾害及气候变暖等领域展开务实合作。韩国一般旅行业协会会长郑宇植对本次会议给予了高度评价，认为会议议题更加务实、成效更加显著。此外，日韩旅游部长对四川灾区旅游业表示关切，大力支持四川地震灾区旅游恢复。

第四届中日韩旅游部长会议于2009年10月17日至18日在日本爱知县名古屋市和岐阜县高山市举办，中国、日本、韩国旅游部门和业界400多位代表参加会议。三国旅游部长就克服当前国际金融危机、甲型H1N1流感等诸多困难恢复国际旅游，迎接东亚地区旅游大交流时代的到来，应对全球变暖问题，下届会议等议题进行探讨。会议发布了《第四届中日韩旅游部长会议联合声明》，达成多项共识。三国表示将克服当前面临的国际金融危机、甲型H1N1流感等困难，努力恢复国际旅游交流；抓住中国2010年上海世博会机遇，积极开发各种世博会旅游产品，促进国际旅游交流；深化旅游界各方合作，迎接21世纪东亚地区旅游大交流的到来；共同推动可持续旅游产品的开发。

2010年8月22日，第五届中日韩旅游部长会议在杭州召开，中日韩三方的旅游企业代表、航空界代表和媒体共 300 余人出席了会议。会议围绕着"交流合作、提升品质、发展共赢"的本届业界交流的主题进行了热烈的探讨。三方嘉宾就"学习友邦的先进经验、提升中国旅行社行业的整体水平""关于交流合作""以中日韩共同观光为主题 FI 大会提案""中日韩三国观光交流对策——BE-SE-TO（北京—首尔—东京）以观光丝绸之路产业来实践的方案""关于提升品质、发展共赢""构建基于亚洲价值观的旅游合作机制"6 个题目进行了演讲。会议一致认为：中日韩旅游市场的进一步繁荣，就是对三方经济发展的促进、就是对三方民间文化交流的促进、就是对三国人民增进了解加深友谊的促进。会议提出了三方业界的合作将向更具体、更深入的领域推进，诸如：风险控制、环境保护、人才培训、专项交流、区域旅游线路开发和促销等。

2011 年 5 月，第六届中日韩旅游部长会议在韩国平昌开幕。三国旅游部长就"对于旅游紧急危机情况的发生共同建立应对体系""为扩大中日韩旅游交流规模，树立并推进 2020 旅游展望""促进签署中日韩诚信旅游倡议书""为扩大中日韩旅游交流，开发共同项目"等议题进行了深入探讨。在达成诸多共识的基础上，三方签署并发布了《第六届中日韩旅游部长会议联合声明》。邵琪伟表示三国旅游业界携手共进、共同发展，成为全球区域旅游交流合作的重要典范，也探索出了一条区域经济一体化背景下国家间产业层面合作的成功之路。韩国文化体育旅游部长官郑炳国在致辞中表示自第一届中日韩旅游部长会议召开以来，三国间的旅游规模从 6 年前的 1 200 万人次增加到 1 665 万人次，旅游业成为三国 21 世纪的重点发展产业。大畠章宏在致辞中表示，三国国民通过旅游途径不仅实现了人员交流数量的增加，也增进了三国人民之间的了解、理解和信任，对东北亚地区的和平、繁荣发展具有深远的意义。

2015 年 4 月，第七届中日韩旅游部长会议在日本东京举行。会议联合声明提出将以开启中日韩旅游交流新时代大幕为契机，作为共同旅游目的地，联合推广"游历东方"旅游活动，以吸引地区外游客。会议上，三国旅游部长就开启中日韩旅游交流新时代、推动"游历东方"活动、提高中日韩旅游交流品质等议题进行了深入探讨，达成了诸多共识，并共同签署和发表了《联合声明》，提出有效提升中日韩旅游便利化，力争到2020年，实现三国往来人数达到3 000万人次的目标。三国旅游部长认为，三国互访人数已达到2 000万人次，中日韩旅游进入了一个新时代。三国将共同深化三方合作，为游客提供更加便捷、友好的旅游环境；联合推出体育旅游产品、节庆旅游产品和世界遗产之旅、古都之旅、美食之旅、邮轮之旅等"一程多站"式旅游产品；共同强化监管，提高旅游交流品质。

五、东亚商务论坛

（一）背景资料

东亚商务论坛是经过外交部和财政部批准的亚洲区域合作专项资金项目之一，是促进中国、日本、韩国与东盟十国经贸交流与合作的一项重要举措，外交部对此高度重视。李克强总理在第16次东盟与中日韩领导人会议上特别强调中方要继续举办东亚商务论坛等活动。在此背景下，中国贸促会负责牵头举办东亚商务论坛，为东盟、中、日、韩、澳大利亚、新西兰和印度的工商界人士提供沟通的平台，并就共同关心的问题展开切实的合作。

（二）往届简况

论坛的规模逐渐扩大、规格逐步提高。一位正部长、三位副部长以及近500名企业代表出席第六届东亚商务论坛，在东亚地区具有一定的影响力。论坛主要包括开幕式、全体会议、专题圆桌会、企业洽谈、产品展示和参观考察等，促进亚洲区域重点领域经贸合作，推进东亚经济一体化进程。论坛通过东亚企业对接网、东亚贸易争端解决机制等项目，利用贸促会的专业优势，给企业提供务实帮助。东亚商务论坛迄今已召开了七次。

2014年5月13日，第6届东亚商务论坛暨第28次东亚商务理事会会议在海南省海口市召开。来自中国、韩国、日本、东盟国家等16个国家的政府官员、国际组织、驻华使节、商协会、学者和工商企业代表近400余人出席论坛。本届论坛以"互利合作引领东亚发展"为主题,旨在加强东亚各国工商界对话交流,促进区域经贸合作。海南省人民政府副省长李国梁在讲话中指出,海南将全面深化与东亚、东南亚、澳大利亚等国家的合作交往,加强在热带高效农业、旅游、清洁能源、海洋渔业等多领域合作,促进多边共赢,力争使海南成为21世纪海上丝绸之路的桥头堡和服务基地。与会的政府官员、工商界、学术界人士围绕"聚焦经济发展扩大互利共赢"和"创新发展模式深化产业合作"等议题进行了讨论。会议期间,中国贸促会副会长于平分别会见了来自柬埔寨、缅甸、菲律宾等的政府官员和工商界人士,就加强中柬、中缅和中菲经贸合作、举办"一带一路"相关活动、首届东亚投资论坛和中菲商务理事会会议等议题进行了深入探讨。

2015年5月13日,第七届东亚商务论坛正式开幕,来自东亚、东南亚、南亚和大洋洲包含中国在内的16国商务机构和企业代表来到杭州出席会议。本届论坛主题为"扩大务实合作,实现共同繁荣",重点就金融合作、中小企业合作等领域展开讨论。中国贸促会副会长于平表示,从现在到2020年,亚洲五年投资需求达8 000亿美元,对企业而言蕴藏无限商机。杭州市市长张鸿铭认为,当前中国提出了建设"一带一路"重要战略构想,东盟也提出了关于地区全面经济伙伴关系合作倡议,这些都为杭州与东亚国家间的经贸合作带来了新的契机。东亚商务论坛为国内企业了解东亚市场搭建了平台,企业借论坛进行品牌展示,不少杭企表示希望进军东亚市场。

东亚商务论坛是我国亚洲区域合作专项商务活动,是促进中国、日本、韩国与东盟十国经贸交流与合作的一项重要举措,为东盟国家及中国、日本和韩国的工商界人士提供沟通的平台。通过东亚商务论坛,东亚国家之间对话与协调日益增强,相互依存不断提高,经贸合作取得了显著成果。此外,不少企业带着自己的优质产品前来展示、宣传。对企业来说,东亚国家作为"一带一路"的重要组成部分,未来发展潜力巨大,而这次论坛为他们熟悉甚至深入东亚市场提供了机会。

六、东亚（辽宁）国际旅游博览会

（一）背景资料

东亚国际旅游博览会是由国家旅游局、辽宁省政府、大连市政府主办，辽宁省旅游局、大连市旅游局承办的专业性国际展会，并得到了国内外 20 余家官方旅游机构鼎力支持，具有较高的权威性和广泛性。东亚国际旅游博览会致力于东亚，尤其是中国东北及环渤海地区出入境旅游市场的推广和交流。

东亚国际旅游博览会在国家旅游局、辽宁省和大连市政府的精心培育下，于 2004 年起至今已举办十二届，先后有近 30 个国家和地区、国内 20 多个省、市、区的 1 000 多家旅游企业参展，近万名海外旅界精英参会，而且呈发展之势。展会立足东亚，关注欧美，是具有强烈国际色彩的区域型专业展会，是东北地区规模最大的国际性展会，辐射国内 30 余个省、市、自治区及海外 20 余个国家和地区。

近年来，辽宁省旅游业以其独特的地域风情和自然环境大力发展温泉、乡村、沟域、滑雪等特色旅游，实现了大发展、快发展，已经成为辽宁省最具活力、发展最快的产业之一。通过举办"东博会"，对推广特色旅游产品、提升服务水平、拉长产业链条、打造旅游品牌等战略，起到强有力的推动作用。

（二）相关成果

2004 年 8 月 5 日至 7 日在大连星海会展中心举行的第一届东亚国际旅游博览会是在辽宁实施老工业基地振兴和进一步扩大开放战略的形势下举办的，也是辽宁首次主办区域性国际旅游展会。

第二届东亚国际旅游博览会于 2005 年 8 月 26 日至 28 日在大连举行。

2006 年 10 月 20 日至 22 日第三届东亚国际旅游博览会在大连市举行。

第四届东亚国际旅游博览会于 10 月 19 日至 21 日在大连市举行，本届东博会将举办专业买家洽谈会、旅行社同业交流会、旅游产品（项目）推介会等一系列高水准的活动。

第五届东亚国际旅游博览会于 2008 年 10 月 10 日至 12 日在大连市举行。

2011 年 9 月 27 日世界旅游日,由辽宁省旅游局和本溪市政府共同举办的第八届东亚国际旅游交易会暨本溪枫叶节在辽宁省本溪市召开。本次交易会更加突出交易功能,交易会还融进了温泉旅游论坛、冰雪旅游论坛、边境旅游高峰论坛等高端活动,成为东亚国家和地区旅游交流与合作的重要载体和依托。另外本届交易会将更新形式,在沈阳、大连、丹东、锦州、盘锦五个城市逐步建立东亚国际旅游交易会的永久性会馆,放大展示辽宁旅游资源的咨询中心功能,以此演绎出四个中心,即辽宁旅游资讯中心、东亚乃至国际旅游资讯中心、辽宁及国际旅游产品销售中心、辽宁纪念品乃至旅游商品销售及展示中心,扩大交易会的功能和影响力。

第九届东亚国际旅游交易会为实现东亚国际旅游交易会的可持续发展,辽宁省旅游局在盘锦市成立了"东亚国际旅游交易会盘锦咨询中心",咨询中心设在盘锦国贸饭店一楼,由旅游咨询中心、旅游销售中心、旅游推广中心和旅游演艺中心组成,常年展示各参展国家或地区以及国内、省内各地的旅游资源和产品,落实和承办各地旅游推介会等活动。本次展会为境内外展商提供了 40 个展位。在东亚国际旅游城市品牌联展中,来自各地的旅游产品、本市旅游产品及"盘锦礼物"特色旅游商品,让市民大饱眼福。这次活动突出了湿地风情、向海发展等特色鲜明的盘锦元素,彰显了旅游搭台、经济唱戏的根本宗旨,一大批重点项目签约落地,签约金额 941.8 万元。

第十届东亚国际旅游交易会于 2013 年 5 月 17 日至 19 日在沈阳举行。本次展区开设了旅游目的地、酒店用品、旅游商品等各类展位 400 余个,举办了旅游产品推介会、旅游商品展、旅游大卖场等活动,有来自韩国、俄罗斯、泰国等十余个国家和地区的旅行商及旅游业界人士千余人以及万余观众参加。本届旅游交易会更重视由过去的旅游专业展示向旅游交易的转变,进一步拓展参展领域,而且还组织旅行社、景区点、酒店等多家旅游企业开展面向公众的展卖活动,这对提升展会服务及创新发展做出了新贡献,同时展会还为加强中、韩、俄之间的旅游交流与合作搭建了业务对接的平台，展示了东亚国家和地区的整体形象和旅游特色产品。

第十一届东亚（辽宁）国际旅游交易会于2014年5月16日至18日在辽宁工业展览馆举办。本届展会展区分为旅游形象、智慧旅游、旅游大卖场、酒店用品及旅游美食展区。来自日本、韩国、朝鲜、美国等12个国家和地区，国内8省区市及省内16个市县200余旅游机构、旅游企业将参加本届交易会。本次交易特设了智慧旅游体验展区，展会形式由旅游形象展示向旅游交易的转变，重点突出与辽宁省主要客源市场的国家和地区及北方十省区基础上，进一步加强与广东等长三角、珠三角等国内重点客源地区的交流与合作，另外媒体宣传形式也有新突破。

以"生态丹东、乐游辽宁、东亚风情、融合共赢"为主题的第十二届东亚（辽宁）国际旅游博览会暨丹东鸭绿江国际旅游节（以下简称"东博会"）于2015年9月10日至12日在中朝边境城市丹东市举办。本届东博会，是国家旅游局2015年确定重点展会，也是辽宁主动融入和对接"一带一路"发展、落实东北老工业基地全面振兴、打造辽宁东北亚旅游集散地和丹东国家级中朝旅游集聚区的一次重要举措，是东亚地区旅游产品展示、销售和交流的平台。来自韩国、日本、俄罗斯、蒙古、朝鲜、新加坡、马来西亚、印度尼西亚以及中国香港、中国澳门、中国台湾等20个东北亚国家和地区参展。展会为期三天，期间将举办16项重要活动，包括中外旅行商合作发展大会、赴朝旅游说明会、辽宁旅游商品创意设计大赛作品展、各参展国家及地区旅游说明会、第三届鸭绿江国际游泳节等重要旅游专业活动，同时丹东还重点推出了"一江四线"旅游产品，游客不但可以欣赏丹东鸭绿江青山绿水生态景观，而且还可以赴朝鲜一日游，一览两国风情。除此之外，本届"东博会"参展的除传统旅行社、酒店、景区等旅游产品外，重点推出了旅游商品、旅游房车、汽车露营、户外用品、旅游装备制造以及游船游艇、航空铁路、特色美食等新兴旅游业态。展会上推出的旅游商品丰富而有特色。

Chapter 1
Prosperous East Asian International Tourism Market

Section 1 Northeast Asian International Tourism Market

Northeast Asian countries have long history, splendid culture, gorgeous sights and huge tourism market demands. With decades of development, Northeast Asia has become an important part of the international tourism market structure, favored by more and more tourists from all over the world. Northeast Asia international tourism market is showing a thriving prosperity.

1.1 The development of Northeast Asia inbound tourism

1.1.1 Inbound tourism growth maintained

Taking the data released by the International Tourism Organization in 2015 as an example, the number of international visitors to Northeast Asia increased by 7%. Japan, the main destination in Northeast Asia, grew by 29% and Korea by 17%. As the largest destination of Northeast Asia, China, received more than 56 million inbound visitors.

1.1.2 Good basis of regional cooperation in Northeast Asia

Northeast Asia is becoming one of the most dynamic regions in the world and has become one of the most promising areas in the tourism industry because of the close economic ties and cultural integration of Northeast Asia. The countries are closely connected with each other, with close cultural exchanges, profound cultural backgrounds, good resource mix, and many world-class resources, which are mutual source markets. In the early 1990s, representatives of the governments of China, Japan and South Korea initiated the establishment of the Association of Northeast Asia Regional Governments and some related tourism organizations. They are committed to expanding the policy dialogue between the member countries and further promoting interregional international tourism exchange. The establishment and effective work of these organizations have effectively promoted the Northeast Asian regional tourism intergovernmental collaboration, information sharing, personnel exchanges and tourism economic development.

The current process of economic globalization and regional integration has also profoundly affected the development of the world tourism industry. Along with Asia-Pacific economic rise, especially China's rise to the world's second economy, the world's tourism hotspot is gradually transferred to the Asia-Pacific region. Northeast Asian tourism market has great potential and broad prospects, where the tendency of tourism cooperation has become increasingly evident. In the near future, Northeast Asia will be the most important tourist area in the Asia-Pacific region.

1.1.3 Northeast Asian countries are main sources and destinations to each other

In recent years, the number of tourists between China, Japan and South Korea is rising, and the three countries are the important sources to each other. Japan and South Korea have been China's two largest sources, while Japan and China are South Korea's two main sources. Such interdependence is a solid foundation for tourism cooperation between the three countries. In 2003, the leaders of the three countries signed the *Joint Declaration on the Promotion of Tripartite Cooperation among Japan, the People's Republic of China and the Republic of Korea*, and proposed a joint tourism promotion plan to enhance the tourism popularity in the world. In 2014, the number of mutual tourists between China, Japan and South Korea reached 20.14 million, among which the number of mutual tourists between China and South Korea reached 10.31 million, and the number of mutual tourists between China and Japan reached 5.03 million.

In 2015, China received 133.8204 million inbound tourists, an increase of 4.14% from previous year. Among them, 4.4444 million tourists were Korean tourists, accounting for 17.10% of total inbound tourists, ranking first, which was followed by

Japan, accounting for 9.61%. Japan's tourism development is robust since the launch of "Nation-building upon Tourism Strategy" in 2003. In recent years, Japan has become a major destination for Chinese tourists, and shopping has also become one of the important purposes for Chinese tourists to travel to Japan. According to the statistics of Japan National Tourism Organization (JNTO), in 2014, the number of inbound tourists to Japan reached 13.41 million, an increase of more than 3 million from previous year, of which the number of Chinese tourists increased from 1.31 million to 2.41 million, ranking the third place, and in 2015, the number of Chinese tourists exceeded 4.90 million, ranking the first. South Korea also put the tourism industry in the key position of the economic development strategy, and in 2015, the per capita consumption value of Chinese tourists to South Korea was about USD2,200 (equivalent to RMB14,283), more than double the per capita consumption of total inbound tourists to South Korea. In 2015, the total number of Chinese tourists to South Korea reached more than 6 million, accounting for more than 40% of the total number of inbound tourists to South Korea. Chinese tourists contributed 1.6% to the GDP of South Korea in 2015.

On April 12, 2015, the 7th China-Japan-South Korea Ministerial Conference on Tourism was held in Tokyo, releasing a joint statement that, in 2020, the number of mutual tourists between the three countries would reach 30 million. By virtue of the Winter Olympics and the Paralympics in Pyeongchang, South Korea from February to March, 2018 and the Summer Olympics and the Paralympics in Tokyo, Japan from July to September, 2020, East Asia would have the opportunity to attract more tourists. The visa conditions would be relaxed to make the travel between the three countries more convenient.

1.2 Challenges to the development of Northeast Asian inbound tourism

Northeast Asian inbound tourism is booming and fruitful, but there are still many challenges that may affect the cooperation of tourism development.

1.2.1 Politics

The political environment in Northeast Asia is complex and volatile. How to coordinate the relationship between the various regions, establish political mutual trust and create a favorable political environment has become a common question for Northeast Asian countries.

1.2.2 Emergencies

Northeast Asia is located in the seismically active zone, with frequent natural disasters, especially the Tohoku earthquake (11 March, 2011 at Kesennuma) that caused tsunami and secondary disasters like nuclear leakage, impacted the tourism market in Northeast Asia at that time.

1.2.3 Economics

In Northeast Asia, economic development is unbalanced, for there are both developed and developing countries. There are big differences in economic system, market mechanism, and economic development strategy etc.

1.2.4 Systems

At present, the cooperation in Northeast Asia has taken on a new pattern in multi-forms, multi-channels, multi-levels and multi-fields, but the bilateral cooperation and multilateral cooperation are in a loose dialogue stage, and the binding force is rather limited. There are many institutions and conferences for cooperation, but their ability to solve practical problems is insufficient, there is not enough guarantee for the agreements passed by them, nor protection for system legislation. Compared with the EU, this region is in lack of a stable and unified organization to develop long-term cooperation plan in the overall interests of the region, restricting the quality and effectiveness of cooperation.

1.3 Potential of Northeast Asian inbound tourism development

As reported in the *Global Tourism Outlook 2020*, Northeast Asian tourism is expected to grow at a rate of 7.2% in the coming years, making it one of the fastest growing regions in the global tourism industry. Therefore, the global tourism is no longer just the cake of Europe and Americas, the Asia-Pacific tourism market will get a large share. According to the World Tourism Organization, in 2012, the number of tourists all over the world reached 1 billion, the number of tourists in Asia-Pacific region increased by 8%, Northeast Asia's total tourism demand grew by 8.6% from the previous year, ranking second in the world. World Tourism Organization predicts that by 2020 the number of international tourists will reach 1.623 billion, of which, the number of tourists in Northeast Asia will reach 223 million, accounting for 15%, so tourism industry will certainly become the emerging industry of the region.

In recent years, as emerging countries become the emerging tourist sources and destinations, the focus of the global tourism is shifting to the east. Northeast Asia is the representative of this trend, with promising tourism market, and expanding tourism development space, which provides a good opportunity for Northeast Asian international tourism market that is already prosperous now.

1.3.1 Special geography drives the development of cruise tourism

Currently, the international tourism consumption demand is in the following basic trend: by organization style, in the tide of personalization, FIT tourism and in particular family tourism becomes the global fashion; by the motif and purpose of tourism, eco-tourism, cultural tourism, incentive tourism, adventure tourism, scientific tourism, submarine tourism, and other various forms of theme tourism, constitute the main theme of tourism.

Northeast Asia is driving the development of global cruise industry. In Northeast Asia, cruise ships are larger, and major cruise operators have the highest marketing budget in China. For example, Xiamen has extended its cruise season; Tianjin has set up a cruise terminal; Qingdao plans to open routes to Dubai; Shanghai plans to set up its own cruise companies; and Nanjing plans to build a cruise terminal. Chinese travel agencies are also seeking the diversified cruise interests, for example, Ctrip purchased some cruise ships, and Spring Airlines also signed contracts with nearly 15 cruise ships. In 2015, the number of Chinese outbound cruise tourists reached 1.9 million, and the market transaction value reached RMB 4.5 billion, including online cruise market value RMB 1.33 billion, up 60.1% year on year, and the cruise tourism is greatly attracting tourists by cost-effective, comfortable cross-border tourism and leisure duty-free shopping and other features. As leisure tourism and outbound tourism continue to rise, China's cruise tourism industry has entered a period of explosive growth. Among the cruise routes, more than 83% of Chinese tourists prefer Japan or South Korea route, followed by Southeast Asia (Vietnam) route. In 2015, Japanese ports played a shining role, plus Japan's visa-free new policy on cruise ships, there were unprecedentedly abundant products of Chinese cruise tourism to Japan. The most favored cruise destinations were Kagoshima, Fukuoka and Nagasaki. The development and rapid growth of cruise products have enriched the experience of Northeast Asian inbound tourism.

1.3.2 The Asia Pacific economic rise lays a solid foundation for regional cooperation of Northeast Asian inbound tourism

Due to geographic proximity, China, Japan and South Korea are closely related to each other, and all the three enjoy a wealth of tourism resources. As Asia Pacific economy is rising, the three countries will work closely with each other in this region, to follow the actual requirement of world tourism development.

Section 2 Southeast Asian International Tourism Market

2.1 Status quo of Southeast Asian inbound tourism

2.1.1 Stable growth

Southeast Asian inbound tourism is growing at a rate higher than world average since 1980s, except the setbacks in 1997 (Asian financial crisis), 2003 (SARS) and 2004 (tsunami). Currently, the number of ASEAN yearly inbound tourists has exceeded 65 million.

2.1.2 Regionality

By geography, the Southeast Asian inbound tourists are mainly from ASEAN countries. In fact, the ASEAN countries become the tourist sources for each other. In 2005, Southeast Asia received 51.2876 million inbound tourists totally, 23.2543 million (or 45.3%) of whom are from inside the ASEAN. In 2006 and 2007, this percentage reduced slightly, but in 2008 and 2009, this percentage increased to 46.3% and 47.1% respectively. Since 2010, this regionality is consolidated and strengthened as the tourism of Southeast Asian countries is furthered developed.

2.1.3 Disparity in development

Different countries in Southeast Asia have different levels of economic development, so their levels of tourism development are also different. Singapore, Thailand and Malaysia are mature in tourism development, which also receive the most inbound tourists. In 2005, Malaysia received the most inbound tourists among ASEAN countries, the number reached 16.431 million, accounting for 32% of all ASEAN inbound tourists; followed by Thailand and Singapore, 11.517 million and 8.942 million respectively, accounting for 22.46% and 17.43% respectively; the number of inbound tourists in Malaysia, Thailand, Singapore, Indonesia, Philippines and Brunei (6 countries) accounted for 87% of the regional total, while the number of inbound tourists in Vietnam, Burma, Laos and Cambodia (4 countries) accounted for the remaining 13%. In 2009, Malaysia still received the most inbound tourists, the number reached historical high, 23.646 million, accounting for 36.14% of the regional total, and the number of inbound tourists in the foregoing 6 countries accounted for 85.87% of regional total. So far, this structure is not much changed, which indicates that the foregoing 6 countries have developed tourism industry earlier, their cultural tourism products are outstanding, and their coastal leisure resort tourism, urban business conference and conference tourism are improved, so they become the famous international tourism destinations of Asia Pacific region. Meanwhile, we should note that the remaining Southeast Asian countries, including the foregoing 4 countries, have developed tourism industry later, but they still have a wealth of characteristic tourism resources, and in recent years, their tourism industry develops fast, and it won't be long for them to catch up with the leading 6 countries.

2.1.4 Competition

Due to the proximity in geography, culture and history, all Southeast Asian countries (excluding Laos and Singapore) have advantageous natural tourism resources, featured by sea islands, sea beach and tropical sights, and advantageous cultural resources featured by historical relics, religious buildings and folk customs. Therefore, their tourism product structure is somewhat the same.

2.2 Advantages for Southeast Asian inbound tourism development

2.2.1 Rich tourism resources

Southeast Asian tourism resources are diversified, colorful, both rich in natural landscape and cultural attractions.

By natural tourism resources, Southeast Asia is full of tropical sights and beautiful beaches and islands, which are of great appeal to tourists. In most areas the climate is humid, with lush vegetation, lush tropical forests and rare birds and animals. Many tropical forests are inaccessible, maintaining the original ecology, which provide inexhaustible tourism resources for forest adventure, scientific expedition and holiday tourism. Moreover, in the Malay Archipelago and Indochina Peninsula, there are many beautiful sights, charming beaches and islands. These beautiful beaches and numerous islands, warm sunshine, azure sea water, soft beaches and tropical rainforest landscape attract a large number of tourists to come here for leisure, vacation; for example, Thailand's Pattaya Beach, Phuket Island, Indonesia's Bali, Singapore's Sentosa Island, the Philippines Cebu Beach, Vietnam's Halong Bay have become world famous tourist destinations. In addition, volcanic and karst landscapes in Southeast Asia provide valuable resources for the development of tourism industry.

By cultural tourism resources, Southeast Asia has numerous historical relics, antiques, and colorful folk customs. Southeast Asia, with a long history, is one of the birthplaces of mankind. The natives have created splendid cultures, and left a large number of historical relics. The imperial palaces and various religious buildings are the most unique historical and cultural heritage of Southeast Asia. For example, Grand Palace (Thailand), Yogyakarta Sultan's Palace (Indonesia), The Malacca Palace (Philippines), Angkor Wat (Cambodia), Reclining Buddha (Thailand), Jade Buddha Temple (Thailand), Borobudur (Indonesia), the National Mosque (Malaysia) etc have become famous tourist attractions. Moreover, there are many ethnic groups and complex religious beliefs in Southeast Asia. All ethnic groups have formed their own unique ethnic culture, folk customs, which are mysterious and attractive to tourists.

In addition, in the modernization of Southeast Asia, there are a variety of conference and exhibition centers, shopping centers and modern recreational facilities becoming important tourist attractions, too.

2.2.2 Governmental support

In Southeast Asia, all governments have fully recognized the importance and contribution of tourism industry to local society and economy, so they are developing tourism industry as their pillar industry. In order to develop inbound tourism, the countries have developed strategies and taken measures in enhancing tourism legislation and management, improving infrastructure, developing and updating tourism projects, strengthening tourism publicity, simplifying entry procedures, and offering policy incentives.

Malaysia has launched the visa on arrival policy since 2006, so that tourists from 23 countries may apply for one-time entry visa on arrival at immigration checkpoint to facilitate the development of inbound tourism. Similarly, in order to promote the development of inbound tourism, Burma with underdeveloped tourism industry has also promoted the visa on arrival policy since 2010.

Thailand implemented a series of measures to stimulate tourism in 2009, requiring hotels and airlines to cut season prices, attract tourists at discounted prices, and shift the slogan from "Magic Thailand" to "Fantastic Thailand, Fantastic Prices"; the Thai government also held a press conference titled "Restart Thai Tourism" in Guangzhou, China.

2.2.3 Good platform for regional cooperation

In the context of economic globalization and regional economic integration, it is necessary for regional cooperation and joint development. Especially for Southeast Asian countries, the increasing cooperation in and out of the region has created a rare opportunity for them to develop inbound tourism.

Within the region, Southeast Asian countries have started regional tourism cooperation since 1970s, so far, they have formed a cooperation mechanism in multi-levels and multi-channels, and their international images are gradually in form, with outstanding effects in tourism cooperation, including regular tourism forums, tourism ministerial summits, visa-free and visa on arrival policies for tourists from some countries, reduction of visa charges and others. Currently, Southeast Asian countries are working hard to improve tourism market within the region, utilize local natural, cultural and historical resources, to integrate the whole region into the world's largest tourism market; at the same time, in order to create better conditions and platform for inbound tourism development, the countries within the region are also jointly developing tourism resources, and building tourism infrastructure in active cooperation.

Outside the region, Southeast Asian countries are working more and more closely with peripheral countries. For example, the ASEAN-China Free Trade Area (ACFTA) is established, the economic and trade cooperation between ASEAN and Japan, South Korea, Australia, India and New Zealand is intensifying, and their communication is becoming more and more frequent, while these countries are also the main sources of Southeast Asian inbound tourism, so Southeast Asia shall use the platform of regional cooperation to expand this tourism market in priority.

2.2.4 Stable source

The main source of Southeast Asian tourism is the countries in this region, in particular, Malaysia, Thailand, Indonesia and Philippines with developed tourism industry. Southeast Asia is a huge market with a population of 560 million. Due to ethnic, cultural and geographical proximity, the tourism psychology is also similar; moreover, the countries are developing fast in good conditions, and the whole region has huge potential of economic growth. Along with local economic rise and people's rising income, the tourism demand will also increase. In addition, they have relaxed immigration policies. Mutual visits between ASEAN people are expanding, so tourism within the region will become the best choice.

In addition, among the main sources of Southeast Asian inbound tourism, China, Japan, Australia, South Korea and Western countries are in recovery or economic boom, with increasing demand for inbound tourism, which is favorable for the expansion of Southeast Asian inbound tourism. In particular, China, closely related with Southeast Asia, has increasing outbound tourism demand, along with booming economy and people's increasing quality of life, and is becoming one of the major sources of ASEAN inbound tourism. It is anticipated that by 2020, China will become the largest source of Southeast Asian inbound tourism.

Chapter 2
International Tourism Market Conditions in Typical Countries of East Asia

Section 1　China

In 2015, China received more than 4.1 billion domestic and foreign tourists, with tourism revenue totaling RMB 4.13 trillion, including 4.0 billion domestic tourists with domestic tourism revenue RMB 3.42 trillion, up 10.5% and 13.1% year on year respectively, and Chinese resident per capita travel frequency was 2.98. In the whole year, China received 133 million inbound tourists, with inbound tourism revenue USD 113.65 billion, increasing by 4.0% and 7.8% year on year respectively. In 2015, 120 million Chinese residents traveled abroad, expending USD 104.5 billion, up 12.0% and 16.7% year on year respectively.

In the first half of 2016, China's tourism market expanded steadily. For example, there were 2.236 billion domestic tourists, up 10.47% from previous year; tourism revenue totaled RMB 2.25 trillion, up 12.4%; there were 67.87 million inbound tourists, with inbound tourism revenue USD 57.0 billion, up 3.8% and 5.3% year on year respectively; and 59.03 million Chinese residents traveled abroad, up 4.3% year on year.

1.1 China inbound tourism market conditions

1.1.1 Inbound tourism market size

In 2006-2015, the number of China's inbound tourists was fluctuating, and the growth rate was fluctuating as well. For example, in 2006, the number of inbound tourists reached 124.942 million, up 3.87% year on year; in 2007, the number rose to 131.8733 million, up 5.55% year on year; in 2008, the number fell to 130.027 million, down 1.40% year on year; in 2009, the number fell further to 126.4759 million, down 2.73% year on year; in 2010, the number recovered to 133.7622 million, up 5.76% year on year; in 2011, the number further rose to 135.4236 million, up 1.24% year on year; in 2012, the number fell to 132.4053 million, down 2.23% year on year; in 2013, the number further fell to 129.0778 million, down 2.51% year on year; in 2014, the number fell to 128.4983 million, down 0.45% year on year; in 2015, the number recovered to 133.8204 million, up 4.14% year on year. In 2015, China's inbound tourism market recovered for the first time after the decline of three consecutive years. It is anticipated that in the future the number of China's inbound tourists will pick up gradually.

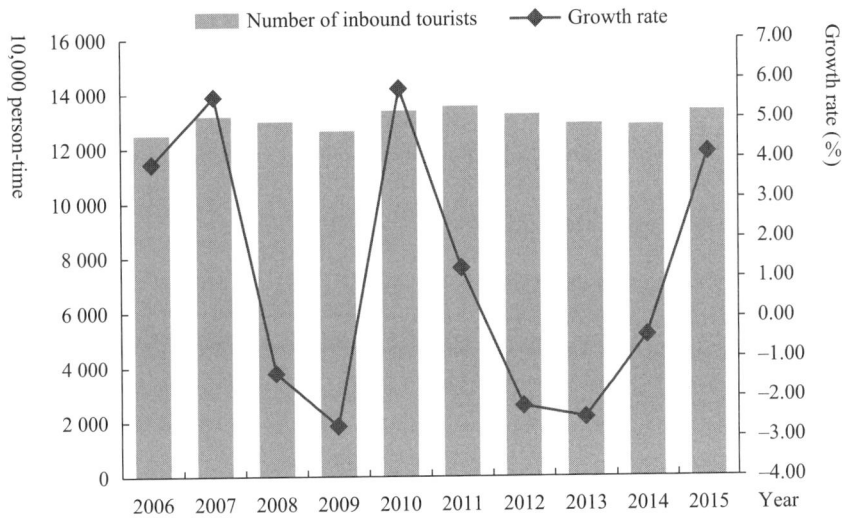

Figure 2-1　China's inbound tourism market size and growth in 2006-2015

1.1.2 The number of China's inbound overnight tourists ranked the fourth, following France, USA and Spain

According to the United Nations World Tourism Organization (UNWTO), in 2015, in the ranking of inbound overnight tourists quantity, China ranked the fourth (56.8857 million inbound overnight tourists). France ranked the first again (84.46 million inbound overnight tourists), while United States (USA) ranked the second (77.51 million inbound overnight tourists), and Spain ranked the third (68.22 million inbound overnight tourists).

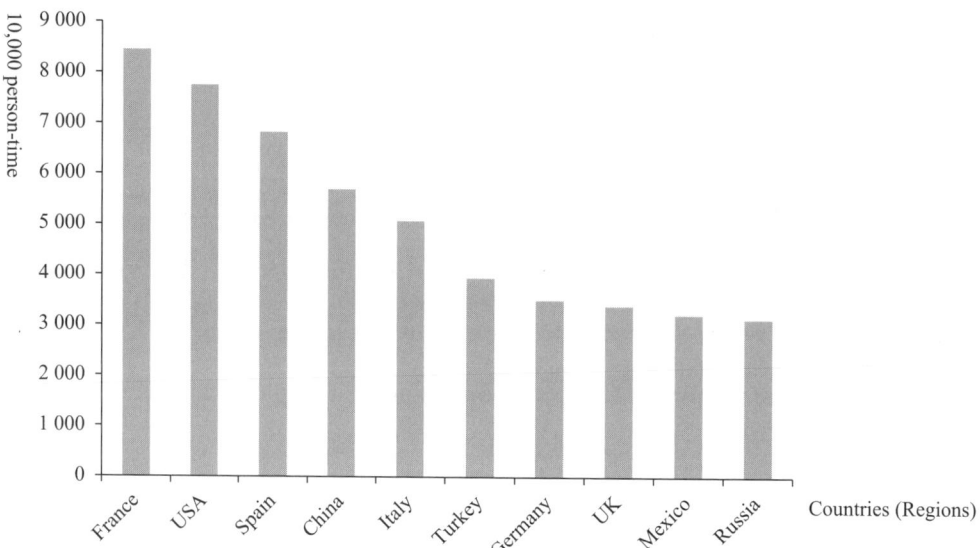

Figure 2-2 Top 10 countries by the number of inbound overnight tourists in 2015

1.1.3 Asian sources in a stable lead

According to statistics in 2011-2015, the main sources of China's inbound tourism were neighboring countries in Asia (62%), the other sources took smaller percentages, including Europe and Americas totaling 33%.

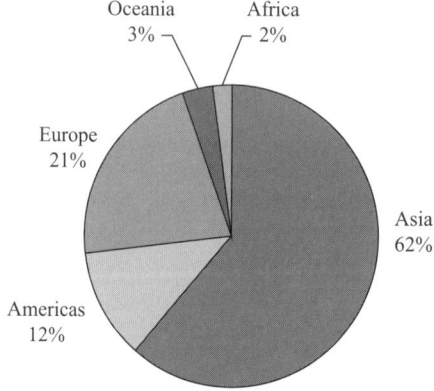

Figure 2-3 Market shares of major sources of China's inbound tourism in 2011-2015

As shown above, the sources in Asia took a large portion of China's inbound tourism market, above 50%, and in recent years, the number of China's inbound tourists from Asia maintained stable, and was much larger than the other sources.

1.1.4 Nearby sources of strategic importance

Regarding the structure of China's inbound tourist sources, in 2015, China received 4.4444 million Korean tourists, accounting for 17.10% of total inbound tourists to China, ranking the first; China received 2.4977 million Japanese tourists, 9.61% of total, ranking the second; 2.1608 million Vietnamese tourists, 8.32% of total, ranking the third (up from the fifth in previous year); 2.0858 million USA tourists, 8.03% of total, ranking the fourth (down from the third in previous year); 1.5823 million Russian tourists, 6.09% of total, ranking the fifth (down from the fourth in previous year). In total, South Korea, Japan, Vietnam, USA and Russia delivered 12.7710 million tourists to China, accounting for 49.15% of total inbound tourists to China. In other words, nearly half of the inbound tourist sources are concentrated on the top 5 countries.

In 2015, other source market conditions were as follows: China received 1.0755 million Malaysian tourists, accounting for 4.14% of total inbound tourists to China, ranking the sixth; 1.0141 million Mongolian tourists, 3.90% of total, ranking the seventh; 1.0040 million Philippine tourists, 3.86% of total, ranking the eighth (up from the ninth in previous year); 0.9053 million Singaporean tourists, 3.48% of total, ranking the ninth (down from the eighth in previous year); 0.7305 million Indian tourists, 2.81% of total, ranking the tenth; 0.6798 million Canadian tourists, 2.62% of total, ranking the eleventh (up from the twelfth in previous year); 0.6415 million Thai tourists, 2.47% of total, ranking the twelfth (up from the fourteenth in previous year); 0.6373 million Australian tourists, 2.45% of total, ranking the thirteenth (down from the eleventh in previous year); 0.6234 million German tourists, 2.40% of total, ranking the fourteenth; 0.5796 UK tourists, 2.23% of total, ranking the fifteenth; 0.5448 million Indonesian tourists, 2.10% of total, ranking the sixteenth; 0.4869 million French tourists, 1.87% of total, ranking the seventeenth; 0.2461 million Italian tourists, 0.95% of total, ranking the eighteenth (up from previous year).

South Korea, Japan, Vietnam, the USA, Russia, Malaysia, Mongolia, the Philippines, Singapore and India together delivered 17.5004 million tourists to China, accounting for 67.35% of the total inbound tourists to China, that is, nearly 70% of the inbound tourist sources are concentrated on the top 10 countries.

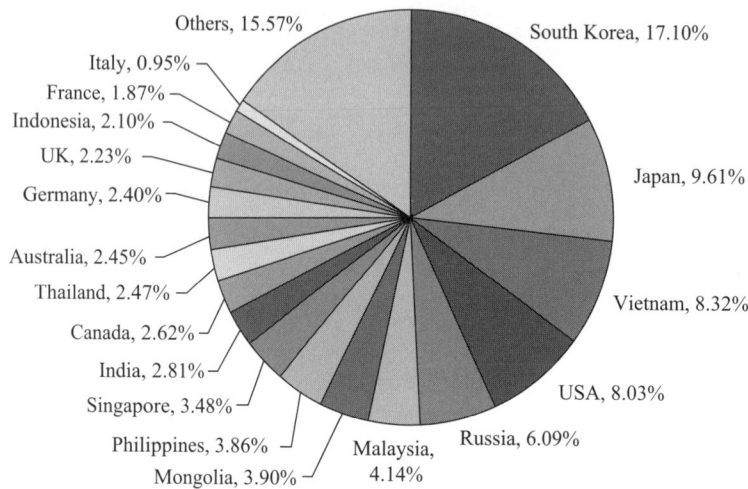

Figure 2-4 Structure of major sources of China's inbound tourism in 2015

1.2 China's outbound tourism market conditions

1.2.1 Outbound tourism market size

In 2015, China's outbound tourism market maintained growth, and in the whole year, the number of China's outbound tourists reached 117 million, up 8.96% year on year.

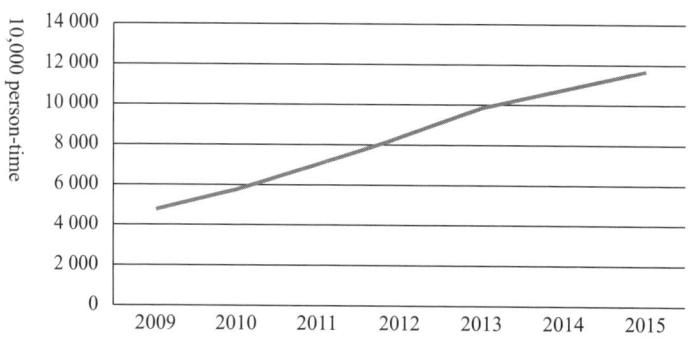

Figure 2-5 China's outbound tourists in history

1.2.2 Nearby destinations in absolute dominance

In 2015, China's outbound tourism destinations were typically nearby destinations. For example, Chinese outbound tourists in Asia accounted for 73.3% of total Chinese outbound tourists, followed by Europe (11.5%), Americas (8.2%), Oceania (3.6%), Africa (2.7%) and others (0.7%). The number of Chinese outbound tourists to Europe grew fast, up 23.8% year on year. In 2015, Chinese outbound tourists to Africa reduced significantly, down 61.8% year on year. The number of Chinese outbound tourists to Oceania grew at a lower rate, reducing from 13.8% in 2014 to 12.4% in 2015.

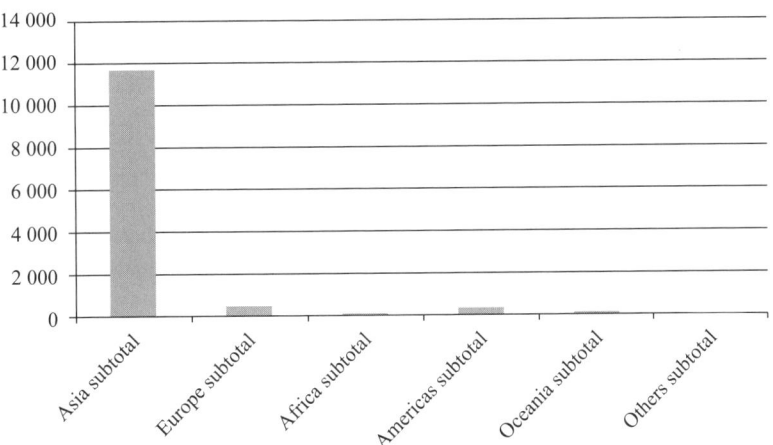

Figure 2-6　Market size of Chinese outbound tourist destinations in 2015

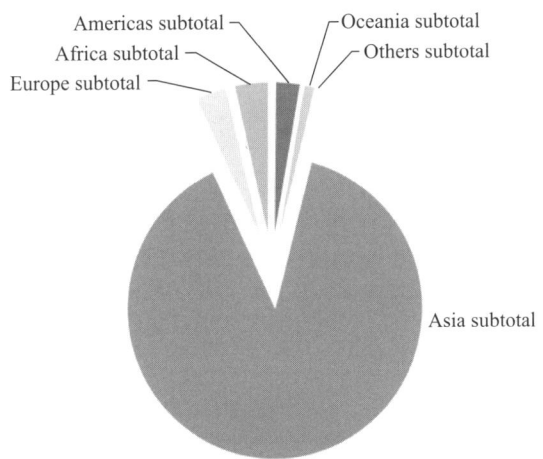

Figure 2-7　Market share of Chinese outbound tourist destinations in 2015

In 2015, the top 10 destinations of Chinese outbound tourists were: Thailand, South Korea, Japan, Vietnam, USA, Singapore, Russia, Australia, Indonesia, and Malaysia.

Section 2　Japan

2.1 Japan's inbound tourism market conditions

Japan's inbound tourism is performing well, because the country is actively performing the "Nation-building upon Tourism Strategy".

2.1.1 Stable structure, outstanding position in Asia market

The sources of Japan's inbound tourists maintained stable structure recently, with little changes. For example, around 70% of Japan's total inbound tourists were from Asia, without large fluctuation even in 2009 (bird flu) and 2011 (Tohoku earthquake). Around 11% were from North America, followed by 10% from Europe, and less than 10% from other regions.

Currently, China in place of South Korea has become the largest source of inbound tourists to Japan. According to Japan National Tourism Organization (JNTO), in 2015, 4.99 million inbound tourists were from China, up 107% year on year, and China became the largest source of Japan's inbound tourists.

There are two reasons for this structure. Firstly, geographical and cultural proximity. Japan is near China and South Korea, their culture and customs are very similar in many aspects, so Chinese tourists may feel home, and prefer Japan. Secondly, Japanese government has launched the entry tourism supporting policies. For example, Japan begins to issue personal travel visa to Chinese tourists since July 2009, largely relaxes the requirements for Chinese tourists to obtain personal travel visa since July 2010, and issues 3-year's multiple entry visa to Chinese tourists who are entering Japan from Okinawa since July 2011. All these preferential policies are stimulating the interest of Chinese tourists in travel to Japan.

2.1.2 Large impact of emergencies

In 2009 and 2011, the number of inbound tourists to China reduced, under the impacts of emergencies, such as bird flu in 2009 and Tohoku earthquake in 2011.

2.1.3 Small percentage of inbound tourism revenue in tourism economy size

According to JNTO, in 2011, Japan's tourism consumption revenue totaled JPY 23.8 trillion, including inbound tourist consumption JPY 1.3 trillion or 5.5% of total. In 2010, Japan's tourism consumption revenue totaled JPY 25.5 trillion, including inbound tourist consumption JPY 1.2 trillion or 4.7% of total.

2.1.4 Scenery concentration

According to JNTO, inbound tourist destinations concentrated on a few big cities. For example, Tokyo ranked the first, as 60.3% inbound tourists visited Tokyo in 2010, and 58.8% in 2009, followed by Osaka, Kyoto, Kanagawa, and Hokkaido among others.

2.2 Japan's outbound tourism market conditions

2.2.1 Stable market size

Japan is economically developed, highly populated, and is one of the major tourist sources of the world. Since Japan launched the "Overseas Travel Double Plan" in 1987, the number of Japanese outbound tourists increased significantly, and exceeded 10 million for the first time in 1990, reaching an unprecedented height, and thence, Japan became a large tourist source country, and Japanese outbound tourism began rapid growth. After 2000, Japanese outbound tourism grew slowly in fluctuation. In 2000, there were 17.82 million Japanese outbound tourists, and in 2014, this number reached 16.90 million. Generally speaking, Japan's outbound tourism market was stable. In recent years, the number of Japanese outbound tourists was in the decline, reducing from 18.4907 million in 2012 to 16.2138 million in 2015, at an average annual decrease of 4.5%.

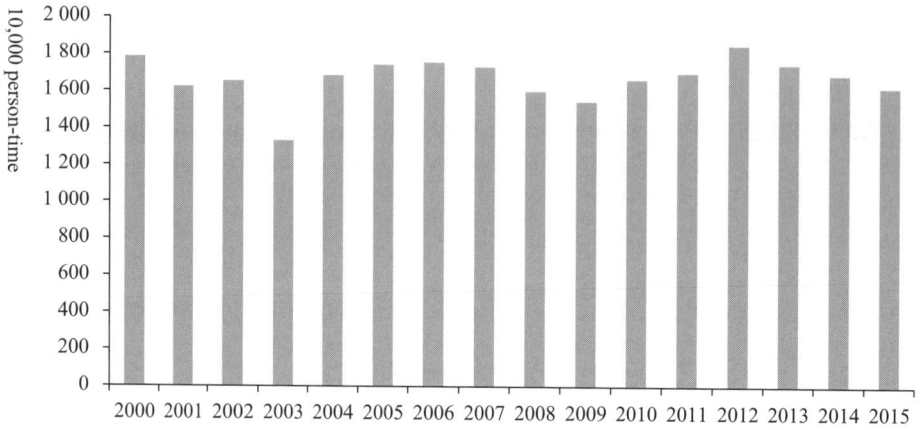

Figure 2-8　Japan's outbound tourism market size in history

2.2.2 Stable market structure

In 2014, the number of Japanese outbound tourists reached 16.9034 million, down 3.3% year on year, including 3.5794 million Japanese outbound tourists to the USA, accounting for 21.18% of total; and 2.7177 million Japanese outbound tourists to China, 16.08% of total.

Table 2-1　Top destinations of Japanese outbound tourists in 2008-2014 (expressed in 10 000 tourists)

Year	Total number of Japanese outbound tourists	Destination	The number of Japanese outbound tourists to destination	Destination	The number of Japanese outbound tourists to destination
2008	1 598.73	China	344.60	USA	325.00
2009	1 544.57	China	331.70	South Korea	305.30
2010	1 663.72	China	373.10	USA	338.60
2011	1 699.42	China	365.82	South Korea	328.91
2012	1 848.97	South Korea	351.87	China	351.82
2013	1 747.27	China	287.75	South Korea	274.78
2014	1 690.34	USA	357.94	China	271.77

Section 3 South Korea

3.1 South Korea inbound tourism market conditions

3.1.1 China is the largest inbound tourist source of South Korea

In 2015, the number of Chinese tourists to South Korea reached 6.11 million, accounting for about 40% of South Korea's total inbound tourists. According to Korea Tourism Organization (KTO), in the whole year of 2015, Chinese tourists contributed USD 22.0 billion or 1.6% of South Korea's GDP, in respect of accommodation, traffic, and shopping. In 2014, KTO and Hana Daetoo Securities announced that the number of Chinese tourists to South Korea was growing at average annual rate of 19.8%, and will reach 14.90 million in 2020, or 3.5 times the current number, when the Chinese tourist consumption in South Korea will exceed KWR 30 trillion (equivalent to RMB180 billion), contributing 8% retail value of South Korea.

3.1.2 Success to attract repeat customers

In 2015, 46.1% of the inbound tourists to South Korea had visited South Korea twice or more, and most inbound tourists were for the purpose of shopping.

53.9% of the inbound tourists visited South Korea for the first time of life, 16.3% twice, 7.9% thrice, and 21.9% four times or even more. The inbound tourists who visited South Korea for twice or more accounted for 46.1% of total. In particular, this percentage was 78.7% for inbound tourists from Japan, followed by Singapore, Hong Kong (China), Russia and China. When asked what they considered most in determining South Korea as the destination, 67.8% of the inbound tourists answered "Shopping", followed by "Foods" (42.8%), Historical and Cultural Relics (27.6%), Clothing and Fashion (23.6%). When asked "What is your favorite tourist site in South

Korea?" most inbound tourists answered "Myeong-dong", followed by Dongdaemun Market, ancient palace, N Seoul Tower and Hongdae-ipgu.

3.1.3 Chinese tourists consumed much in South Korea

The per capita inbound tourist consumption in South Korea was USD 2 127.4, and Chinese tourist consumption per capita was the highest, USD 2 204.5.

By field, inbound tourists consumed the most in shopping, USD 983 per capita, followed by accommodation (USD 417.7), foods (USD 291.1), and travel agency cost (USD 120.0), travel expense in South Korea (USD 109.4).

By source, per capita Chinese tourist consumption in South Korea was the highest, USD 2 204.5, followed by Europe and USA (USD 2 066.9 per capita) and Southeast Asia (USD 1 852.2 per capita).

By age, the smaller the age, the higher the tourist spent. The inbound tourists aged 15-20 spent the most, USD 2 527.1 per capita, followed by those aged 20-29 (USD 2 092.5 per capita), aged 30-39 (USD 2 074.1 per capita), and aged 41+ (USD 1 075.5 per capita).

3.2 South Korea's outbound tourism market conditions

In 2005, the number of Korean outbound tourists exceeded 10 million for the first time, reached 10.08 million, and this number increased to 11.61 million in 2006 and 13.325 million in 2007 respectively. This number dropped significantly by 10% in 2008 and 20.9% in 2009 respectively, under the impacts of financial crisis and bird flu (H1N1). The number started to recover since 2010, and the annual growth rate was 31.5% in 2015.

In recent years, although South Korea is in depression for a long time, such as the 3-year low of GDP in 2015, the number of Korean outbound tourists reached 19.3143 million, a historical new high, up 20.1% from 16.0807 million in 2014.

Section 4   Vietnam

4.1 Rapid growth of inbound tourism market in Vietnam recently

Vietnam National Administration of Tourism was established in 1960s, however, Vietnam tourism industry developed slowly before 1980s, under the influence of many factors, at that time, tourism industry served for the reception of Soviet and East European visitors. In 1981, Vietnam officially joined the UNWTO. Although Vietnam tourism industry started late, after many years of efforts, Vietnam tourism industry made remarkable progress. In 1990s, Vietnam tourism industry developed fast. Recently, the number of inbound tourists to Vietnam is increasing significantly.

In January-September 2016, Vietnam received 7.265380 million inbound tourists, up 25.7% year on year.

By source, inbound tourists from different countries have different stay length in Vietnam. Tourists from remote countries stayed longer in Vietnam, while those from nearby countries stayed in a less length of time.

4.2 Inbound tourist consumption level to be improved

Vietnam is rich in tourism resources, distributed around the country, suitable for various tourism products catering to different market demands. However, because human resources are not enough for international tourism, tourism resources are pending further development, and others, the number of inbound tourists and the revenue of Vietnam inbound tourism have a large space for improvement.

Section 5　Malaysia

5.1 High quality tourism resources

Malaysia is a tropical island near the equator, and the pleasant climate and excellent geography give Malaysia unique natural tourism resources. In Malaysia, there are bright sunshine, beautiful beaches, scenic islands, lush primeval forests, various caves, high mountains, highlighting the tropical characteristics. At the same time, long history, distinctive ethnic groups and colorful cultures have created numerous charmful human and cultural attractions of Malaysia.

Recently, Malaysia tourism industry develops fast, and its position and reputation in the global tourism market is increasing fast. For example, Kuala Lumpur, Malacca, Penang, Genting Resort City, Sabah, Langkawi, Redang Island etc have become world famous tourist destinations; Malaysia has also won the titles of "World's Best Tourist Destination", "Best Eco-tourism Destination", "Best Brand Promotion and Best Eco-tourism Destination", "Best Tourism Organization" in Asia, and "One of the Most Expensive Tourist Destinations" rated by the World Economic Forum. The titles or honors have added to Malaysia's appeal. Shopping Malaysia has eventually become a well-known brand associated with top-end shopping. National and international tourism delegations, dialogues and conferences are constantly promoting and advertising shopping in Malaysia. This is an important part of the *Malaysia Tourism Transformation Plan (MTTP:2020:36:168)* where the country has set a target of 36 million tourist arrivals with RM 168 billion tourist receipts in the year 2020. The Ministry of Tourism and Culture Malaysia (MOTAC) is put in the frontier of encouraging innovation and creativity.

5.2 Inbound tourism market is promising

In addition to the rich tourism resources, good business environment and infrastructure, the correct formulation and implementation of tourism policy is another important reason for the rapid development of Malaysia's tourism industry. Malaysian tourism policy is to propose the tourism development objectives and main measures in the national economic program, and to design national tourism development policies and special tourism policies. The government has formulated and implemented special tourism policies, including rural tourism master plan, national eco-tourism program, student tourism project, and the second home project, etc.

In order to promote the development of inbound tourism, Malaysia Tourism Promotion Board (MTPB) was established in 1992, committed to the development of Malaysia into a famous international tourist country. In addition to the launch of the "Tourism Year", the MTPB has been focusing on tourism overseas marketing, and has to set up offices in some major source countries, to carry out tourism promotion, advertising activities, so that more and more people will get to know Malaysia. It is reported that as early as in 2000, the Malaysian government broadcast travel advertising in CNN television program, which was the first example in Asian countries. In recent years, Malaysian tourism industry is an identity of Malaysia built by the government. The MOTAC is to put forward the "Malaysia, Charm of Asia" tourism slogan. In order to better promote tourism, the MTPB employed 13 PR companies and 11 advertising companies from worldwide, and carry out public relations activities according to the characteristics of different countries.

Most inbound tourists to Malaysia come from Asia Pacific region, in particular the Southeast Asian countries with the most developed tourism industry. The ASEAN is now trying to promote the integration of regional tourism, the countries actively develop the tourism market within the region, and strive to integrate the Southeast Asian region into the world's largest tourism market, which undoubtedly provides a good opportunity for the development of Malaysia's inbound tourism market.

The main sources of Malaysia's inbound tourism - China, Japan, Australia, South Korea, European and American countries - have gradually recovered or developed rapidly, and the demand for outbound tourism has increased, which will be conducive to the development of inbound tourism in Malaysia. Especially in China, closely related to Malaysia, due to rapid economic development and significant improvement in people's lives, Chinese residents are increasingly interested in travel abroad, so China and Malaysia have become mutual sources of tourism, and China is one major source of tourism in Malaysia. In 2013, 1.8 million Chinese tourists traveled to Malaysia, accounting for more than 30% of total inbound tourists to Malaysia.

Malaysia expects to attract 36 million tourists by 2020 and generate at least RM 168 billion of revenue. On February 17, 2016, Deputy Prime Minister of Malaysia Ahmad Zahid Hamidi attended the 19th Malaysia Tourism Awards 2014/2015 Ceremony, saying that the government hopes that with the visa-free policy to Chinese tourists, Malaysia strives to attract 8 million Chinese tourists to visit Malaysia.

5.3 Tourism cultural brand headed by Year of Tourism

Malaysia Year of Tourism was first held in 1990 with the theme of "Charming Malaysia, Year of Festivals". Since then, Malaysia has hosted the "Charming Malaysia, Nature First" in 1994 and "Malaysia 50th Anniversary" in 2007, among a series of activities. In 2014, the Government of Malaysia put forward higher requirements and expectations on the fourth Malaysia Year of Tourism.

5.4 Visa facilitation

In order to facilitate the entry of tourists to the greater extent, the Government of Malaysian has also introduced new measures in the immigration system. The government has implemented a "paperless entry system" at 44 major checkpoints across the country. Foreigners are not required to fill in a white card when entering Malaysia. At the same time, the government has also enabled the "e-visa". Foreign tourists to Malaysia can apply for entry visas via Internet, by simply submitting personal information online.

Malaysia electronic visa launch ceremony & press conference was held in Beijing on March 1, 2016. The Government of Malaysia announced the implementation of visa-free and e-visa policies for Chinese tourists to facilitate Chinese tourists' travel to Malaysia.

Section 6   Philippines

6.1 Rich tourism resources

The Philippines, a country with 7,107 beautiful islands, has magnificent natural landscape, long history and passionate people. More than a hundred ethnic tribes, exotic styles, integrated culture and art ... all these have co-created the Philippine unique human arts and natural landscape.

The Philippines can be entered from five international gateways, namely, Manila, Laoag, Subic, Cebu and Davao. Manila is the first gateway to the Philippines, and the capital of the country; Laoag is an international gateway in the province of Ilocos Norte located at the northwest corner of Luzon Island; Subic recently becomes an international port, with all kinds of leisure, recreational and adventure facilities; Cebu is the largest capital of number one capital of the South, dubbed the imperial capital of the South; Davao is full of strong local colors, forms, flavors and combinations, marking the Philippines and Malaysia's cultural customs. Other popular tourist destinations are Batangas City, The Dolphin Bay, Legazpi City, Boracay Island, Palawan etc. Among them, Boracay Island, Cebu and Bohol Island are the most desirable international tourist destinations of the Philippine coastal tourism. Boracay Island is famous for its 4 km long white sand beach. The USA famous tourism magazine *Travel+Leisure* has named Boracay Island as the "World's Best Beach Resort 2012".

The theme of the Philippine tourism is mainly for outdoor adventure, sunshine coast, water sports, diving tour, cultural experience, Philippine uncommon education, honeymoon choice, incentive travel and enjoying life.

6.2 Inbound tourism relying on nearby sources

In 2015, the Philippines received 5.36 million inbound tourists, up 10.9% year on year, with tourism revenue USD5 billion, up 5.9% year on year, accounting for 8% of GDP. The inbound tourism employed 5 million people, accounting for 12.7% of total labor force. South Korea, the United States and Japan are the top 3 sources of inbound tourists to the Philippines, and in that year, 1.34 million, 0.779 million and 0.496 million tourists were from South Korea, United States and Japan respectively. China is the fourth largest source of inbound tourists to the Philippines, the number of Chinese tourists to the Philippines reached 491,000, up 24.3% year on year, accounting for 9.2% of total.

According to the data of July 2016 released by Philippine Department of Tourism, in January-May 2016, there were 2.52 million inbound tourists to the Philippines, up 13% year on year, with tourism revenue PHP106.6 billion, up 14% year on year. In May 2016, there were 0.445 million inbound tourists to the Philippines, up 8% year on year; with tourism revenue PHP 20 billion, up 19% year on year. In January - May 2016, South Korea, United States, and China are the top 3 sources of inbound tourists to the Philippines, the number of Chinese tourists to South Korea grew by 81% year on year, so China becomes the fastest growing source.

6.3 Tourism development driven by international conferences

The development of the tourism industry in the Philippines is also related to many international conferences held in the Philippines. As a member of the United Nations and a member of many international organizations, the Philippines has often sought to host delegates to Manila for international conferences such as the International Monetary Fund Conference, the International Law Conference, the ASEAN Summit and Ministerial Meetings, the World Medical Conferences, the Pacific Regional Tourism Conference and the United Nations Conference on Trade and Development.

Section 7　Indonesia

Indonesia's tourism industry started late, but developed fast since mid-1970s, with increasing number of inbound tourists and tourism revenue. The rapid development of tourism industry has not only brought a lot of foreign currency revenue for the national economy, promoted the development of related industries, especially has brought vitality for the commercial, hotel and tourism goods production, but also employed a large number of people. Tourism has become a pillar industry of the Indonesian national economy, and is the second largest foreign currency earner in the non-oil and gas industry (the largest is electronics export industry). The Government has long attached great importance to the development of tourist attractions, the construction of hotels, the training of staff and the streamlining of entry procedures in order to speed up the development of the tourism industry.

7.1 Diversity of tourism resources

Indonesia consists of 17,508 islands between the Pacific Ocean and the Indian Ocean, of which about 6,000 are inhabited. There are more than 400 volcanoes, including 77 active volcanoes. Java is the center of Indonesia, also the most populous island, and the capital of Jakarta is located in the island's northwest coast.

Indonesia is also very rich in animal resources. It is estimated that there are more than 200,000 animal species, of which 525 species are protected rare animals. Indonesia has a vast expanse of sea, numerous lakes and rivers, so it is rich aquatic resources, abundant in various fish, shrimp, crab, snail, shellfish, sea cucumber, pearl, edible algae and bird's nest etc.

Indonesia is rich in cultural resources. The Borobudur Stupa and the Candi Prambanan in Central Java are listed on the UNESCO World Heritage List. In addition, the traditional clothing, cuisine, traditional dance and music performances in various regions are well-known tourist attractions.

Table 2-2 World heritages of Indonesia

Name	Type	Location
Borobudur Stupa	Cultural heritage	Central Java
Candi Prambanan	Cultural heritage	Yogyakarta
Sangiran Early Man Site	Cultural heritage	Aceh
Tropical Rainforest Heritage of Sumatra	Historical heritage	North Sumatra
Ujung Kulon National Park	Historical heritage	West Java
Komodo National Park Lorentz National Park	Historical heritage Historical heritage	East Nusa Tenggara Papua

Indonesia is a country with the largest number of islands in the world, whose most fascinating place is Bali. Bali is famous for its natural seaside scenery and unique local customs. Here all the water-related leisure activities can be found. Water skiing, windsurfing, diving, surfing, water motoring, speed boating, rafting, and popular mineral hot spring baths. As the coastline is long, the island is very rich in tourism resources, with beautiful tropical scenery that is most memorable. There are wood carvings, silverware and batik souvenirs on sales at the scenic spots. Coffee in Indonesia is the best for shopping, and KapalApi is the most popular coffee brand.

7.2 Large growth potential of inbound tourism

In 2000, the number of inbound tourists to Indonesia reached 5.06 million. Since then, the number of inbound tourists to Indonesia fluctuated, the highest decline occurred in 2003, when only 4.46 million tourists visited Indonesia. In 2010, Indonesia's inbound tourism was on the rise again.

Although the number of inbound tourists to Indonesia reached 8.8 million in 2013, there was still a larger room for growth, especially China source market had great potential. Since July 1, 2015, Indonesia is implementing the visa-free policies to Chinese tourists, which has greatly contributed to the number of Chinese tourists to Indonesia.

Table 2-3　The number of Indonesia's inbound tourists in 2000-2013

Year	The number of inbound tourists	Growth (%)	Revenue (USD1 million)	Growth (%)
2000	5 064 217		5 748.80	
2001	5 153 620	1.77	5 396.27	-6.13
2002	5 033 400	-2.33	4 305.56	-20.21
2003	4 467 021	-11.25	4 037.02	-6.04
2004	5 321 165	19.12	4 797.88	18.85
2005	5 002 101	-6.00	4 521.90	5.75
2006	4 871 351	-2.61	4 447.98	-1.63

Continued

Year	The number of inbound tourists	Growth (%)	Revenue (USD1 million)	Growth (%)
2007	5 505 759	13.02	5 345.98	20.19
2008	6 234 497	13.24	7 347.60	37.44
2009	6 323 730	1.41	6 297.99	-14.29
2010	7 002 944	10.74	7 603.45	20.73
2011	7 649 731	9.24	8 554.39	12.51
2012	8 044 462	5.16	9 120.89	6.62
2013	8 802 129	9.42	—	—

7.3 Interaction with neighboring countries

Indonesia plans to focus on strengthening tourism cooperation with neighboring ASEAN countries to attract more tourists from Thailand, the Philippines and Vietnam to Indonesia. By country, Indonesia has reached an agreement with Singapore and Malaysia to jointly invest USD 570 million, to develop their coastal areas into an international tourist resort, named "Eastern Caribbean Tourist Area". Indonesia is also in consultation with the Thai and Malaysian tourism authorities to establish a permanent tourism alliance with coordinating function, to strengthen tourism cooperation between the three countries, joint use and joint development. Historically, Indonesia and Burma have had good cooperation in politics, economy, society, military and security. According to the friendly investment agreement signed in 1951, Indonesia has defined Burma s a free and friendly country. In order to promote tourism cooperation, the two countries held a seminar on trade and tourism in Yangon, Burma, in late June 2009, to explore the possibility of further promoting trade and business ties between the two countries and enhancing tourism exchanges and cooperation.

7.4 Tourism recovery plan

As part of the plan to revitalize the tourism industry, the Indonesian government is trying to promote traditional tourism market. The focus of the marketing is on attracting tourists from China, Japan, Southeast Asian countries, Australia and Middle East. The tourism recovery plan first started from the neighboring areas, in turn developed other markets. These countries are also the main source of Indonesian tourism in previous decades. To implement the recovery plan, the Indonesian Ministry of Tourism has set up a working committee comprising five groups for different markets, each group organizing a series of activities such as participation in tourism exhibitions.

Chapter 3
Sharing of Development Bonus from Chinese Outbound Tourism Market

Section 1　Chinese Outbound Tourism Market Behavior Survey

1.1 Influencing factors for outbound tourists' consumption decision-making

According to the survey results[①], most of respondents enjoyed outbound tourism for the first time, accounting for 46.3%. "Visit and Sightseeing" and "Leisure and Vacation Enjoyment" were outbound tourists' main purposes, accounting for 56.2% and 37.3% of total respondents, respectively. 61.7% of respondents considered outbound tourism as major spending decision. According to questionnaire results of travel frequencies and importance of decision-making, outbound tourism was still generally a difficult consumption choice for people to make.

1.1.1 Most of Chinese Mainland tourists enjoyed outbound tourism for the first time

Most of respondents, who enjoyed outbound tourism for the first time, were in the majority, accounting for 46.3% of total respondents, followed by respondents enjoying outbound tourism for the second time, for the third time or for the more times, accounting for 26.0%, 12.25% and 15.4% of total respondents, respectively. This proves that most of Chinese Mainland outbound tourists were not frequent travelers.

[①]　These results contained herein were those of 2015.

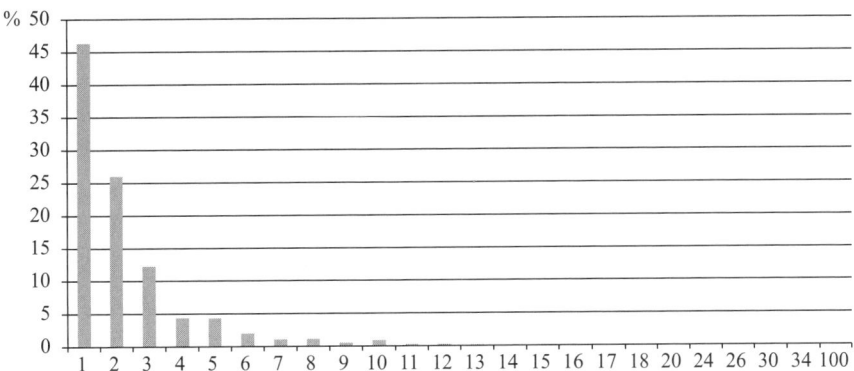

Figure 3-1 Distribution of outbound tourism times by Chinese Mainland outbound tourists (respondents) in 2015

1.1.2 Outbound tourism was major spending for most of consumers

In 2015, 59.8% of the respondents considered outbound tourism as a major spending decision, which decreased compared with the proportion of 61.7% in 2014.

1.1.3 Outbound tourism information was mainly obtained from the internet, introduction from close relatives and friends or travel agencies

Before travel, most of respondents obtained relevant tourism information from Website/BBS/Forum, relatives and friends or travel agencies, accounting for 60.5%, 56.2% and 49.7% of total respondents, respectively. Few responders took advantage of information channel.

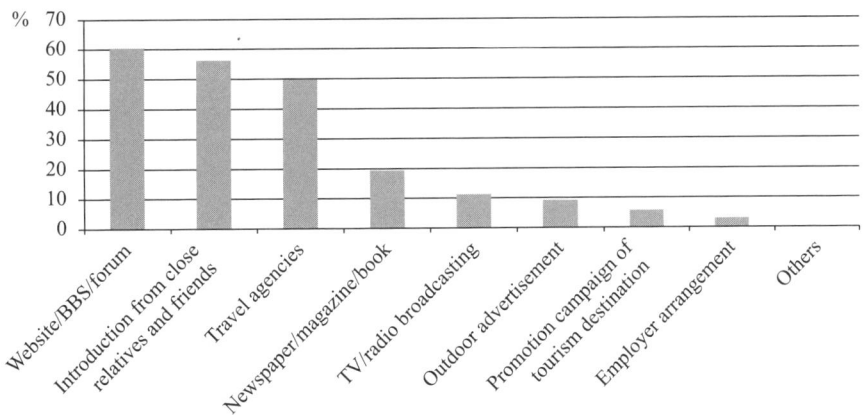

Figure 3-2 Outbound tourism information sources for Chinese Mainland outbound tourists (respondents) in 2015

1.1.4 Information on scenic area, tour prices and folk customs was mainly searched before travel

According to the survey results, outbound tourists mainly searched for information on scenic area / tourist attractions (69.8%), information on tour prices (56.2%), information on folk customs of tourist destination (32.8%) and information on transportation (31.9%), respectively.

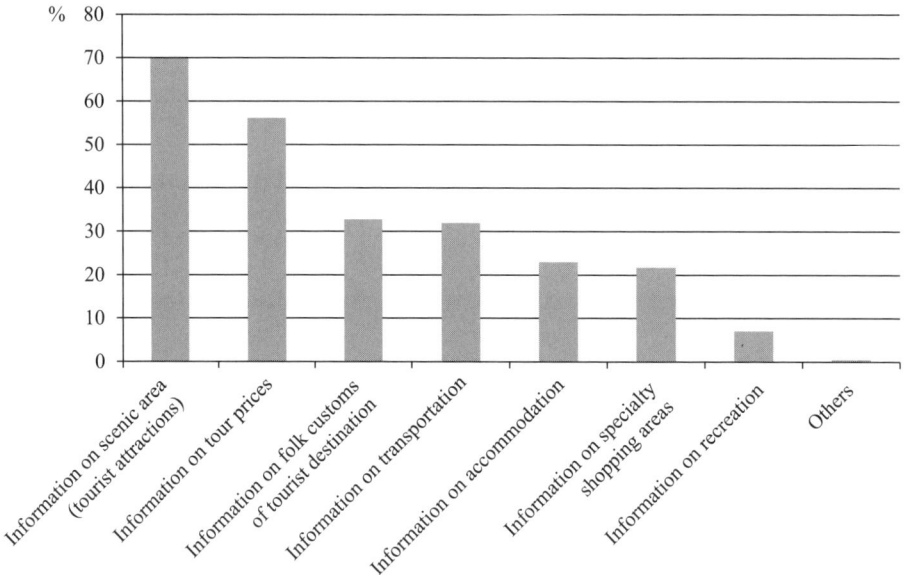

Figure 3-3   Information obtained by Chinese Mainland outbound tourists (respondents) before travel in 2015

1.2 Characteristics of outbound tourists' consumption decision-making (other than group tour)

Most of respondents travelled together with their families or friends. When choosing outbound tourism destinations, they emphasized "attraction of scenic area / tourist destination" to the utmost extent. 77.2% of respondents were willing to take outbound travel under arrangement of travel agencies. When choosing travel agencies, reputation and credibility of travel agencies and recommendation from friends were top priorities for consideration. When choosing outbound hotels, respondents preferred medium-priced hotels and budget hotels. The number of outbound attractions respondents visited generally ranged 3-9, and most of respondents visited 10 or more outbound attractions. Most of respondents spent less than two weeks in travelling, and outbound tourists who spent less than one week in travelling were in the majority, accounting for 52.7% of total respondents.

1.2.1 Most of outbound tourists travelled together with their families or good friends

Most of outbound tourists travelled together with their families, accounting for 59.9% of total respondents, followed by outbound tourists travelling together with good friends, accounting for 26.8% of total respondents. These two types of respondents were far more than those travelling together with other travelling companions.

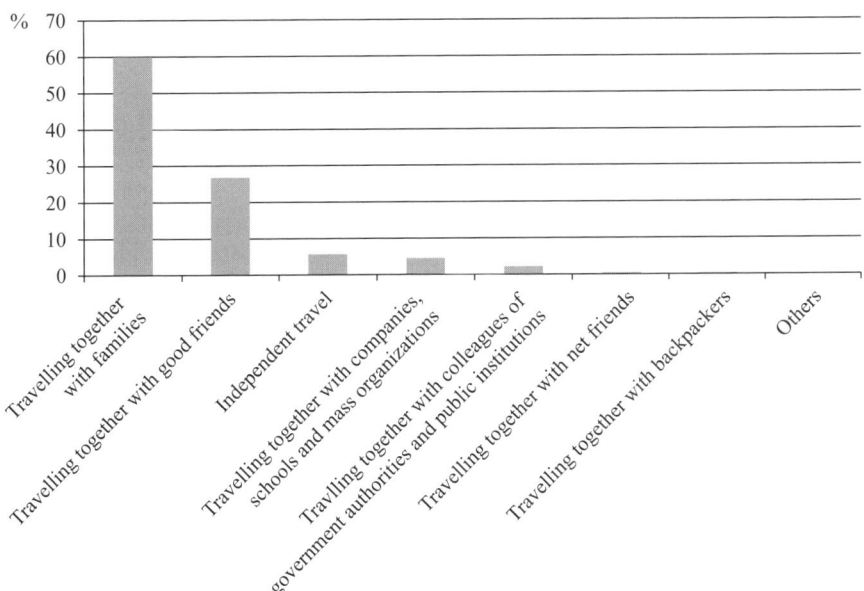

Figure 3-4 Traveling companions for Chinese Mainland outbound tourists (respondents) in 2015

1.2.2 The greatest influencing factor for outbound tourists' choice for outbound tourism destination was "attraction of scenic area / tourist destination"

When choosing outbound tourism destinations, 46.6% of respondents placed top priority over "attraction of scenic area / tourist destination", and 28.4% of respondents placed top priority over "Travel Expense". Few respondents chose other influencing factors.

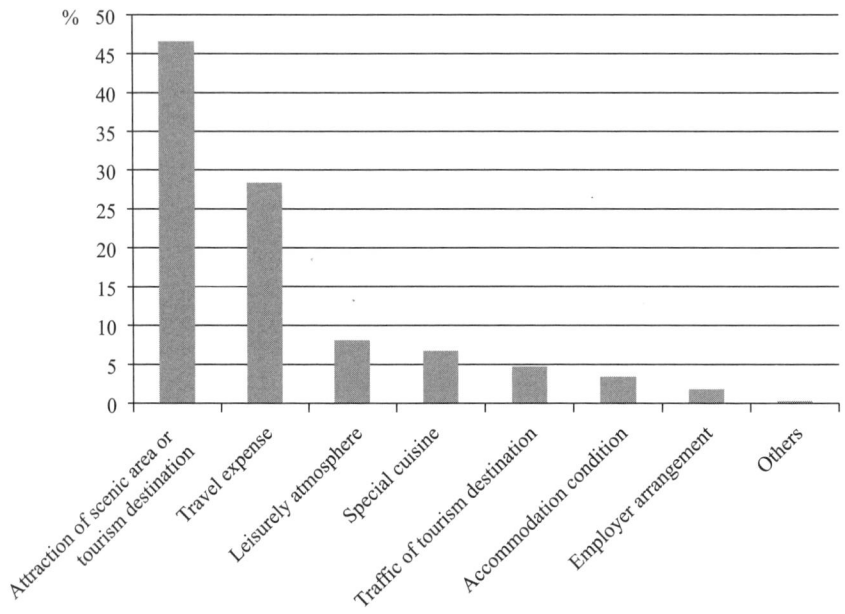

Figure 3-5 Influencing factors for Chinese Mainland outbound tourists (respondents) in choices for outbound tourism destinations in 2015

1.2.3 Outbound tourists taking group tour accounted for high proportion

77.2% of respondents took group tour under arrangement of travel agencies, higher than the proportion of 76.6% in 2014. This proves that most of respondents preferred outbound tourism products of travel agencies, with which they were unfamiliar.

1.2.4 Brand Awareness played the more important role in the choice of travel agencies

Outbound tourists mainly chose travel agencies to enjoy their outbound travel.

Influencing factors for outbound tourists for choosing travel agencies included brand awareness, credibility and fee scale of travel agencies and recommendation from friends. Respondents, who chose "brand awareness", "recommendation from friends", "credibility" and "fee scale" of travel agencies, accounted for 49.1%, 43.3%, 39.9% and 34.3% of total respondents.

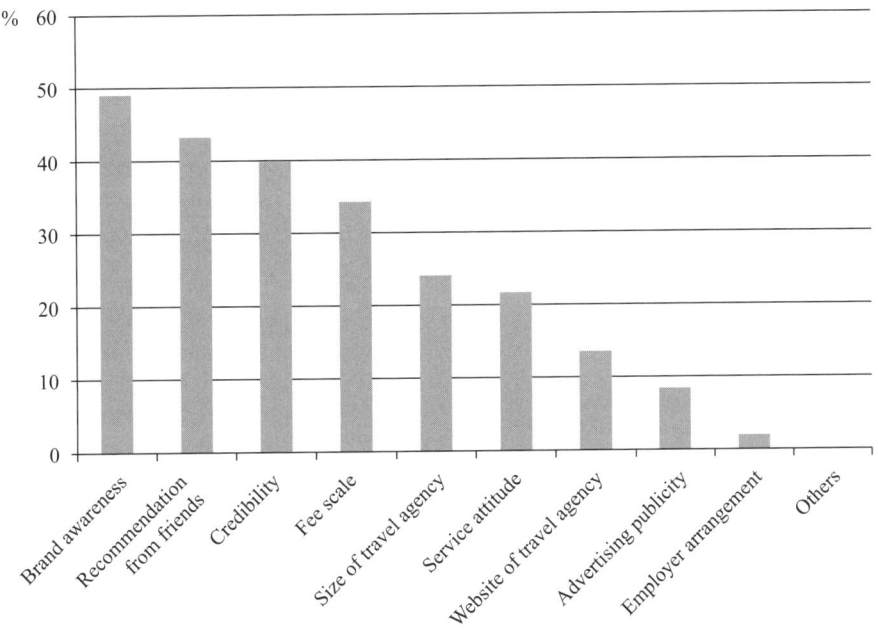

Figure 3-6　Influencing factors for Chinese Mainland outbound tourists (respondents) in choices for travel agencies in 2015

1.2.5 Medium-priced hotels were the most important choices of outbound tourists

Outbound tourists preferred medium-priced hotels and budget hotels, accounting for 45.4% and 31.0% of total respondents, respectively, which basically remained unchanged compared with those in 2014. Meanwhile, most of outbound tourists chose luxury hotels, who accounted for 16.3% of total respondents. Relatively few chose other types of accommodation facilities.

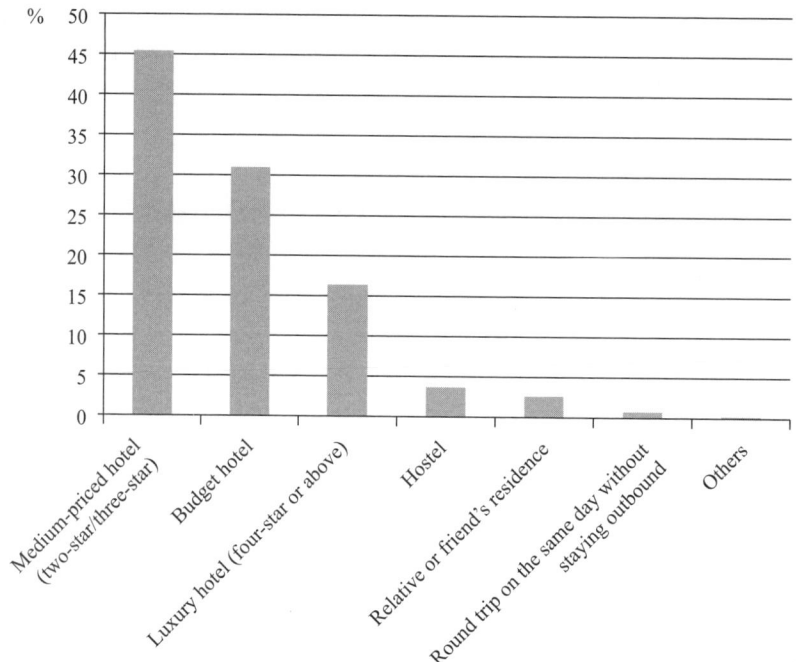

Figure 3-7　Distribution of accommodation choices made by Chinese Mainland outbound tourists (respondents) in 2015

1.3 Consumption structure characteristics of outbound tourists

Most of outbound tourists spent 5,000-10,000 yuan, accounting for 31.5% of total respondents. Outbound tourism spending items were mainly "shopping", "group tour expense", "catering" and "scenic spot ticket". "Shopping" saw the highest spending amount.

1.3.1 Medium-end and high-end consumers presented ever-increasing ratio

Chinese outbound tourism highlighted the feature of medium-end and high-end consumption. 60.5% of respondents' spending amount in a single outbound tour exceeded 10,001 yuan, and this proportion was far higher than that in 2014. Most of outbound tourists spent 5,001-10,000 yuan, accounting for 31.5% of total respondents. Outbound tourists, who spent 5,000 yuan and lower, accounted for only 8.0% of total respondents.

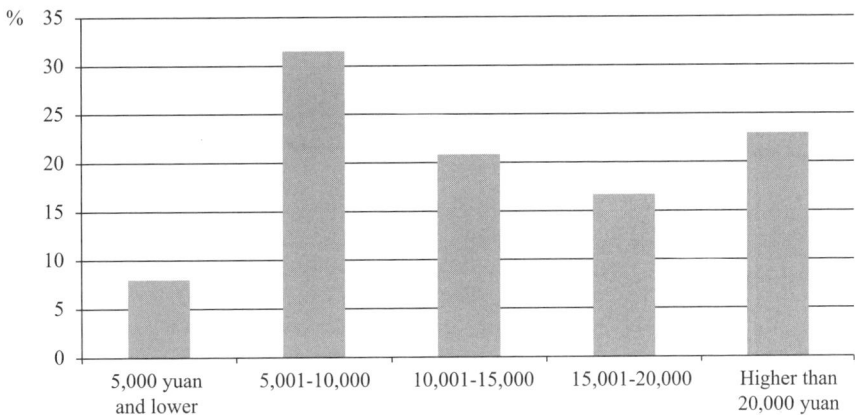

Figure 3-8　Distribution of outbound tourism spending by Chinese Mainland outbound tourists (respondents) in a single outbound tour in 2015

1.3.2 Shopping was still the most important outbound tourism spending item

Respondents, who chose "shopping", accounted for the highest proportion up to 85.9% of total respondents. Respondents, who chose "group tour expense" and "catering", accounted for 61.8% and 58.7% of total respondents, respectively.

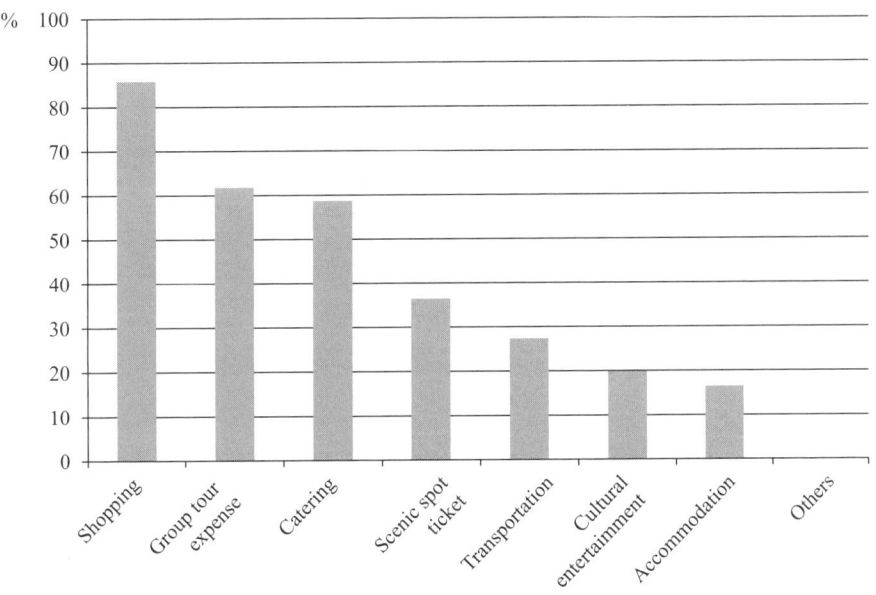

Figure 3-9　Distribution of outbound tourism spending items chosen by Chinese Mainland outbound tourists (respondents) in 2015

1.3.3 "Shopping" and "group tour expense" were primary outbound tourism spending items with the highest amount

42.5% of respondents thought that they spent most on "shopping". 40.33% of respondents thought that they spent most on "group tour expense". Respectively less than 6% of respondents thought that they spent heavily on other items on average. This proves that "shopping" and "group tour expense" were primary outbound tourism spending items and most spent items for Chinese Mainland outbound tourists.

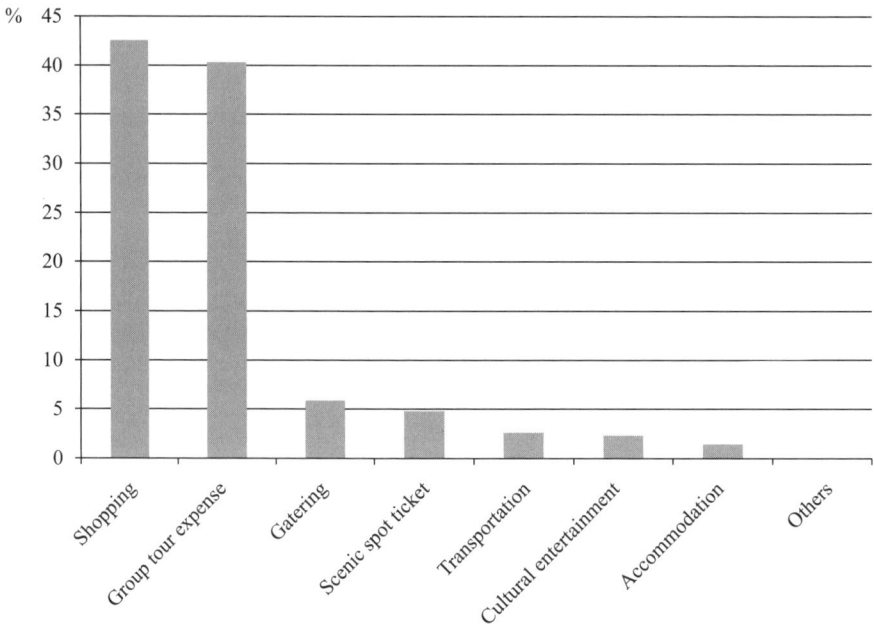

Figure 3-10 Average amounts of outbound tourism spending items for Chinese Mainland outbound tourists (respondents) in 2015

1.4 Reservation channels of outbound tourists' spending (other than group tour)

According to data statistics, outbound tourists (other than group tour) mainly made online reservation for flight, hotel or route arrangement. The Internet was more frequently applied by the Chinese outbound tourists.

1.4.1 Outbound flight reservation channels

Among respondents, 65.1% of outbound tourists (other than group tour) reserved and bought air tickets via the Internet, far more than those who bought air tickets via other channels. 11.4% of outbound tourists directly bought air tickets at ticket office. Outbound tourists, who reserved air tickets by phone and according to employer arrangement, accounted for 9.91% and 7.8%, respectively.

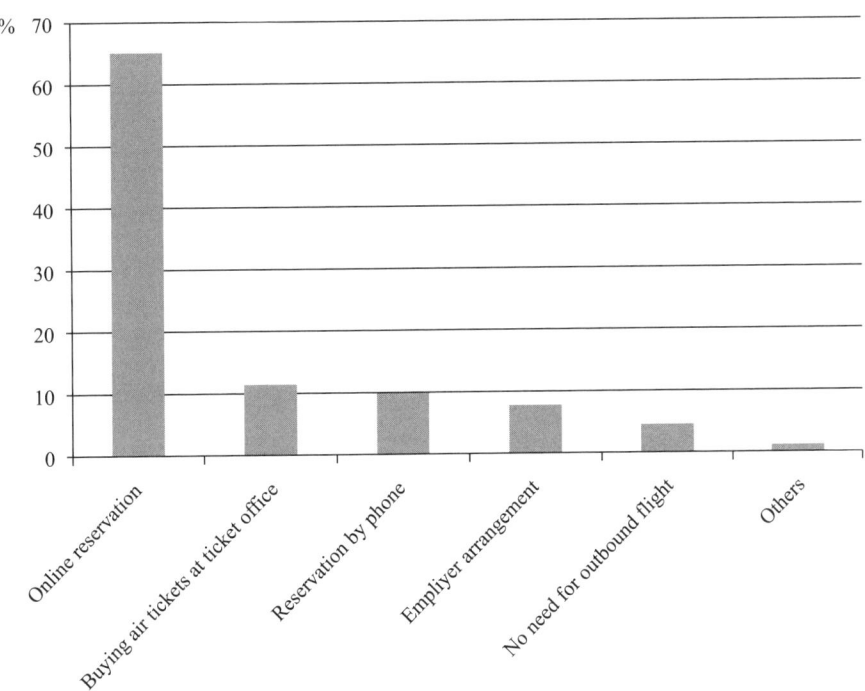

Figure 3-11 Outbound flight reservation channels for Chinese Mainland outbound tourists (respondents) in 2015

1.4.2 Outbound hotel reservation channels

Among respondents, 56.5% of outbound tourists (other than group tour) reserved and paid for hotels via the Internet, followed by those who directly checked in outbound hotels (13.5%). Less than 10% of outbound tourists reserved and paid for accommodation facilities via other channels.

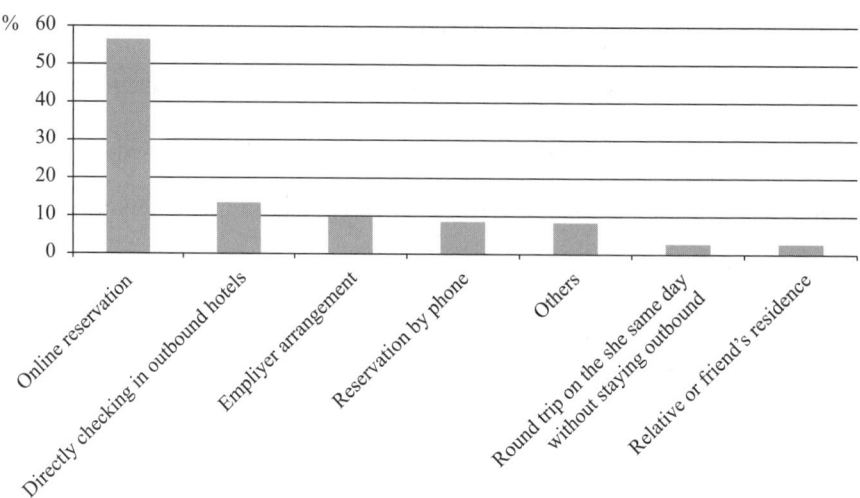

Figure 3-12 Outbound hotel reservation channels for Chinese Mainland outbound tourists (respondents) in 2015

1.4.3 Channels for obtaining information on tourist routes

Among respondents, 57.7% of outbound tourists (other than group tour) arranged for tourist routes through online search. Moreover, outbound tourists, who arranged for tourist routes through recommendation from relatives and friends, temporary arrangement and employer arrangement, accounted for 18.0%, 15.4% and 8.6%, respectively.

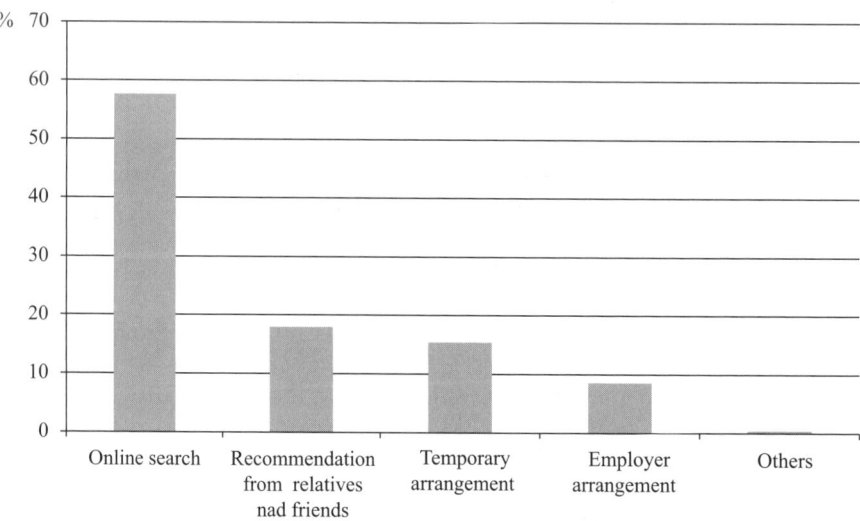

Figure 3-13 Tourist route arrangement channels for Chinese Mainland outbound tourists (respondents) in 2015

1.4.4 Channels for choice for dining places in the process of outbound tourism

Among respondents, outbound tourists (other than group tour) mainly had meals in dining places they randomly encountered, who accounted for 40.4%. Outbound tourists (other than group tour), who chose dining places through online search, recommendation from locals and recommendation from relatives and friends, accounted for 25.0%, 20.9% and 11.8% of total respondents, respectively. This proves that in the choice for dining places, outbound tourists (other than group tour) were not as dependent on online search and reservation as they chose flights, hotels and tourist routes.

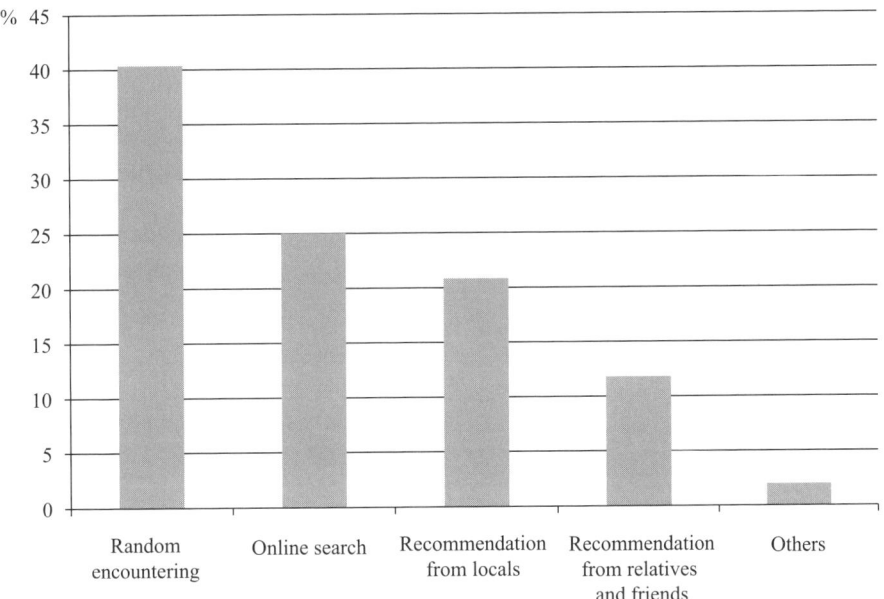

Figure 3-14　Dining place choice channels for Chinese Mainland outbound tourists (respondents) in 2015

1.5 Outbound tourists' future spending preferences

1.5.1 Group tour was still an important choice for outbound tourism

70.0% of respondents said that they were willing to join group tour for outbound tourism. 24.0% of respondents thought that "it doesn't matter". Only 6.0% of respondents expressed unwillingness to join group tour for outbound tourism.

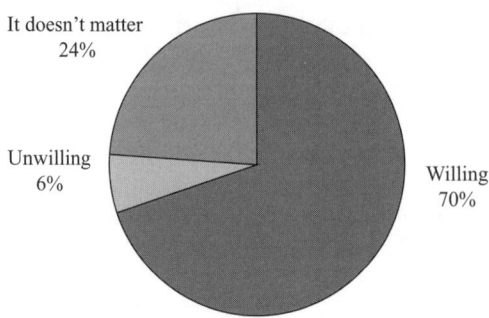

Figure 3-15 Attitudes of Chinese Mainland outbound tourists (respondents) for group tour for outbound tourism in 2015

1.5.2 Outbound tourists' future overseas tourism preferences kept stable and concentrated on "visit and sightseeing"

According to the questionnaire statistics results, "visit and sightseeing" was the most desired tourism items in the future overseas travel for outbound tourists, as 66.0% of respondents chose this item. Outbound tourists, who chose "participatory recreational activities", "adventure" and "understanding of local resident's livelihood", accounted for 10% of total respondents, respectively.

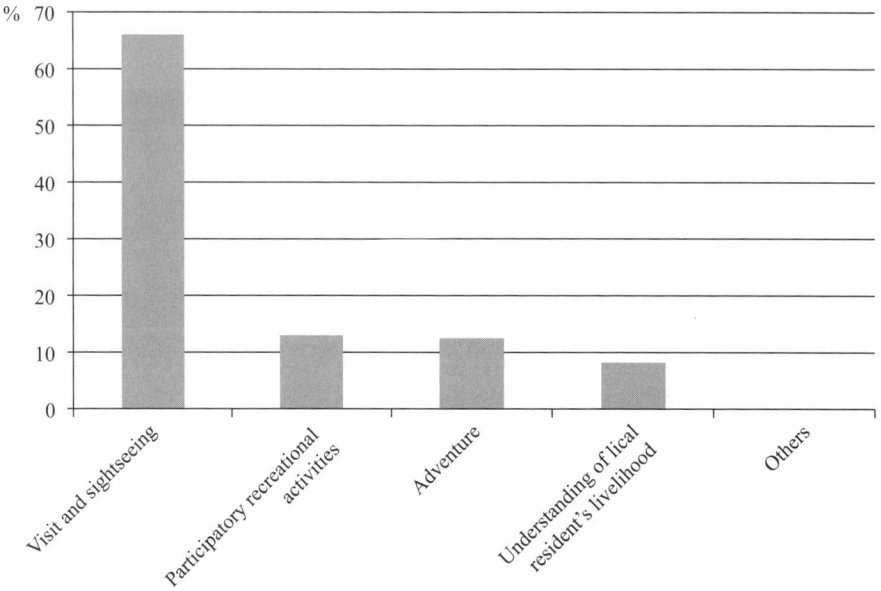

Figure 3-16 Distribution of future spending preferences of Chinese Mainland outbound tourists (respondents) for outbound tourism in 2015

Section 2 Evaluation for Chinese Outbound Tourists' Satisfaction Degrees of East Asian Countries

2.1 Japan

2.1.1 Score and ranking of satisfaction degree

In 2015, Chinese outbound tourists' satisfaction degree of Japan was 78.07, ranking 9th among 24 sample destination countries.

2.1.2 Analysis of questionnaire survey

The average score for Satisfaction Degree in the questionnaire survey was 8.12 points, 0.18 point higher than the average score of 7.94, ranking 7th among 24 sample destination countries. The top-ranking three items were "degree of beauty", "sanitation facility" and "informationization level", with scores of 8.49, 8.45 and 8.43, respectively. The lowest-ranking items were "foreign tour guide", "signs, information and service in Chinese" and "travel price", with scores of 7.77, 7.72 and 7.70, respectively.

2.1.3 Analysis of web comments

In 2015, Chinese Outbound Tourist Satisfaction Degree Index of Japan under comment survey was 80.86, 1.07 higher than average value of overall satisfaction degree for outbound tourism. Satisfaction degrees of all single items exceeded 73 points. Among them, "attitude of local residents" got the highest scores of 88.99 points. Item with the lowest satisfaction degree was "tourism industry management", which was 73.13 points.

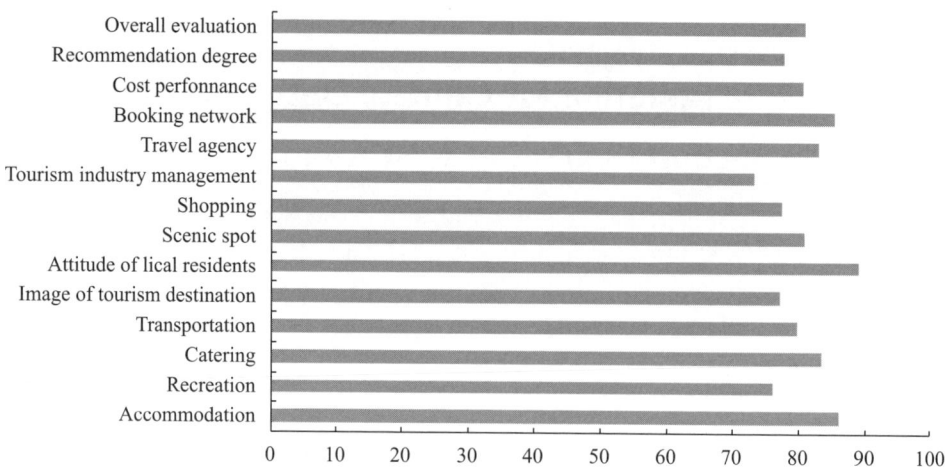

Figure 3-17　Chinese outbound tourists' web comments for Japan

2.2 South Korea

2.2.1 Score and ranking of satisfaction degree

In 2015, Chinese outbound tourists' satisfaction degree of South Korea was 77.58, ranking 11th among 24 sample destination countries.

2.2.2 Analysis of questionnaire survey

The average score for Satisfaction Degree in the questionnaire survey was 7.94 points, the same as the average score of 7.94, ranking 12th among 24 sample destination countries. The top-ranking three items were "degree of beauty", "reputation" and "convenience of swiping bank card", with scores of 8.32, 8.28 and 8.21, respectively. The lowest-ranking items were "signs, information and service in Chinese", "agricultural modernization" and "industrial travel", with scores of 7.59, 7.58 and 7.56, respectively.

2.2.3 Analysis of web comments

In 2015, Chinese Outbound Tourist Satisfaction Degree Index of South Korea under comment survey was 81.21, 1.42 higher than average value of overall satisfaction degree for outbound tourism. Satisfaction degrees of all single items exceeded 75 points. Among them, "attitude of local residents" got the highest scores of 89.39 points. Item with the lowest satisfaction degree was "tourism industry management", which was 75.90 points.

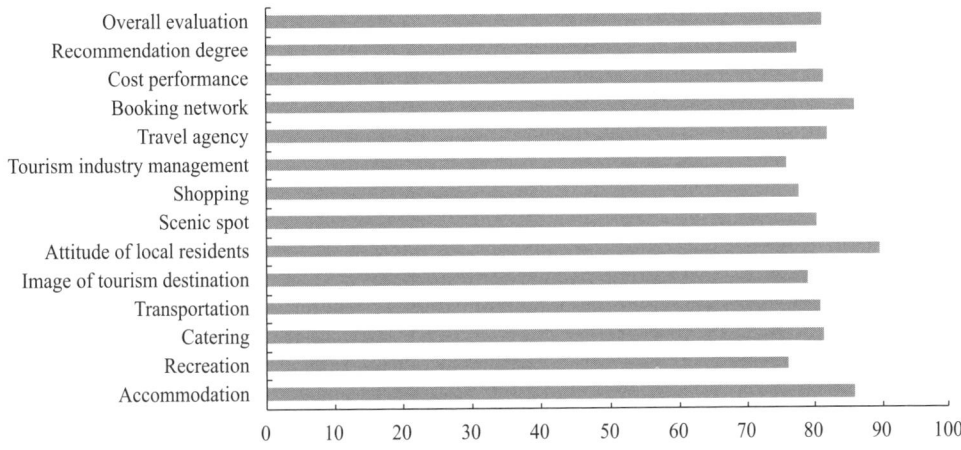

Figure 3-18 Chinese outbound tourists' web comments for South Korea

2.3 Malaysia

2.3.1 Score and ranking of satisfaction degree

In 2015, Chinese outbound tourists' satisfaction degree of Malaysia was 77.01, ranking 15th among 24 sample destination countries.

2.3.2 Analysis of questionnaire survey

The average score for Satisfaction Degree in the questionnaire survey was 7.94 points, the same as the average score of 7.94, ranking 12th among 24 sample destination countries. The top-ranking three items were "natural ecology", "degree of beauty" and "air quality", with scores of 8.30, 8.29 and 8.26, respectively. The lowest-ranking items were "long-distance passenger transportation", "signs, information and service in Chinese" and "industrial travel", with scores of 7.69, 7.57 and 7.55, respectively.

2.3.3 Analysis of web comments

In 2015, Chinese Outbound Tourist Satisfaction Degree Index of Malaysia under comment survey was 78.86, 0.93 lower than average value of overall satisfaction degree for outbound tourism. Satisfaction degrees of all single items exceeded 73 points. Among them, "attitude of local residents" got the highest scores of 89.24 points. Item with the lowest satisfaction degree was "tourism industry management", which was 73.69 points.

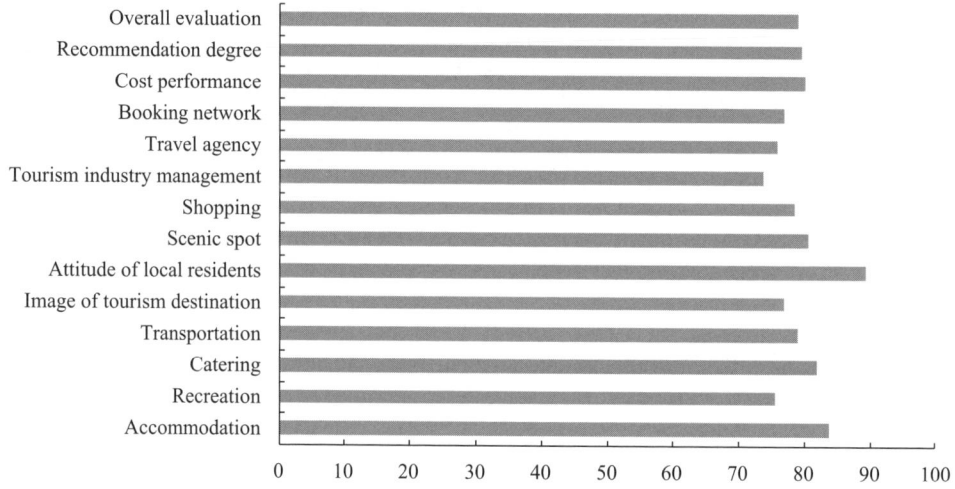

Figure 3-19　Chinese outbound tourists' web comments for Malaysia

2.4 Vietnam

2.4.1 Score and ranking of satisfaction degree

In 2015, Chinese outbound tourists' satisfaction degree of Vietnam was 74.70, ranking 22nd among 24 sample destination countries.

2.4.2 Analysis of questionnaire survey

The average score for Satisfaction Degree in the questionnaire survey was 7.62 points, 0.32 point lower than the average score of 7.94, ranking 22nd among 24 sample destination countries. The top-ranking three items were "natural ecology", "air quality" and "gardening and afforestation", with scores of 7.96, 7.96 and 7.93, respectively. The lowest-ranking items were "accessibility facility", "sanitation facility" and "signs, information and service in Chinese", with scores of 7.37, 7.34 and 7.25, respectively.

2.4.3 Analysis of web comments

In 2015, Chinese Outbound Tourist Satisfaction Degree Index of Vietnam under comment survey was 80.26, 0.47 higher than average value of overall satisfaction degree for outbound tourism. Satisfaction degrees of all single items exceeded 75 points. Among them, "attitude of local residents" got the highest scores of 88.70 points. Items with the lowest satisfaction degree were "shopping" and "tourism industry management", which were 75.91 points and 75.01 points, respectively.

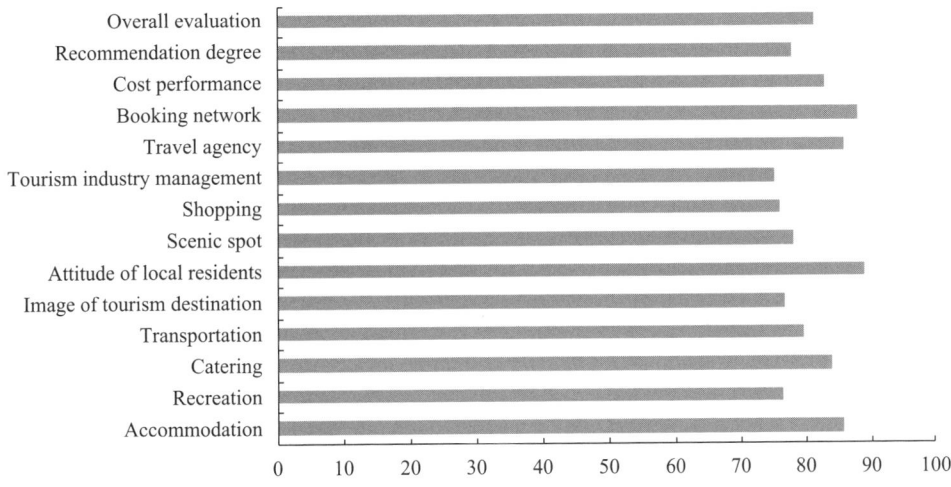

Figure 3-20 **Chinese outbound tourists' web comments for Vietnam**

2.5 Philippines

2.5.1 Score and ranking of satisfaction degree

In 2015, Chinese Citizens' Satisfaction Degree of the Philippines was 75.24, ranking 19th among 24 sample destination countries.

2.5.2 Analysis of questionnaire survey

The average score for Satisfaction Degree in the questionnaire survey was 7.73 points, 0.21 point lower than the average score of 7.94, ranking 18th among 24 sample destination countries. The top-ranking three items were "natural ecology", "degree of beauty" and "air quality", with scores of 8.04, 8.04 and 8.03, respectively. The lowest-ranking items were "sense of safety", "industrial travel" and "signs, information and service in Chinese", with scores of 7.52, 7.50 and 7.40, respectively.

2.5.3 Analysis of web comments

In 2015, Chinese Outbound Tourist Satisfaction Degree Index of the Philippines under comment survey was 79.09, 0.70 lower than average value of overall satisfaction degree for outbound tourism. Satisfaction degrees of all single items exceeded 71 points. Among them, "attitude of local residents" got the highest scores of 88.33 points. Item with the lowest satisfaction degree was "tourism industry management", which was 71.57 points.

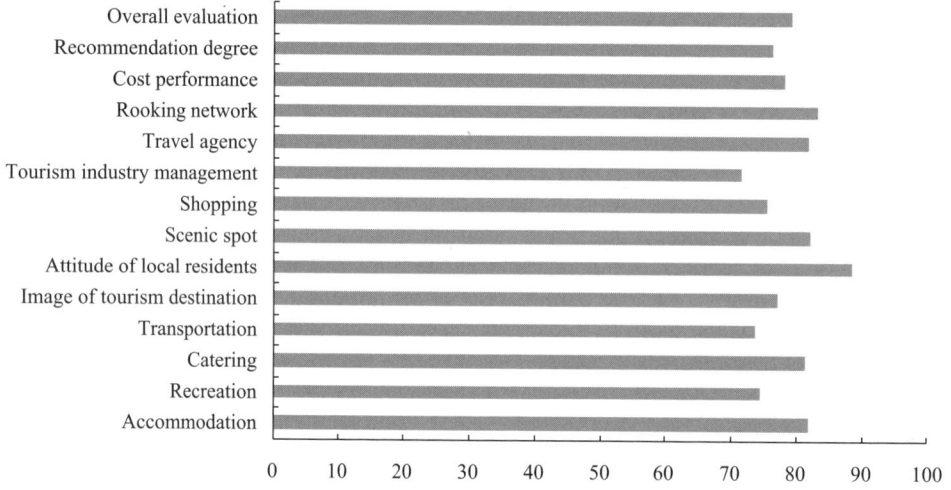

Figure 3-21 Chinese outbound tourists' web comments for the Philippines

2.6 Indonesia

2.6.1 Score and ranking of satisfaction degree

In 2015, Chinese outbound tourists' satisfaction degree of Indonesia was 76.80, ranking 16th among 24 sample destination countries.

2.6.2 Analysis of questionnaire survey

The average score for Satisfaction Degree in the questionnaire survey was 7.71 points, 0.23 point lower than the average score of 7.94, ranking 19th among 24 sample destination countries. The top-ranking three items were "air quality", "degree of beauty" and "natural ecology", with scores of 8.16, 8.10 and 8.07, respectively. The lowest-ranking items were "construction management", "long-distance passenger transportation" and "signs, information and service in Chinese", with scores of 7.44, 7.42 and 7.32, respectively.

2.6.3 Analysis of web comments

In 2015, Chinese Outbound Tourist Satisfaction Degree Index of Indonesia under comment survey was 80.34, 0.55 higher than average value of overall satisfaction degree for outbound tourism. Satisfaction degrees of all single items exceeded 71 points. Among them, "attitude of local residents" got the highest scores of 88.77 points. Item with the lowest satisfaction degree was "tourism industry management", which was 71.31 points.

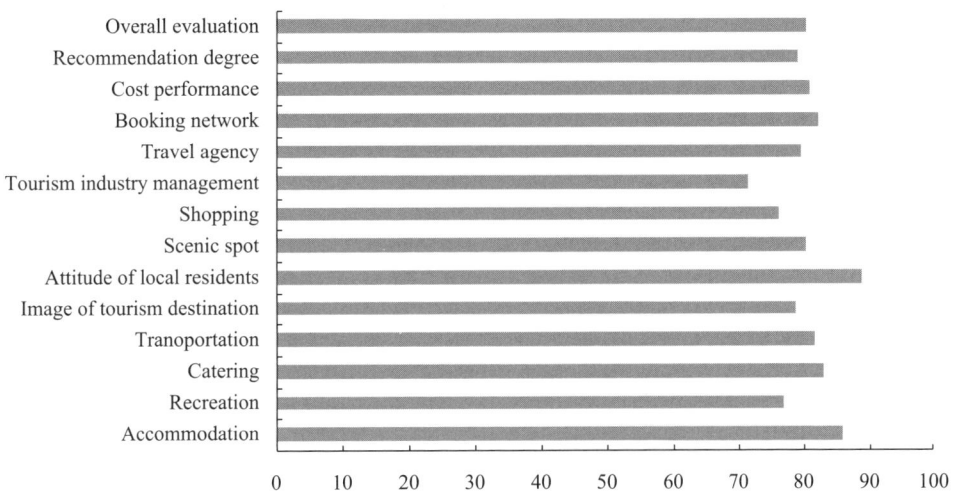

Figure 3-22 Chinese outbound tourists' web comments for Indonesia

Chapter 4
Basic Status and Behavioral Characteristics of East Asia on Chinese Inbound Tourism Market

Section 1 Aggregate Market Size of East Asian Inbound Tourism to China

1.1 Japan

In 2011-2015, the number of Japanese inbound tourists to China continued to decline. In 2013, growth rate of the number of Japanese inbound tourists to China dropped sharply, which began to rebound in 2014 and continuously declined in 2015. In 2011, the number of Japanese inbound tourists to China totaled 3.6582 million, down 1.96% on a year-on-year basis. In 2012, the number of Japanese inbound tourists to China totaled 3.5182 million, down 3.83% on a year-on-year basis. In 2013, the number of Japanese inbound tourists to China totaled 2.8775 million, down 18.21% on a year-on-year basis. In 2014, the number of Japanese inbound tourists to China totaled 2.7176 million, down 5.60% on a year-on-year basis. In 2015, the number of Japanese inbound tourists to China totaled 2.4977 million, down 8.10% on a year-on-year basis. In view of the current development trend, the future market of Japan's inbound tourism to China is expected to continuously present a slight decline.

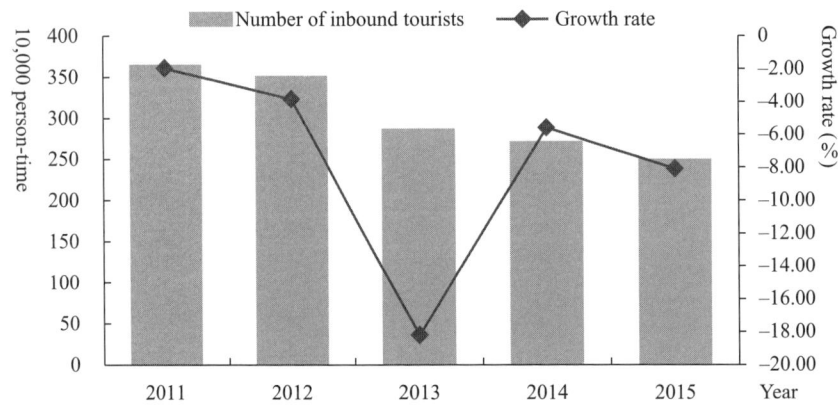

Figure 4-1 Aggregate market and growth of Japan's inbound tourism to China in 2011-2015

1.2 South Korea

In 2011-2015, the number of South Korean inbound tourists to China and its growth rate continued to fluctuate. In 2011, the number of South Korean inbound tourists to China totaled 4.1854 million, up 2.67% on a year-on-year basis. In 2012, the number of South Korean inbound tourists to China totaled 4.0699 million, down 2.76% on a year-on-year basis. In 2013, the number of South Korean inbound tourists to China totaled 3.9690 million, down 2.48% on a year-on-year basis. In 2014, the number of South Korean inbound tourists to China totaled 4.1817 million, up 5.36% on a year-on-year basis. In 2015, the number of South Korean inbound tourists to China totaled 4.4444 million, up 6.30% on a year-on-year basis. On the whole, the number of South Korean inbound tourists to China showed an increasing trend, in which a substantial increase happened in 2014. It is expected that the number of South Korean inbound tourists to China will grow steadily.

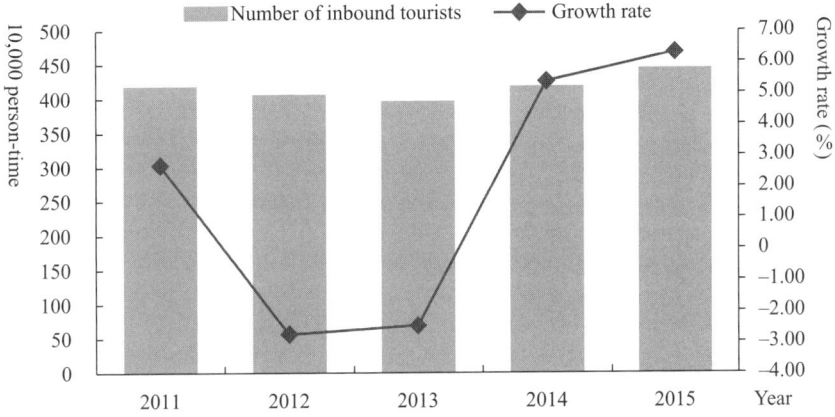

Figure 4-2 Aggregate market and growth of South Korea's inbound tourism to China in 2011-2015

1.3 Vietnam

In 2011-2015, the number of Vietnamese inbound tourists to China continued to rise, while growth rate of the number of Vietnamese inbound tourists to China kept sustained growth. In 2011, the number of Vietnamese inbound tourists to China totaled 1.0065 million, up 9.40% on a year-on-year basis. In 2012, the number of Vietnamese inbound tourists to China totaled 1.1372 million, up 12.99% on a year-on-year basis. In 2013, the number of Vietnamese inbound tourists to China totaled 1.3654 million, up 20.07% on a year-on-year basis. In 2014, the number of Vietnamese inbound tourists to China totaled 1.7094 million, up 25.19% on a year-on-year basis. In 2015, the number of Vietnamese inbound tourists to China totaled 2.1608 million, up 26.41% on a year-on-year basis. In view of the current development trend, the future market of Vietnam's inbound tourism to China is expected to continuously grow steadily.

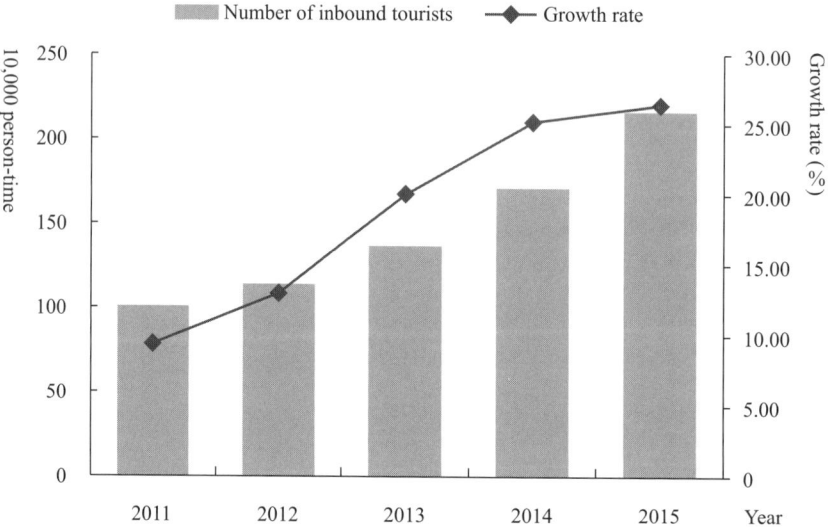

Figure 4-3 Aggregate market and growth of Vietnam's inbound tourism to China in 2011-2015

1.4 Malaysia

In 2011-2015, the number of Malaysian inbound tourists to China continued to decline. In 2015, growth rate of the number of Malaysian inbound tourists to China showed an increasing trend. In 2011, the number of Malaysian inbound tourists to China totaled 1.2451 million, down 0.01% on a year-on-year basis. In 2012, the number of Malaysian inbound tourists to China totaled 1.2355 million, down 0.77% on a year-on-year basis. In 2013, the number of Malaysian inbound tourists to China totaled 1.2065 million, down 2.35% on a year-on-year basis. In 2014, the number of Malaysian inbound tourists to China totaled 1.1296 million, down 6.37% on a year-on-year basis. In 2015, the number of Malaysian inbound tourists to China totaled 1.0755 million, down 4.79% on a year-on-year basis. The future market of Malaysia's inbound tourism to China is expected to rebound.

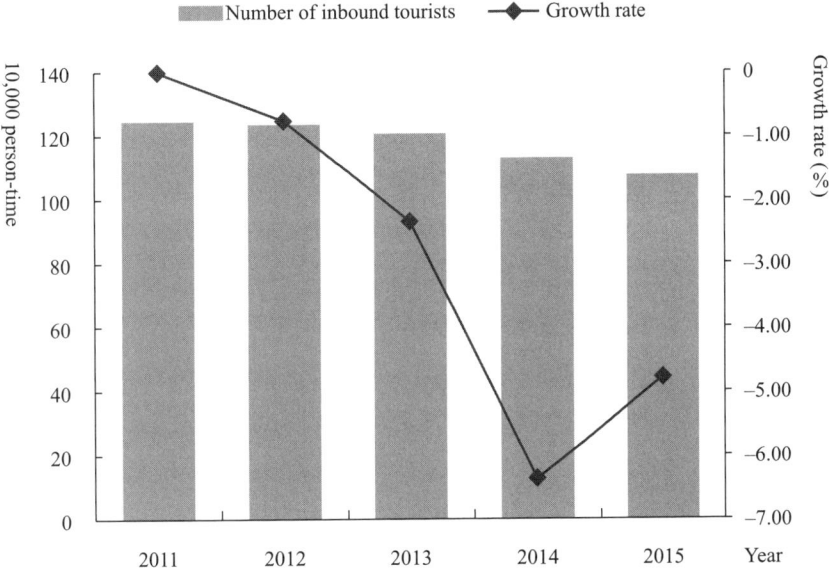

Figure 4-4 Aggregate market and growth of Malaysia's inbound tourism to China in 2011-2015

1.5 Philippines

In 2011-2015, the number of Philippine inbound tourists to China continued to fluctuate. Before 2015, growth rate of the number of Philippine inbound tourists to China continuously declined, which began to rebound in 2015. In 2011, the number of Philippine inbound tourists to China totaled 893,400, up 7.97% on a year-on-year basis. In 2012, the number of Philippine inbound tourists to China totaled 962,000, up 7.57% on a year-on-year basis. In 2013, the number of Philippine inbound tourists to China totaled 996,700, up 3.61% on a year-on-year basis. In 2014, the number of Philippine inbound tourists to China totaled 967,900, down 2.89% on a year-on-year basis. In 2015, the number of Philippine inbound tourists to China totaled 1.004 million, up 3.73% on a year-on-year basis. In view of the current development trend, the future number of Philippine inbound tourists to China is expected to rise.

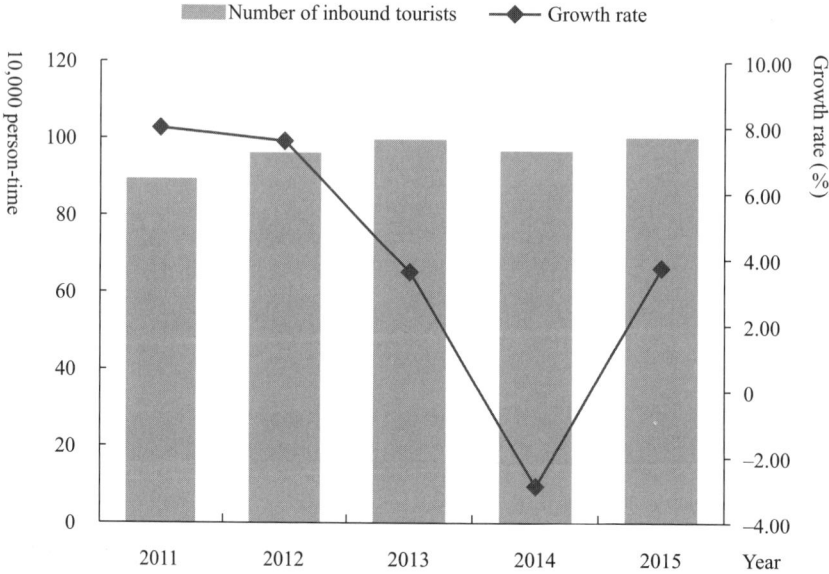

Figure 4-5 Aggregate market and growth of the Philippines' inbound tourism to China in 2011-2015

1.6 Indonesia

In 2011-2015, the number of Indonesian inbound tourists to China showed a decreasing trend. Before 2015, growth rate of the number of Indonesian inbound tourists to China continuously declined, which began to slightly rebound in 2015. In 2011, the number of Indonesian inbound tourists to China totaled 608,700, up 6.15% on a year-on-year basis. In 2012, the number of Indonesian inbound tourists to China totaled 622,000, up 2.18% on a year-on-year basis. In 2013, the number of Indonesian inbound tourists to China totaled 605,300, down 2.68% on a year-on-year basis. In 2014, the number of Indonesian inbound tourists to China totaled 566,900, down 6.34% on a year-on-year basis. In 2015, the number of Indonesian inbound tourists to China totaled 544,800, down 3.90% on a year-on-year basis. The future number of Indonesian inbound tourists to China is expected to gradually rise.

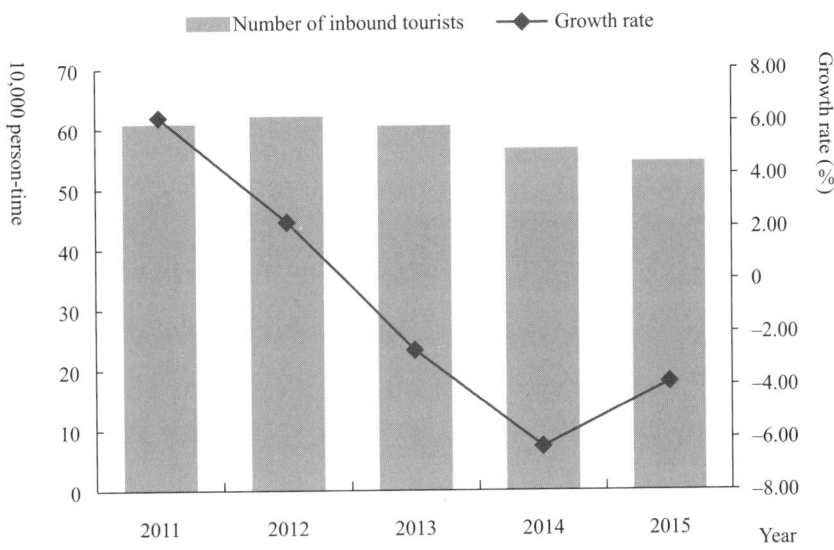

Figure 4-6 Aggregate market and growth of Indonesia's inbound tourism to China in 2011-2015

Section 2　Market Structure of East Asia Inbound Tourism to China

2.1 Japan

2.1.1 Analysis for transport means of Japanese inbound tourists to China

Among Japanese inbound tourists to China in 2015, 59.92% of them went by plane; 9.64% of them went by boat; 16.18% of them went by foot; 12.50% of them went by car; and 1.75% of them went by train.

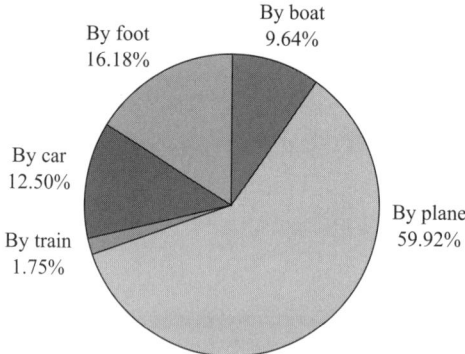

Figure 4-7　Transport means of Japanese inbound tourists to China in 2015

2.1.2 Analysis for age structure of Japanese inbound tourists to China

Among Japanese inbound tourists to China in 2015, 3.74% of them were aged under 14; 2.98% of them were aged 15-24; 38.43% of them were aged 25-44; 46.31% of them were aged 45-64; and 8.54% of them were aged over 65.

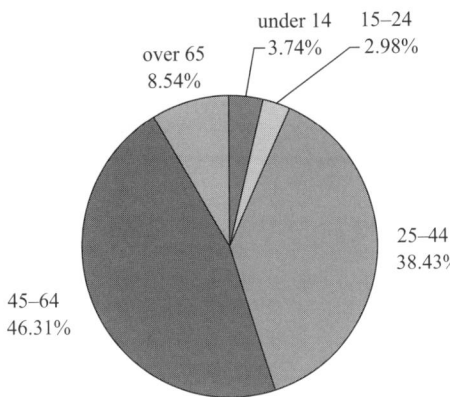

Figure 4-8　Age structure of Japanese inbound tourists to China in 2015

2.1.3 Analysis for gender structure of Japanese inbound tourists to China

Among Japanese inbound tourists to China in 2015, 79.89% of them were male, and 20.11% of them were female.

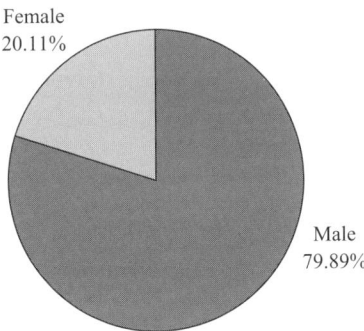

Figure 4-9　Gender structure of Japanese inbound tourists to China in 2015

2.1.4 Analysis for purpose structure of Japanese inbound tourists to China

Among Japanese inbound tourists to China in 2015, 15.73% of them went for sightseeing and leisure; 31.15% of them went for conference/business; 4.69% of them were service staffs; 2.14% of them went for visiting relatives and friends; and 46.29% of them went for other purposes.

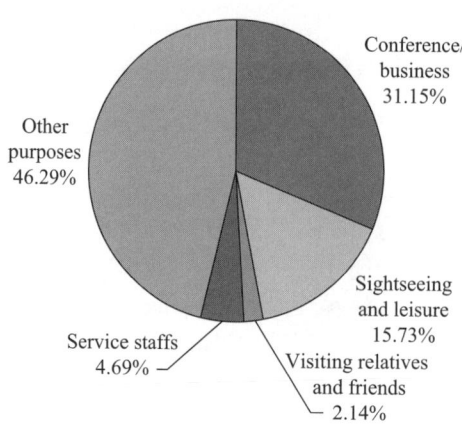

Figure 4-10　Purpose structure of Japanese inbound tourists to China in 2015

2.2 South Korea

2.2.1 Analysis for transport means of South Korean inbound tourists to China

Among South Korean inbound tourists to China in 2015, 84.96% of them went by plane; 4.98% of them went by foot; 7.43% of them went by boat; 2.22% of them went by car; and 0.41% of them went by train.

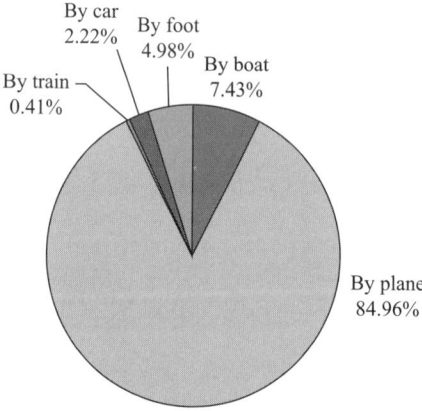

Figure 4-11　Transport means of South Korean inbound tourists to China in 2015

2.2.2 Analysis for age structure of South Korean inbound tourists to China

Among South Korean inbound tourists to China in 2015, 3.86% of them were aged under 14; 6.75% of them were aged 15-24; 37.66% of them were aged 25-44; 43.35%

of them were aged 45-64; 8.38% of them were aged over 65.

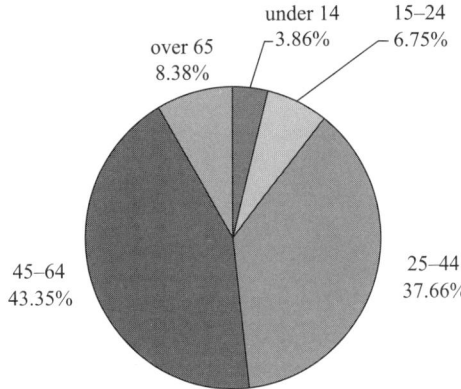

Figure 4-12　Age structure of South Korean inbound tourists to China in 2015

2.2.3 Analysis for gender structure of South Korean inbound tourists to China

Among South Korean inbound tourists to China in 2015, 61.42% of them were male, and 38.58% of them were female.

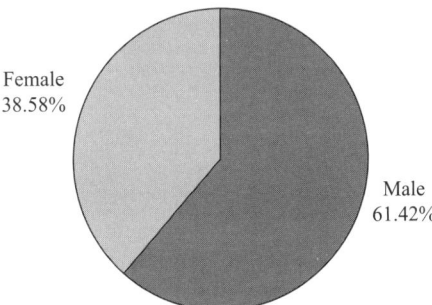

Figure 4-13　Gender structure of South Korean inbound tourists to China in 2015

2.2.4 Analysis for purpose structure of South Korean inbound tourists to China

Among South Korean inbound tourists to China in 2015, 45.50% of them went for sightseeing and leisure; 24.88% of them went for conference/business; 9.15% of them were service staffs; 0.77% of them went for visiting relatives and friends; and 19.69% of them went for other purposes.

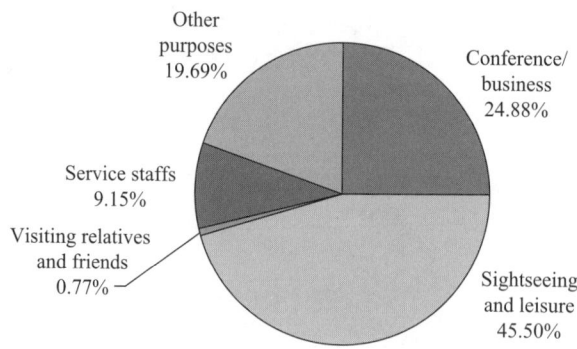

Figure 4-14 Purpose structure of South Korean inbound tourists to China in 2015

2.3 Malaysia

2.3.1 Analysis for transport means of Malaysian inbound tourists to China

Among Malaysian inbound tourists to China in 2015, 74.16% of them went by plane; 15.50% of them went by foot; 3.69% of them went by boat; 5.71% of them went by car; and 0.94% of them went by train.

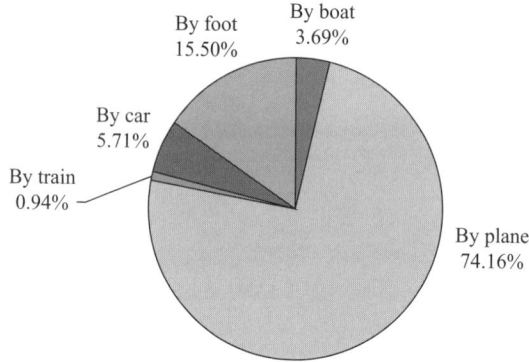

Figure 4-15 Transport means of Malaysian inbound tourists to China in 2015

2.3.2 Analysis for age structure of Malaysian inbound tourists to China

Among Malaysian inbound tourists to China in 2015, 3.90% of them were aged under 14; 7.89% of them were aged 15-24; 45.57% of them were aged 25-44; 36.55% of them were aged 45-64; 6.08% of them were aged over 65.

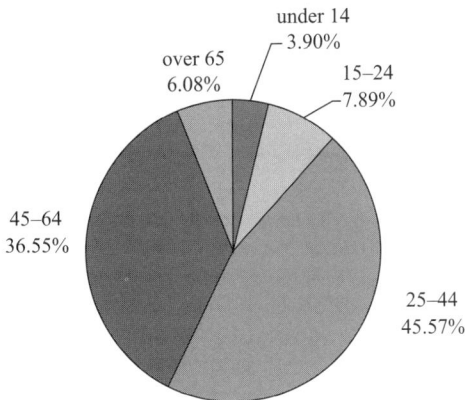

Figure 4-16　Age structure of Malaysian inbound tourists to China

2.3.3 Analysis for gender structure of Malaysian inbound tourists to China

Among Malaysian inbound tourists to China in 2015, 61.65% of them were male, and 38.35% of them were female.

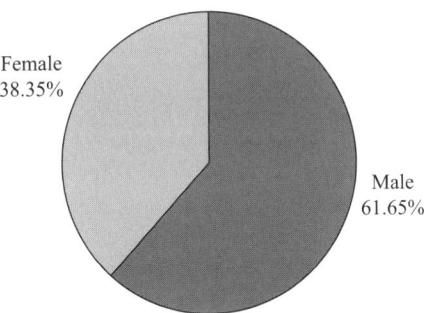

Figure 4-17　Gender structure of Malaysian inbound tourists to China

2.3.4 Analysis for purpose structure of Malaysian inbound tourists to China

Among Malaysian inbound tourists to China in 2015, 59.69% of them went for sightseeing and leisure; 14.71% of them went for conference/business; 8.90% of them were service staffs; 1.29% of them went for visiting relatives and friends; and 15.41% of them went for other purposes.

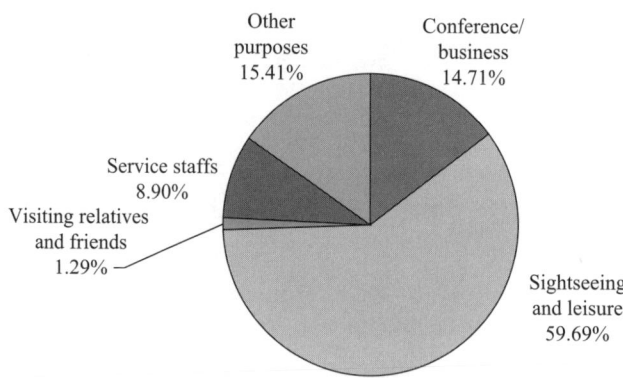

Figure 4-18 Purpose structure of Malaysian inbound tourists to China in 2015

2.4 Philippines

2.4.1 Analysis for transport means of Philippine inbound tourists to China

Among Philippine inbound tourists to China in 2015, 20.62% of them went by plane; 10.04% of them went by foot; 65.06% of them went by boat; 3.63% of them went by car; and 0.66% of them went by train.

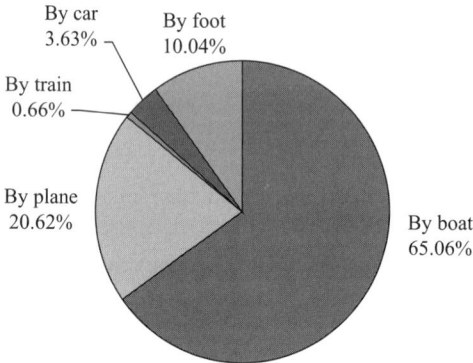

Figure 4-19 Transport means of Philippine inbound tourists to China in 2015

2.4.2 Analysis for age structure of Philippine inbound tourists to China

Among Philippine inbound tourists to China in 2015, 1.34% of them were aged under 14; 7.19% of them were aged 15-24; 64.10% of them were aged 25-44; 25.78% of them were aged 45-64; 1.58% of them were aged over 65.

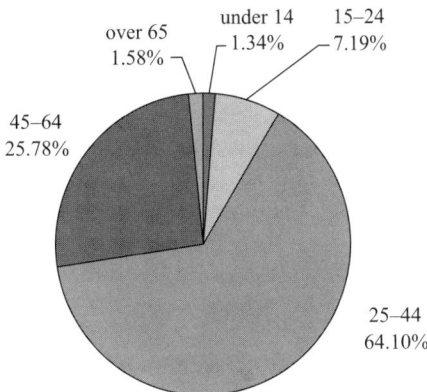

Figure 4-20　Age structure of Philippine inbound tourists to China

2.4.3 Analysis for gender structure of Philippine inbound tourists to China

Among Philippine inbound tourists to China in 2015, 79.17% of them were male, and 20.83% of them were female.

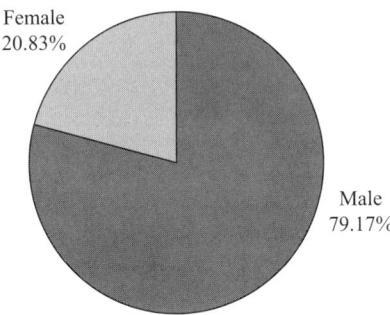

Figure 4-21　Gender structure of Philippine inbound tourists to China

2.4.4 Analysis for purpose structure of Philippine inbound tourists to China

Among Philippine inbound tourists to China in 2015, 19.26% of them went for sightseeing and leisure; 3.21% of them went for conference/business; 67.41% of them were service staffs; 0.27% of them went for visiting relatives and friends; and 9.85% of them went for other purposes.

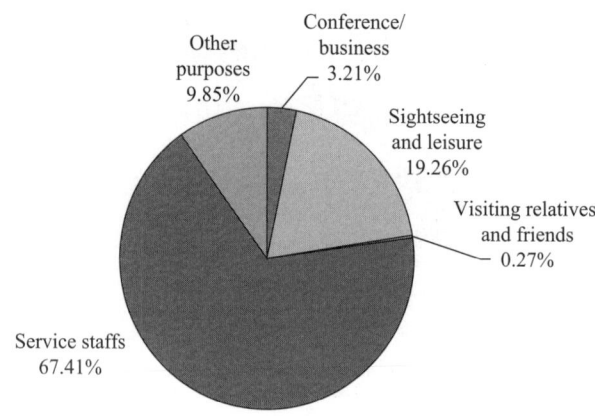

Figure 4-22　Purpose structure of Philippine inbound tourists to China in 2015

2.5 Indonesia

2.5.1 Analysis for transport means of Indonesian inbound tourists to China

Among Indonesian inbound tourists to China in 2015, 43.60% of them went by plane; 19.31% of them went by foot; 25.21% of them went by boat; 10.04% of them went by car; and 1.84% of them went by train.

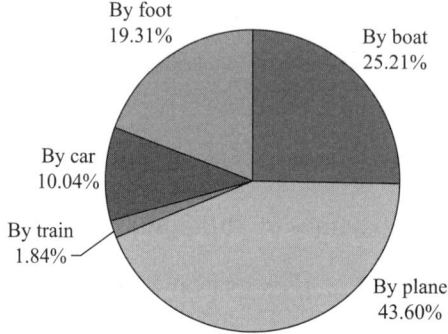

Figure 4-23　Transport means of Indonesian inbound tourists to China in 2015

2.5.2 Analysis for age structure of Indonesian inbound tourists to China

Among Indonesian inbound tourists to China in 2015, 3.05% of them were aged under 14; 10.87% of them were aged 15-24; 52.29% of them were aged 25-44; 27.46% of them were aged 45-64; 6.33% of them were aged over 65.

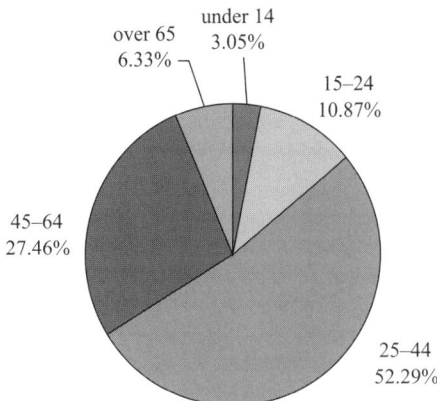

Figure 4-24 Age structure of Indonesian inbound tourists to China

2.5.3 Analysis for gender structure of Indonesian inbound tourists to China

Among Indonesian inbound tourists to China in 2015, 57.30% of them were male, and 42.70% of them were female.

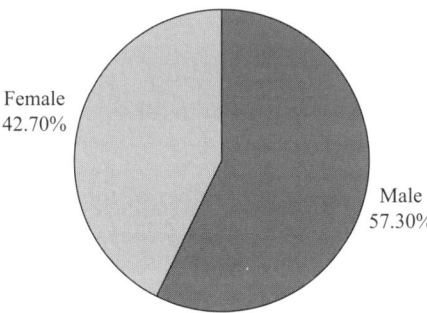

Figure 4-25 Gender structure of Indonesian inbound tourists to China

2.5.4 Analysis for purpose structure of Indonesian inbound tourists to China

Among Indonesian inbound tourists to China in 2015, 57.42% of them went for sightseeing and leisure; 5.34% of them went for conference/business; 26.69% of them were service staffs; 0.68% of them went for visiting relatives and friends; and 9.88% of them went for other purposes.

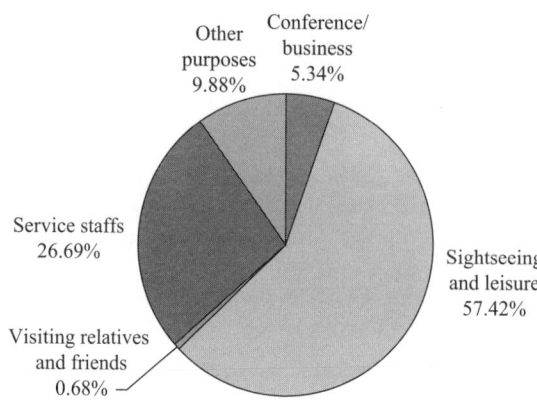

Figure 4-26 Purpose structure of Indonesian inbound tourists to China in 2015

Section 3 Investigation on Market Behavior of East Asian Inbound Tourism to China

3.1 Inbound tourists' consumption decision-making influence characteristics

According to the survey results[①], the number of inbound tourists visiting China for the first time was significantly higher than that of tourists visiting China many times. In terms of the purposes of inbound tourists, "understanding of Chinese characteristic culture" and "visit and sightseeing" were still the main purposes.

3.1.1 Over 50% of inbound tourists visited China for the first time

Among inbound tourists to China, 58.19% of them visited China for the first time.

---

① These results contained herein were those of 2015.

第四章　东亚在中国入境旅游市场中的基础地位与行为特征
Chapter 4 Basic Status and Behavioral Characteristics of East Asia on Chinese Inbound Tourism Market

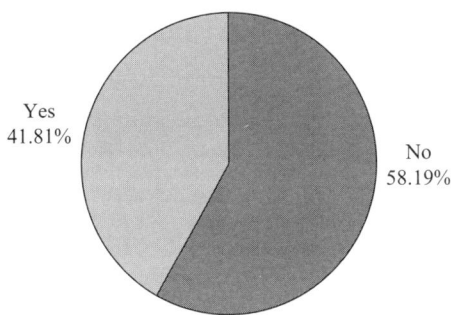

Figure 4-27 Frequency of inbound tourists (respondents) visiting China

3.1.2 Chinese characteristic culture and sightseeing attracted inbound tourists most

Among inbound tourists to China, 55.56%, 28.24%, 5.09% and 3.61% of them toured for "understanding of Chinese characteristic culture", "visit and sightseeing", "leisure and vacation enjoyment" and "business", respectively.

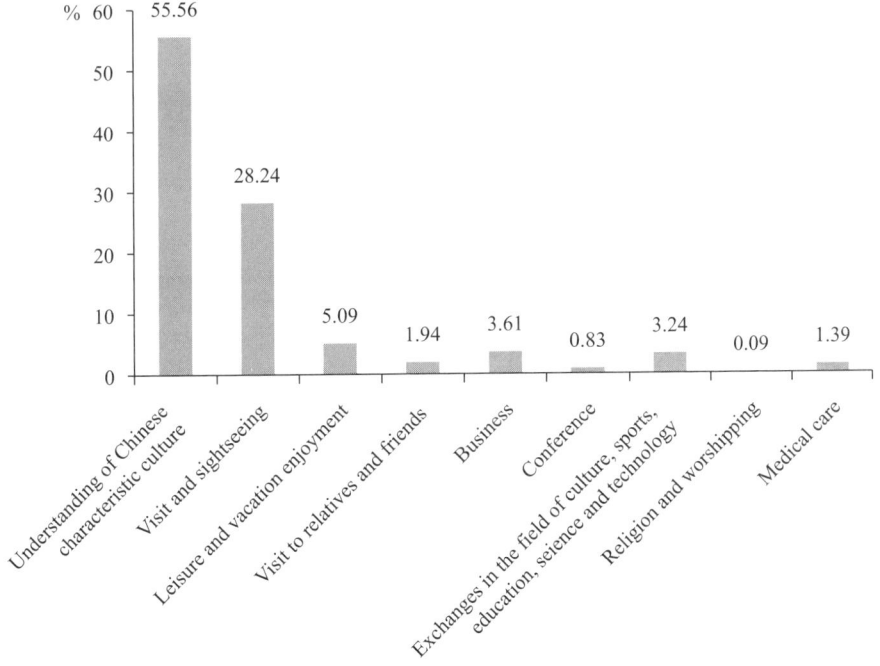

Figure 4-28 Purposes of inbound tourists to China (respondents) in 2015

183

3.2 Inbound tourists' consumption decision-making characteristics

According to the survey results, "Introduction from Friends and Relatives" is currently main information source access channel for inbound tourists to China. 20.49% of the inbound tourists are influenced by "introduction from friends and relatives" prior to travel. Prior to travel, inbound tourists mainly obtain the information on the characteristic cultural and recreational activities, tourism and shopping environment, traffic and weather of tourism destination, etc. In the choice of destinations and tourist attractions, travel expense is the most concerned issue, followed by destination traffic, travel safety and leisure environment influencing the choice of destination. In the choice of traveling companions, 34.58% of inbound tourists choose to travel with their friends, and 33.39% of inbound tourists choose to travel with their families. The main tourist attractions include landscape, art and culture and cuisine and cooking, accounting for 16.75%, 15.08% and 13.88%, respectively. In terms of the number of scenic spots, 27.32% of inbound tourists visit 3-5 tourist attractions, with the highest representativeness. 30.26% of inbound tourists stay in China for 8-15 days, with the highest representativeness. In the choice of accommodation, budget hotel is preferred by inbound tourists, followed by medium-priced hotel.

3.2.1 Inbound tourism information was mainly obtained from introduction from relatives and friends or outdoor advertisement

Among inbound tourists to China, 20.49% of them obtained relevant tourism information from introduction from relatives and friends; 15.75% of them obtained relevant tourism information from outdoor advertisement; 13.19% of them obtained relevant tourism information from Website/BBS/Forum; and 9.72% of them obtained relevant tourism information from TV/radio broadcasting.

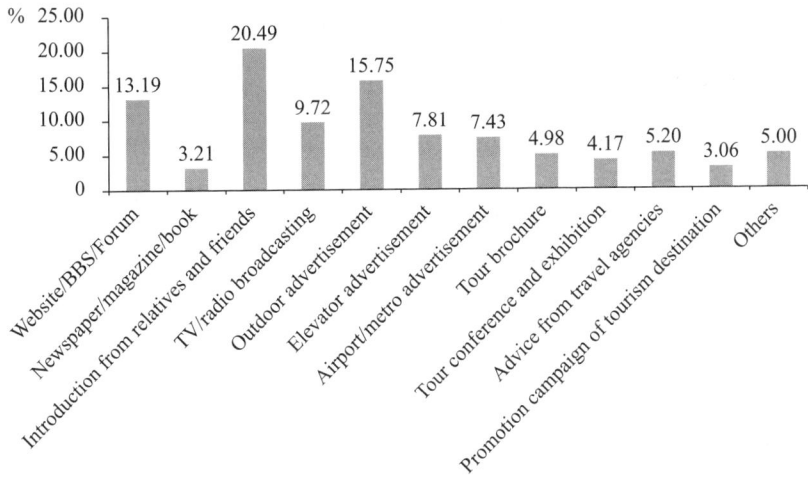

Figure 4-29 Information access channels of inbound tourists to China (respondents) in 2015

3.2.2 Characteristic cultural and recreational activities, tourism and shopping environment, traffic and weather of tourism destination and other daily life information attracted the most attention from inbound tourists

Among inbound tourists to China, 19.30% of them searched information on characteristic cultural and recreational activities; 15.71% of them searched information on tourism and shopping environment; 14.46% of them searched information on traffic and weather of tourism destination; 13.73% of them searched information on tour price; and 12.42% of them search information on tourism products and services.

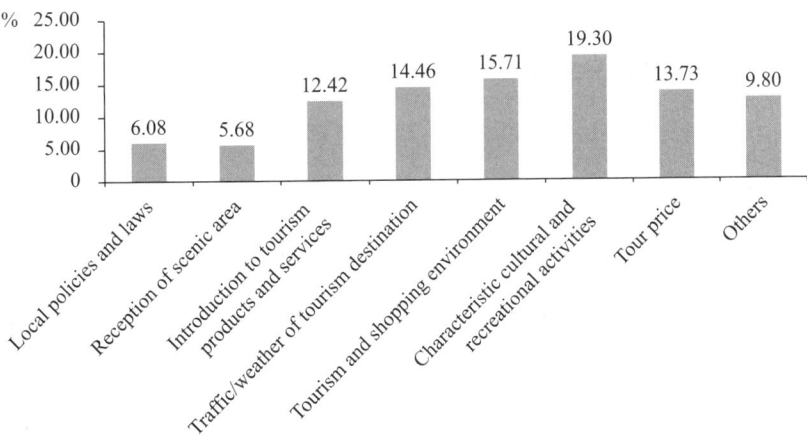

Figure 4-30 Information search contents of inbound tourists to China (respondents) in 2015

3.2.3 Tour expense and traffic/weather of tourism destination had the greatest influence in the choice of tourism destination

Among inbound tourists to China, 15.44% of them placed top priority over tour expense; 15.12% of them placed top priority over traffic of tourism destination; 9.51% of them placed top priority over tour safety; and 7.93% of them placed top priority over leisure environment.

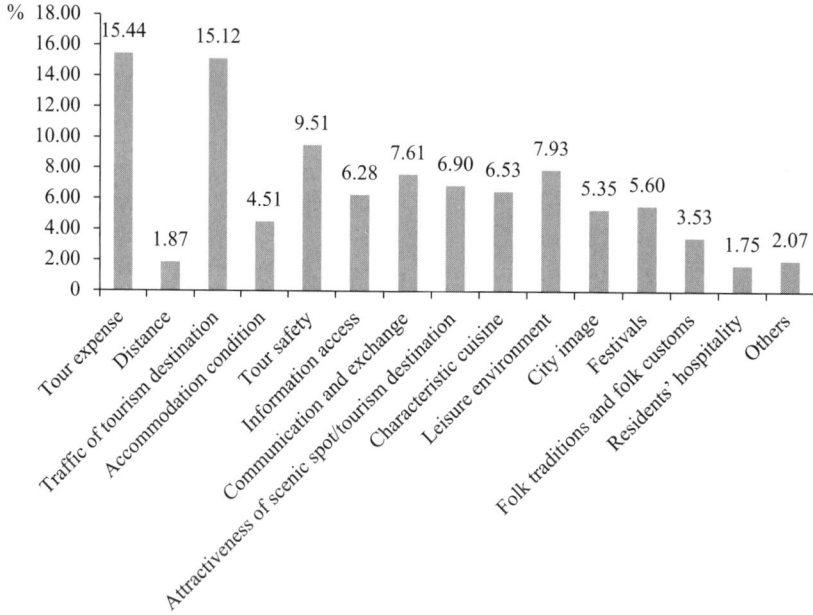

Figure 4-31 Influencing factors for inbound tourists to China (respondents) in the choice for tourism destinations in 2015

3.2.4 Most of inbound tourists travelled together with their families or good friends

Among inbound tourists to China, 34.58% of them travelled together with friends; 33.39% of them travelled together with families; 12.81% of them traveled alone; 10.10% of them travelled together with companies, schools and mass organizations; and 3.81% of them travelled for business activities/conference, training and tourism.

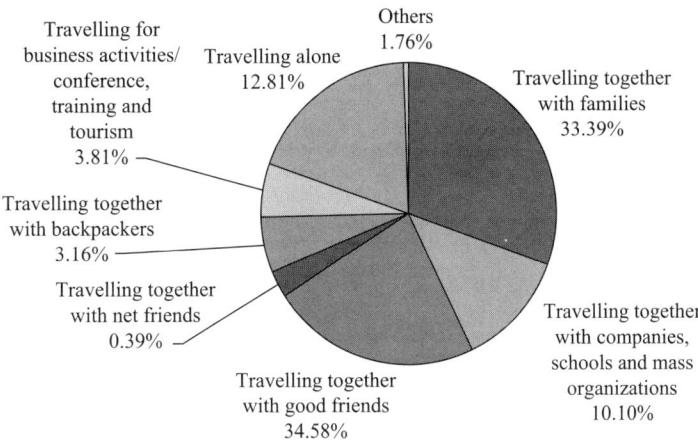

Figure 4-32 Traveling companions for inbound tourists (respondents) in 2015

3.2.5 Landscape, art and culture, cuisine and cooking were main tour items

Among inbound tourists to China, 16.75% of them toured for landscape; 15.08% of them toured for art and culture; 13.88% of them toured for cuisine and cooking; and 13.59% of them toured for health care.

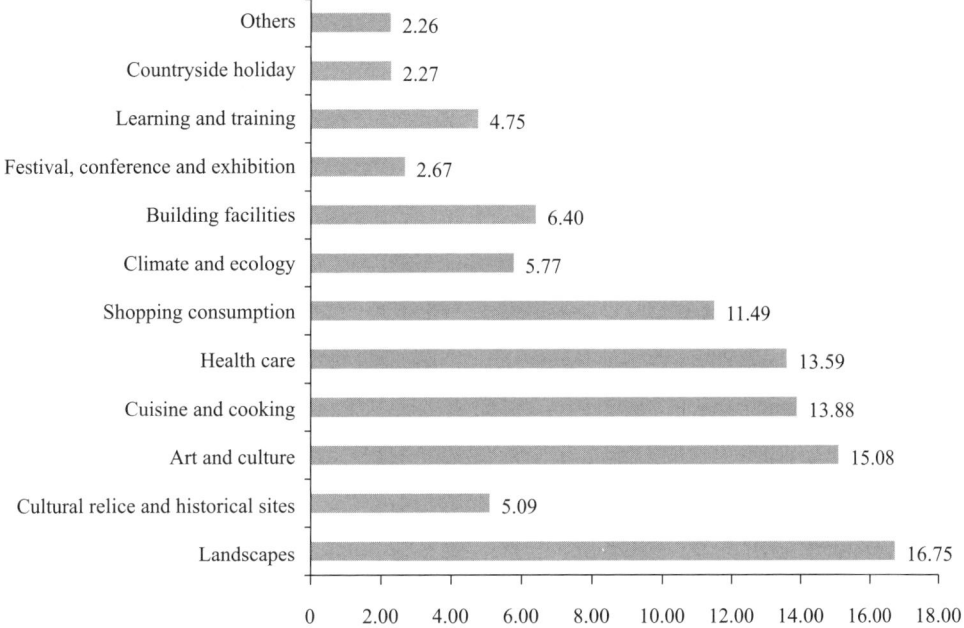

Figure 4-33 Tour items of inbound tourists to China (respondents) in 2015

3.2.6 Tour line design with 3-5 tourist attractions was the most popular

Among inbound tourists to China, they mainly visited 3-9 tourist attractions. 27.32% of them made tour line design with 3-5 tourist attractions; and 25.79% of them made tour line design with 6-9 tourist attractions.

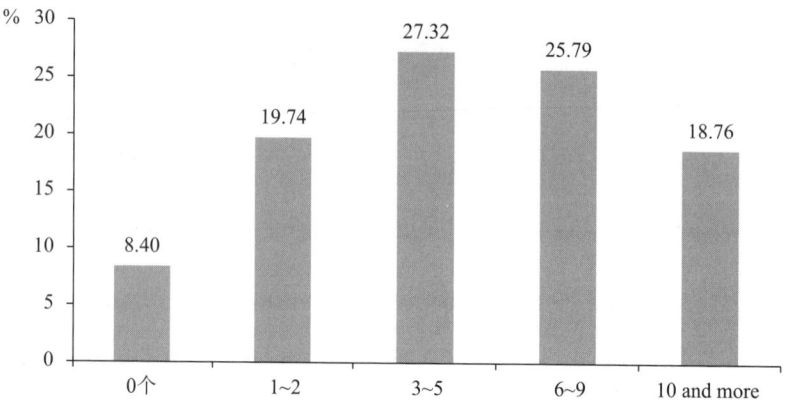

Figure 4-34 Number of tourist attractions visited by inbound tourists to China (respondents) in 2015

3.2.7 Duration for staying in tourist destination was mainly 8-15 days

Among inbound tourists to China, 30.26% of them chose to stay for 8-15 days in tourist destinations; and 29.77% of them chose to stay for 4-7 days in tourist destinations.

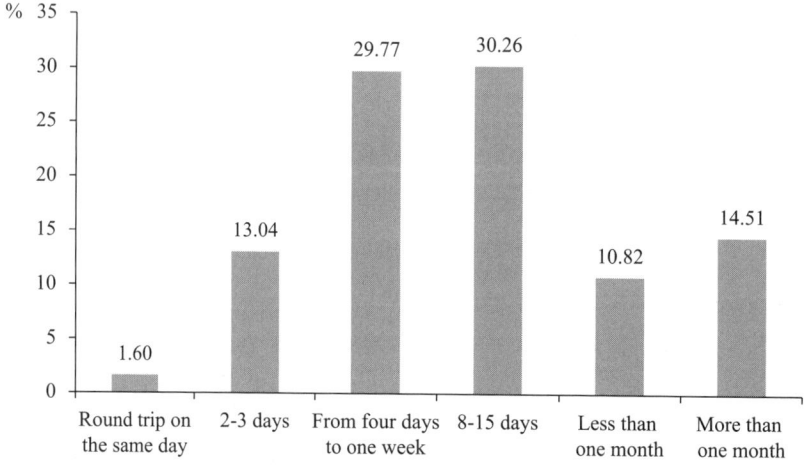

Figure 4-35 Duration of inbound tourists to China (respondents) staying in tourist destinations in 2015

3.2.8 Budget hotel was favored by the most tourists

Among inbound tourists to China, 35.69% of them preferred budget hotels; 25.08% of them preferred medium-priced hotel (two-star/three-star or similar level); and 22.88% of them preferred luxury hotel.

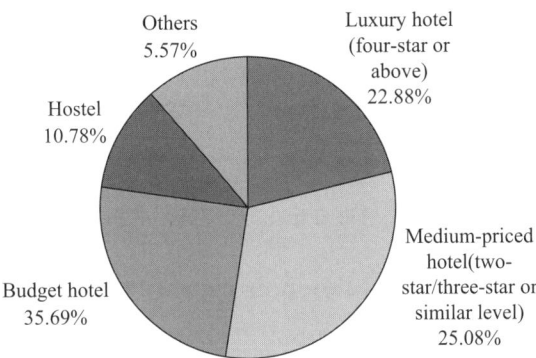

Figure 4-36 Accommodation choice of inbound tourists to China (respondents) in 2015

3.3 Inbound tourists' consumption structure characteristics

According to the survey results, per capita consumption of inbound tourists to China showed normal distribution, with high amount in the middle and low amount at both ends. Over 60% of inbound tourists spent from $1 001 to $5 000. 14.82% of inbound tourists spent $501 to $1 000. 14.03% of inbound tourists spent less than $500. 9.38% of inbound tourists spent more than $5,000. In terms of consumption items, 22.88% of inbound tourists said that transportation expense was the largest consumption items, followed by shopping consumption (accounting for 20.94% of total consumption expenditure).

3.3.1 Middle-class consumer group accounted for over 50%

For inbound tourists to China, the main distribution range of per capita expenditure were $1,001-2,000 (27.48%), $2,001-3,000 (18.81%) and $3,001-5,000 (15.51%), respectively.

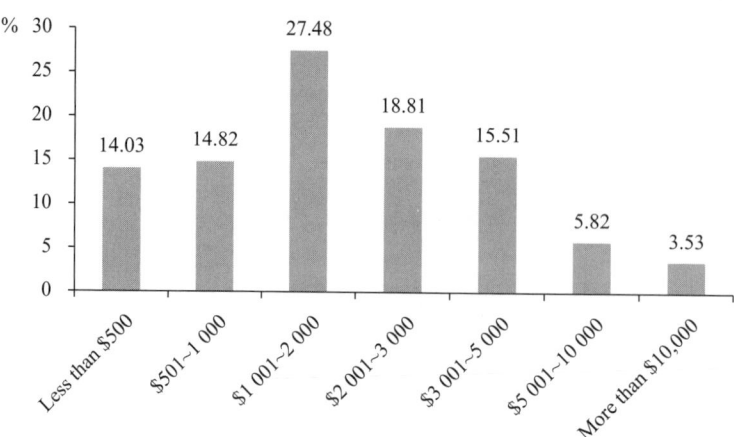

Figure 4-37　Per capita consumption of inbound tourists to China (respondents) in 2015

3.3.2 Transportation expense and shopping expense presented the highest proportion

For inbound tourists to China, the highest-amount spending items were transportation (22.88%), shopping (20.94%), catering (20.70%) and accommodation (11.86%), respectively.

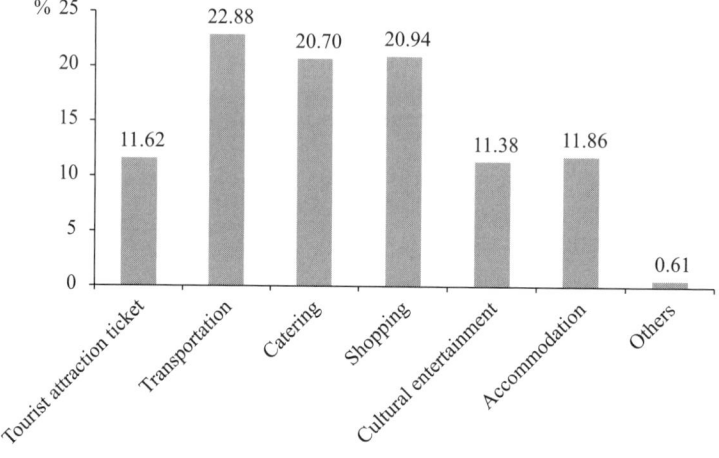

Figure 4-38　The highest-amount spending items of inbound tourists to China (respondents) in 2015

3.4 Consumption evaluation of inbound tourists

According to the survey results, inbound tourists to China gave favorable evaluation in all aspects. In terms of overall image of tourist destination, urban construction, urban management, public sector services and window services, inbound tourists basically gave the average evaluation score of more than 8. But some aspects revealed shortcomings, such as air quality (components of urban construction), mobile phone signal coverage and the Internet coverage (components of public sector services), transportation and catering services (components of window services), with respective scores of 8.17, 8.28, 8.36, 8.17 and 8.30 below the averages.

3.4.1 Informatization level and openness were the favorite indicators of inbound tourists

Inbound tourists to China spoke highly of various indicators of tourist destination on the whole, among which informatization level and openness were the favorite indicators, with respective scores of 8.90 and 8.87.

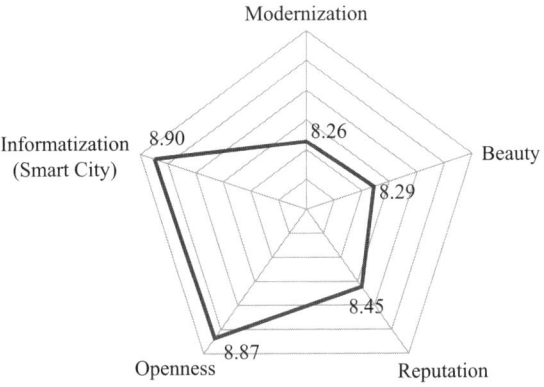

Figure 4-39 Overall evaluation of inbound tourists to China (respondents) for China's tourist destinations in 2015

3.4.2 Poor evaluation results of air quality and sanitation facilities

Inbound tourists to China gave respective scores of 8.17 and 8.21 for air quality and sanitation facilities in tourist destination, which were lower than the average.

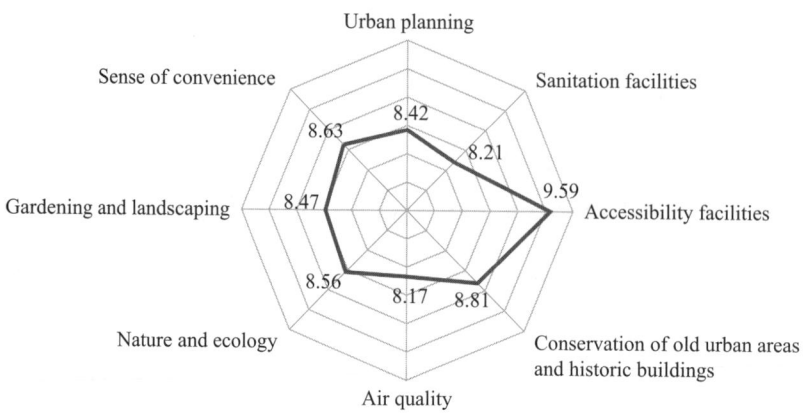

Figure 4-40   Evaluation of inbound tourists to China (respondents) for urban construction of China's tourist destinations in 2015

3.4.3 Emergency rescue system was praised, whereas sense of security got low evaluation score

The scores, given by inbound tourists to China for urban construction of China's tourist destinations, quite differed. Among them, emergency rescue system (health system and weather forecast) saw the highest score of 9.59. Sense of security (safety and first aid information) saw the lowest score of 8.27.

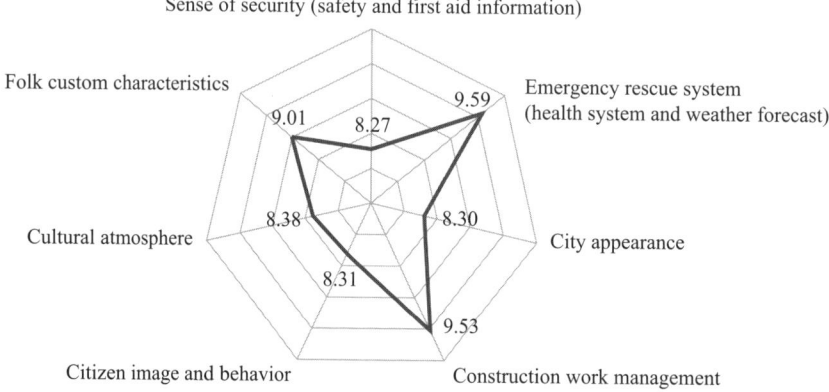

Figure 4-41   Evaluation of inbound tourists to China (respondents) for urban management of China's tourist destinations in 2015

3.4.4 Mobile phone signal coverage and the Internet coverage saw low scores

Inbound tourists to China gave low scores for mobile phone signal coverage and the Internet coverage, which were 8.28 and 8.36, respectively.

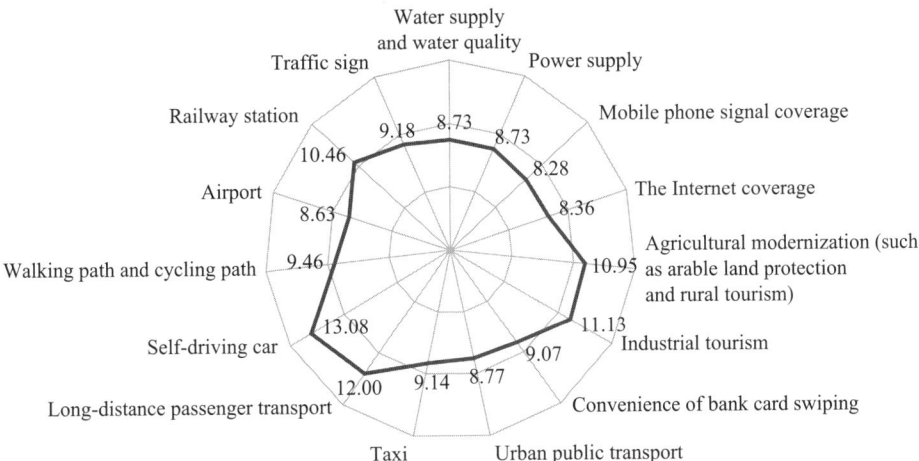

Figure 4-42 Evaluation of inbound tourists to China (respondents) for public sector services of China's tourist destinations in 2015

3.4.5 Transportation and catering services were poorly evaluated

Inbound tourists to China gave low scores for transportation and catering services, which were 8.17 and 8.30, respectively.

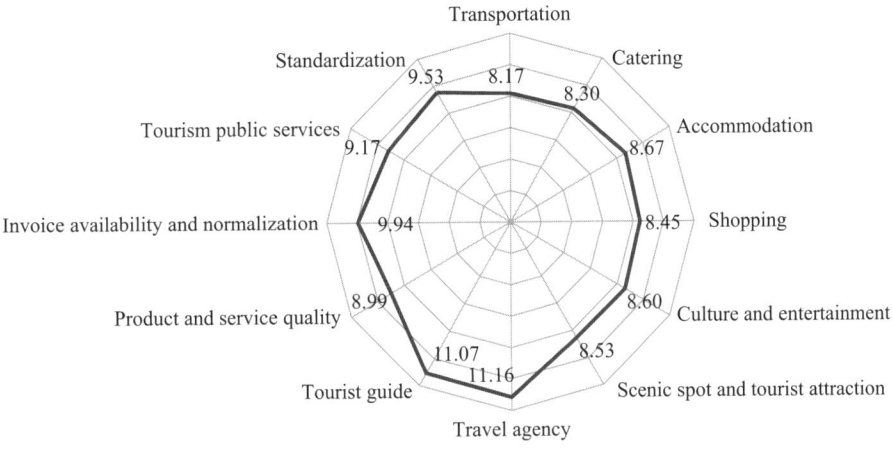

Figure 4-43 Evaluation of inbound tourists to China (respondents) for window services of China's tourist destinations in 2015

Chapter 5
Ushering in Bright Future for International Tourism Cooperation in East Asia

Section 1 Prospects for International Tourism Cooperation in East Asia

Tourism cooperation development trend of East Asia is not only influenced by global economic globalization and regionalization environment, but also is closely tied with the geographical connection and similarity, richness and complementarity of natural, human and other tourism resources in East Asian countries, as well as the support of East Asian governments for tourism development and cooperation.

1.1 Remarkable regional integration advantages of East Asian countries are demonstrated from geographical and cognitive perspectives

Among ten Southeast Asian countries, seven countries are located in peninsula. Countries mostly borders on each other in Indochina Peninsula. In addition to Singapore, other countries border on at least two countries. Thailand borders on more countries, i.e., Myanmar, Laos, Cambodia and Malaysia are its neighbors. Size of such countries in the peninsula is generally small. Thus, the spatial distance from one country to another in Southeast Asia is relatively short. In Northeast Asia, China and South Korea also border on each other. Japan is across the sea. Sea, land and air transportation is convenient. Therefore, geographically connected or similar characteristics are favorable contributor for East Asian countries to carry out tourism cooperation.

In terms of cognition, international tourists have integrated image cognition of East Asia. Westerners are traditionally accustomed to regarding East Asia as a whole. This is a prerequisite for the establishment and dissemination of regional tourism image, which is also an important foundation for tourism cooperation in East Asia.

1.2 Abundant tourism resources of East Asia show typical complementary advantages

There are obvious differences in the social and economic development of East Asian countries. In East Asian countries, their tourism development is at varying degree and the tourism market sharply differentiates. However, abundant tourism resources of East Asia have some common complementarities, which constitute the basis and foundation for the regional tourism cooperation in East Asia.

East Asia is rich in natural tourism resources, and features vast territory, a variety of natural sceneries and broad natural landscape difference, which is one of the tourist areas with the most magnificent scenic landscape in the world. The ocean landscape, the forest landscape, the grassland and wetland landscape, the volcanic lava landscape, the ice and snow landscape and the frigid zone and polar landscape give sharp contrast to the utmost extent. These landscapes demonstrate the coarse and primitive characteristics, and boast unparalleled natural, authentic, perfect and mysterious styles compared with other landscapes.

East Asia has a long history and splendid culture. For example, China gives birth to one of the "Four Great Ancient Civilizations". Buddhist culture prospers in Thailand. East Asia is a multicultural hub, where the representatives of worldwide major cultural patterns can be found: Indochina Peninsula takes pride in Buddhist culture. Singapore is representative of social tourism resources of East Asian countries, as its residents are mostly the Chinese and reflect the characteristics of Confucian culture. Japan is the embodiment of Shinto culture. The cultural interdependence and complementarity of East Asian countries lay an important cultural foundation for the cultural exchange (especially tourism activities) in East Asia. This is undoubtedly a very favorable condition for the development of regional tourism cooperation in East Asia. Many East

Asian countries are reputed as "Country of Etiquette and Ceremonies" or "Country of Smile", and their oriental-style considerate services are highly praised by European and American tourists. East Asia comprises sub-frigid and subtropical regions, where the natural landscapes are very diverse. With its uniform cultural origin, colorful and orderly tourist destination landscapes are formed. This is the material condition for tourism cooperation in East Asia.

1.3 Governmental support vigorously ensures international tourism cooperation in East Asia

East Asian governments attach great importance to the development of tourism industry. Well-known for tradition of tourism economy development, Singapore worked out *Vision Planning for Tourism Economy in the 21st Century* in 1996. Japan set forth Nation-building upon Tourism Strategy in 2003. South Korea promulgated *Tourism Industry Promotion Act* in 1961, and developed *Prospects for Tourism in the 21st Century*. In recent years, China has promulgated *Law on Tourism*, and defines tourism industry as a strategic pillar industry and modern service industry for making common people more satisfied. Malaysia increases its infrastructure investment in tourism sector. Vietnam developed Tourism Development Strategy 2010. At the same time, the governments of the East Asian countries attach great importance to cooperation in the tourism fields, such as bilateral, multilateral, sub-regional and regional tourism. They convene meetings on tourism cooperation at all levels, conduct discussions and research, establish regional tourism cooperation mechanisms, sign tourism cooperation agreements, and jointly organize a number of tourism promotion events. The tourism cooperation mechanism between ASEAN and China, Japan and South Korea within the framework of "10+3", established in 2002, marks a new historical stage in the development of tourism cooperation in East Asia.

Section 2 Policy Recommendations for International Tourism Cooperation in East Asia

In the tourism sector, East Asia is one of the fastest developing regions in the world. The friendly relations among East Asian countries are time-honored, and the friendly exchanges have a long history. East Asia boasts vast territory, rich tourism resources and rapid economic development. It shoulders responsibility and mission to take more active actions and cooperation by seizing new development opportunities. To this end, it is hereby recommended that East Asian countries shall strengthen negotiation and collaboration at the following aspects:

2.1 It is necessary to attach importance to the leading role of local governments in international exchanges, and promote bilateral and multilateral tourism exchanges in pragmatic manner

It is necessary to take full advantage of existing ASEAN and China-Japan-South Korea (ASEAN Plus Three, APT) Summit, East Asia Summit, ASEAN and China-Japan-South Korea (10+3) Tourism Ministers' Meeting, China-Japan-South Korea Tourism Ministers' Meeting, East Asian Business Forum and East Asia International Tourism Expo and other communication and exchange mechanisms, follow the philosophy of "government guidance, enterprise participation and public support", and gradually improve and expand international tourism cooperation mechanism of East Asia. With stress on the high-level exchanges and exchanges of East Asian countries, it is necessary to attach more importance to the leading role of East Asian governments in international tourism cooperation in East Asia, explore for the establishment of international tourism exchange and cooperation platform of East Asian countries with local and urban cooperation units, actively seek for normalized operation, and promote bilateral and multilateral tourism exchanges and information sharing in pragmatic manner. On this basis, it is necessary to give full consideration to local and regional characteristics. It is advised that local governments may take a lead role, explore for the establishment of regional integrated cooperative development mechanism, and actively pursue closer connectivity and more in-depth bilateral and multilateral policy exchanges.

2.2 It is necessary to begin with improvement of convenience, and take the initiative to explore for market openness and sharing

Most of East Asian countries are both tourists market and primary tourist destinations. In view of current trend of international tourism development, upgrading the openness of the domestic tourism market is not only the basic law of the development of tourism market, but also the basic premise of carrying out bilateral and multilateral tourism market cooperation. It is hereby recommended that East Asian countries should begin with improvement of convenience, take the initiative and mutually work hard for visa, air traffic rights, tax rebate, rapid customs clearance, market access and movement of natural persons, and further lift the obstacles to the flow of tourists in East Asia. In the implementation process of relevant facilitation measures, it is necessary to actively raise the level of connectivity with the relevant countries, bravely eliminate regional protectionism, put facilitation policies into practice, and effectively promote the two-way and multi-way tourism market openness and sharing.

2.3 It is necessary to jointly develop top-quality tourism products and cross-border quality tourist routes

It is necessary to take into account current characteristics of the international tourism market demand, and jointly develop top-quality tourism products (in particular cross-border quality tourist routes). In view of strategic opportunities from the rapid development of international cruise industry at present, it is necessary to jointly develop Circum-Yellow Sea top-quality tourist route and Circum-Japan Sea top-quality tourist route in Northeast Asia and top-quality island tourist route in Southeast Asia. According to different characteristics of tourism market demand, it is necessary to jointly design cross-border thematic tourist routes, such as business / conference / exhibition tourism products, cultural tourism products, religious tourism products, shopping tourism products and other special tourism products. It is necessary to push forward the cooperation of special tourism products, and jointly launch development of popular tourism products. The cooperation can be strengthened in youth study tour, golf tourism, ice tourism, pension tourism and other fields with great potentials in East Asian countries, with a view to expanding profound exchanges of East Asian countries in the tourism sector.

2.4 It is necessary to kick off more liberalized industrial policy, and guide and encourage tourism industry cooperation

It is necessary to make use of golden opportunities and contributors from the construction of free trade zones and cross-border tourism cooperation zones. Under the premise of policy permission and no jeopardy to respective interests, it is necessary to actively pioneer in the introduction and implementation of industry openness policies in terms of market access, tax, land, capital, information, franchise and other aspects, formulate catalog of tourism investment guidance in East Asia, strive to promote the expansion of tourism openness in East Asian countries, and fully arouse the enthusiasm of tourism enterprises to participate in international tourism cooperation in East Asia. It is necessary to give full play to functions and roles of tourism industry organizations in the international tourism cooperation, and make them have the ability to represent the tourism industry to communicate with governments and render services to enterprises.

2.5 It is necessary to pay more attention to basic supporting role of education, science, technology and talent

It is necessary to strengthen cooperation among East Asian countries for tourism education and scientific research, and further strengthen resource input and organizational guarantee for tourism talent cultivation, tourism research investment, tourism expert and think tank debate, special tourism policy reserve etc. It is necessary to innovate the human resources development mechanism of international tourism in East Asia, and comprehensively cultivate the language ability of tourism practitioners so as to enhance the reception ability. It is necessary to encourage the tourism practitioners to exchange in East Asian countries or the cities with developed tourism, and improve the quality and ability of the talents. It is necessary to improve overall quality of tourism practitioners in East Asian countries, and upgrade taste and level of East Asian tourism by means of high-quality services. It is necessary to set up a wider range of personnel exchange and training mechanisms, focus on movement of natural persons, commercial presence and emergency ambulance guarantee, and strive to expand the scope of movement of natural persons from senior managers and senior technical staffs to tour guides, chefs and health care personnel.

Appendix 1　East Asian Tourism Cooperation

East Asian tourism cooperation is an important part of the East Asian regional cooperation. Its origin can be traced back to "Kunming Conference" in 2000. Advocated by China, Tourism Ministers' Meeting of Thailand, Singapore and Malaysia was convened in Kunming on August 21, 2000. They signed *Minutes of Ministerial Meeting on the Joint Governance of Regional Tourism in Four Countries*, which jointly rectified non-standard behaviors on outbound tourism market (such as zero package tour fee), and effectively standardized the tourism market. Covering the maximum range, "10+3" Regional Tourism Cooperation makes a late start, but it takes skyrocketing development pace. At present, East Asian tourism cooperation mainly includes four parts, i.e., intra-ASEAN tourism cooperation, ASEAN-China-Japan-South Korea tourism cooperation, bilateral tourism cooperation and sub-regional tourism cooperation.

1. Intra-ASEAN Tourism Cooperation

ASEAN tourism cooperation was kicked off by establishment of ASEAN Tourism Working Committee in 1976. In 1979, the "ASEAN Tourism Association (ASEANTA)" was established, followed by the ASEAN Hotel & Restaurant Association, the ASEAN Travel Agent Association and other industry organizations. On September 26, 1998, the ASEAN member states signed an agreement in the Kuala Lumpur (capital of Malaysia) to establish the ASEAN Tourism Information Centre. The ASEAN Tourism Information Centre is mainly responsible for ten tasks, including introduction and announcement of tourism resources and tourism investment opportunities of the ASEAN member states, coordination and implementation of short-term and long-term market projects contributing to inbound and outbound tourism in the ASEAN.

At present, intra-ASEAN tourism cooperation has been institutionalized. Since 1998, the ASEAN Tourism Ministers' Meetings have been held regularly every year. Special meetings are also held under special circumstances. The ASEAN Tourism Ministers' Conference has become a system since it was first held in 1998, which is held every January during the "ASEAN Tourism Forum (ATF)". In recent years, ASEAN has accelerated tourism cooperation and harvests plentiful fruits. Ten ASEAN member countries plan to establish a single Asian market similar to the European Union by 2020.

2. Tourism Cooperation between Southeast Asia and China-Japan-South Korea

The cooperation between ASEAN, China, Japan and South Korea under the framework of "10+3" is an integral part of East Asian tourism cooperation in East Asia regional cooperation, which makes a late start. ASEAN-China-Japan-South Korea Tourism Ministers' Conference is one of the seven ministerial-level meetings under the framework of "10+3" Cooperation. Since 2002, in echo with the ASEAN Tourism Ministers' Conference and the ASEAN Tourism Forum, ASEAN-China-Japan-South Korea "10+3" Tourism Ministers' Meeting (ASEAN Plus Three Tourism Ministers' Meeting) is simultaneously held every year, with a view to strengthen ASEAN-China-Japan-South Korea cooperation in the tourism sector.

3. Bilateral Tourism Cooperation with Other Parts of East Asia

Bilateral cooperation among countries in East Asia also develops rapidly. Compared with multilateral cooperation, bilateral tourism cooperation is often more operable with greater substantive significance.

In recent years, the ASEAN countries have signed a series of bilateral cooperation agreements on the issues with respect to regional tourism cooperation, such as improvement of the level of tourism services, simplification of entry and exit procedures and joint development of tourism resources. For example, Vietnam and Cambodia agree to strengthen cooperation for simplifying transit procedures, launching more powerful tourism promotion and unveiling new tourist routes. With a view to development of the "Golden Triangle" Tourist Area, Thailand and Laos sign *Laos-Thailand Tourism Cooperation Agreement*, while Thailand and Myanmar sign *Myanmar-Thailand Tourism Cooperation Agreement*. Thailand has also signed tourism cooperation agreements with Vietnam, Cambodia, Indonesia and Malaysia. After setting forth Strategy of Revitalizing the State with Tourism, Japan gradually attaches importance to bilateral tourism cooperation with other East Asian countries. In May 2005, Japan signed a bilateral tourism cooperation agreement with Vietnam in Tokyo, and both parties will formulate reciprocal tourism policy. In July 2005, Japan executed a tourism decision with China to kick off Chinese citizens' group tour to Japan on the basis of access to residents of Beijing, Shanghai, Guangdong and other five Chinese provinces and cities. Japan and China sign *Memorandum of Understanding on Negotiation for Further Strengthening Tourism Cooperation and Exchange*, and reach a consensus on further strengthening tourism exchange and cooperation, thereby setting a new milestone of tourism exchange and cooperation between both countries. China also sign treaties, agreements and memorandums of understanding on bilateral tourism cooperation with ten ASEAN countries, which provides framework and guarantee for tourism cooperation between China and ASEAN countries. In addition, China and South Korea agree to strengthen exchange and cooperation, and join hands to promote the development of tourism industry in China and South

Korea.

4. Sub-regional Tourism Cooperation in East Asia

At present, sub-regional tourism cooperation in East Asia mainly refers to Lancang-Mekong sub-regional tourism cooperation. Since the 1990s, with the end of the Cold War and the relaxation of international relations, the cooperative development of Mekong River Basin attracts wide attention from the international community. Lancang-Mekong Sub-regional Tourism Cooperation was initiated and formed by the Asian Development Bank (ADB) in 1992. The relevant countries of Mekong River Basin participate in Economic Cooperation Program thanks to the support of the Asian Development Bank (ADB).

Sub-regional countries put forward the idea of taking tourism industry as cooperation pacesetter, and suggest the measures to promote tourism cooperation. Based on sub-regional economic cooperation mechanism, Lancang-Mekong Sub-regional Tourism Cooperation is dominated and driven by international organizations such as the United Nations Economic and Social Commission for Asia and the Pacific (ESCAP), the Asian Development Bank (ADB) and other international organizations, which is a new cooperation mechanism committed to making joint efforts to develop this sub-region as a complete tourism destination, building the overall image, and unveiling on the global tourism market.

Appendix 2 East Asia Local and Regional Government Congress

Since 2010, the East Asia Local and Regional Government Congress has been held for six times. The year 2010 is the 1300th anniversary of Heijyokyo becoming the capital of Japan. Japan hopes to build the foundation, taking this conference as an opportunity for the future development of East Asia as did like their pioneers who made Japan's basic framework. To this end, as an important link of the 1300th anniversary of Heijyokyo becoming the capital of Japan, the "East Asia Local and Regional Government Congress" is held by local governments of Japan, China and South Korea. This congress is aimed to frankly exchange the situation and topics among the representatives of local governments, discuss the common topics and deepen mutual understanding.

I. Sponsor Conference of the East Asia Local and Regional Government Congress

The Sponsor Conference of the East Asia Local and Regional Government Congress was held in Nara Prefecture on October 25-28, 2009, aiming to establish the 2010 East Asia Local and Regional Government Congress, negotiate the *Charter* and prepare for some work. Totally 19 local governments from China, South Korea and Japan participated in this conference.

The local governments include: 19 local governments

China (6): Shaanxi Province, Henan Province, Jiangsu Province, Xi'an City, Luoyang City and Yangzhou City

South Korea (6): South Chungcheong Province, Gongju, Seosan, Buyeo County, North Gyeongsang Province and Gyeongju

Japan (7): Gifu Prefecture, Shizuoka Prefecture, Nara Prefecture, Nara, Tenri,

Kashihara and Asuka

In the sponsorship conference, all the present local governments reported their "real conditions and topics". Meanwhile, they discussed the *Nara Charter of East Asia Local and Regional Government Congress (Draft)* as a rule operating the East Asia Local and Regional Government Congress and adopted the *Nara Statement regarding Establishment of East Asia Local and Regional Government Congress (Draft)*.

In the sponsorship conference on October 26, 2009, the representatives from the 19 local governments introduced the current conditions and topics of their respective region. Mr. Shogo Arai, Governor of Nara Prefecture said, Nara Prefecture bounds in rich natural and cultural heritage and tourism, plays an important role in this prefecture. In order to strengthen the tourist activity, Nara Prefecture formulated 5A (Accommodation, Access, Appetite, Attraction and Amity) strategy. Mr. Gen Nakagawa, Mayor of Nara also introduced the cultural heritage protection in Nara for the purpose of sustainable natural development and promotion of urban construction. Mr. ZHOU Yuming, Deputy Secretary of Shaanxi Province, generally introduced Shaanxi. According to his words, Shaanxi has its own advantages both in terms of natural resources, history and transportation. According to the introduction of Mr. Heita Kawakatsu, Governor of Shizuoka Prefecture, the "Land of Mount Fuji", among the foreigners traveling in Shizuoka Prefecture, 70% were Asians and the Chinese and South Korea tourists accounted for a large ratio; also, he proposed to embrace the new era of East Asia. Mr. Koh Youngchi, Deputy Governor of North Gyeongsang Province, introduced the development with China and Japan and suggestions on cultural exchanges of the three sides. Other local governments made an introduction about cultural heritage, urban construction, ecological protection and agricultural and industrial development by combining their own development and put forward a strategic objective.

In the conference, the governments participated in the dialogue and the experts in the fields of economy and trade also actively interacted with the local governments, discussing the future development of East Asia. Mr. Matsushita Masako, Corporation Aggregate and Vice Chairman of Kansai Economic Federation and International Chairman, Mr. Shogo Arai, Governor of Nara Prefecture, and Mr. Kim Mo-hwan, Procurator of Buyeo County, reviewed the exchanges among China, Japan and South Korea in terms of economy and history, analyzed the economic development and issues of East Asia. All of them hoped to build a close economic tie among China, Japan and South Korea.

In order to more directly understand the concerns of the people in the East Asia region and strengthen diverse exchanges in various fields in this region, it was determined to establish the "East Asia Local and Regional Government Congress" according to the result of the sponsorship conference and to hold the first congress in Nara in 2010. In addition, they endeavored to adopt the *Nara Charter of East Asia Local and Regional Government Congress (Draft)* in the first congress, which was confirmed by all parties. The local governments reached the consensus: to call on other related local governments in East Asia to participate in the "East Asia Local and Regional Government Congress".

II. The 1st East Asia Local and Regional Government Congress

The 1st East Asia Local and Regional Government Congress was held on October 6-8, 2010 in Nara. The representatives from totally 34 local governments of 6 countries i.e. Japan, China, South Korea, Philippines and Indonesia exchanged their opinions on deepening cooperation between local governments and promoting stable development of East Asia. The 1st East Asia Local and Regional Government Congress was held to celebrate the 1300th anniversary of Heijyokyo becoming the capital of Japan.

The local governments include: 34 local governments

China (5): Anhui Province, Henan Province, Shaanxi Province, Yangzhou City and Dunhuang City

India (1): Varanasi City (Isipatane Migadaye)

Indonesia (1): Special Region of Yogyakarta

Philippines (1): Aurora

South Korea (8): Gyeonggi Province, South Chungcheong Province, Gongju, Seosan, Buyeo County, South Jeolla Province, North Gyeongsang Province and Gyeongju

Japan (18): Aomori Prefecture, Yamagata Prefecture, Fukushima Prefecture, Niigata Prefecture, Toyama Prefecture, Fukui Prefecture, Gifu Prefecture, Shizuoka Prefecture, Mie Prefecture, Shimane Prefecture, Kōchi Prefecture, Kumamoto Prefecture, Nara Prefecture, Niigata, Nara, Tenri, Kashihara and Asuka

This congress was a peace and development platform between Japan and other countries in East Asia and also an exchange and long-term cooperation mechanism among local governments. Based upon the achievements of 2009 sponsorship conference of East Asia Local and Regional Government Congress, the *Nara Charter of East Asia Local and Regional Government Congress (Draft)* would be decided by vote to establish the East Asia Local and Regional Government Congress.

The first East Asia Local and Regional Government Congress unanimously approved the text of *Nara Charter of East Asia Local and Regional Government Congress (Draft)*, decided and explained its logo. The agreement to the *Nara Charter (Draft)* covered the main content of the East Asia Local and Regional Government Congress for reporting the regional conditions and the common topics, exploring the resolution approach about these topics. The uninterrupted conference year by year facilitated building a friendly and trustworthy relation among local governments so as to make contributions to the stable development among the countries, even in

East Asia. In addition, the agreement elaborated the activities, members and guest composition as well as the expense of the East Asia Local and Regional Government Congress.

The 1st East Asia Local and Regional Government Congress also unanimously approved the *Joint Statement (Draft)*. According to the *Joint Statement (Draft)*, the congress is held on an annual basis to jointly solve the common problems and the reports as well as the contents discussed in the congress shall be published. In addition, all parties call on actively participation of the local governments outside East Asia in this congress to commonly build a cooperation framework among local governments. According to the *Joint Statement (Draft)*, the 2011 East Asia Local and Regional Government Congress will be held in Nara.

In terms of regions, the representatives from local governments of China, Japan and Korea made a keynote speech on "cultural heritage protection to promote tourism" and "youth exchange". In the speech on "cultural heritage protection to promote tourism", the representative of each local government discussed the approaches to protect and preserve their own cultural heritage, put forward some new elements such as festival, arts and technology for their development, so as to attract more tourists and promote the economic development. At last, in the speech on celebrating establishment of the first East Asia Local and Regional Government Congress, the representative of Associates, Mr. Yukio Okamoto and Mr. Lee O-young, the first Minister of Ministry of Culture of the Republic of Korea discussed the current status and future of East Asia. Mr. Yukio Okamoto said," technology changes the development of the world. As long as we combine the traditional things with the new technology and the local governments work together, can we constantly promote the social progress and peace." Mr. Lee O-young said, the relations among China, Japan and South Korea have a common historical origin, each party should set aside prejudice, support each other, play an active role and avoid disadvantage, to form an East Asian cultural community with sustainable relationship.

III. The 2nd East Asia Local and Regional Government Congress

The 2nd East Asia Local and Regional Government Congress was held on October 18-26, 2011 in Nara. The representatives from totally 44 local governments of 6 countries, i.e. China, India, Philippines, South Korea, Vietnam and Japan attended the congress and deeply exchanged their ideas on such topics as "crisis management" and "regional promotion".

The local governments include: 44 local governments

China (7): Anhui Province, Shandong Province, Henan Province, Shaanxi Province, Xi'an City, Yangzhou City and Huangshan City

India (1): Varanasi City

Philippines (2): Benguet, Aurora

South Korea (7): Gyeonggi Province, South Chungcheong Province, Gongju, Buyeo County, South Jeolla Province, North Gyeongsang Province and Gyeongju

Vietnam (3): Thừa Thiên Thuận, Thuận Hóa, Hội An

Japan (24): Aomori Prefecture, Yamagata Prefecture, Fukushima Prefecture, Niigata Prefecture, Toyama Prefecture, Fukui Prefecture, Gifu Prefecture, Shizuoka Prefecture, Mie Prefecture, Wakayama Prefecture, Shimane Prefecture, Kagawa Prefecture, Kōchi Prefecture, Kumamoto Prefecture, Nara Prefecture, Tagajō, Niigata, Dazaifu, Nara, Tenri, Kashihara, Ikaruga, Asuka and Shimoichi

The congress this year covered discussion among the leaders of local governments and included the discussion of administrative personnel into the agenda, thereby achieving great results. Through the conference in a consecutive manner, while improving the administrative capacity of local governments, the friendly and trustworthy relationship among them can be boosted and more local governments are willing to participate in this congress to realize its purpose.

In the 2nd East Asia Local and Regional Government Congress, another 12 new local governments became its members, including 2 from China, i.e. Shandong Province and Weifang City. In the congress, the representatives of the local governments discussed "political institution and role of local governments" under the network framework of local governments and analyzed the "practice, responsibility and function of local governments in managing crisis" while dealing with disasters. In addition, before the discussion, with the assistance of experts, the responsible persons of this congress carried out research of such topics as "tourism", "urban and rural development" and "safeguarding of cultural property". In addition, they agreed to set up an East Asia summer school.

IV. 3rd East Asia Local and Regional Government Congress

The year 2012 ushered in the 3rd East Asia Local and Regional Government Congress. The members increased to 64 local governments of 7 countries, including China's 14 provinces and cities.

In 3rd East Asia Local and Regional Government Congress held in 2012, the 4 well received topics in the last congress derived their group discussions covering these topics as the common topics of local governments: "Think over the Social Security in the Era of Ageing with Fewer Children", "Actions Taken to Ensure Tax Revenue", "Regional Revitalization" and "Talent Training". The discussion result (outline) of each topic was generalized as the following two points: 1. Concrete measures made by local governments (best practice); 2. Specific measures made for further improvement in the future (in terms of application and system). In the discussion of the third topic "Regional Revitalization", the present representatives put forward specific measures and form of regional revitalization in the future at five aspects: transportation for revitalizing tourism, cooperation with personnel in the non-tourism industry, make flexible use of regional features and culture, industrial integration and responsibility sharing of administrative organs.

V. 4th East Asia Local and Regional Government Congress

The 4th East Asia Local and Regional Government Congress was held in Nara Prefecture in January 20-22, 2014, when were present 39 local governments of 5 countries.

The local governments include: 39 local governments

China (1): Shandong Province

Philippines (1): Baler

South Korea (7): Gyeonggi Province, South Chungcheong Province, Seosan, Buyeo County, South Jeolla Province, North Gyeongsang Province and Gyeongju

Vietnam (2): Phú Tho Province, Viet Tri

Japan (28): Yamagata Prefecture, Fukushima Prefecture, Niigata Prefecture, Fukui Prefecture, Yamanashi Prefecture, Nagano Prefecture, Gifu Prefecture, Shizuoka Prefecture, Mie Prefecture, Kyoto Prefecture, Wakayama Prefecture, Tottori Prefecture, Shimane Prefecture, Tokushima Prefecture, Kagawa Prefecture, Kōchi Prefecture, Nara Prefecture, Tagajō, Niigata, Dazaifu, Nara, Tenri, Kashihara, Gose, Ikaruga, Asuka, Kōryō and Shimoichi

※ Special guest: Myanmar (Rangoon and Mandalay Governments)

In the plenary session held on January 21, 2014, Mr. Toshihiro Nikai (member of the House of Representatives of Japan) made a speech celebrating the congress. The representatives of local governments put forward measures towards the two topics and the form in the future through group discussion and Mr. Shogo Arai, Governor of Nara Prefecture delivered his report.

In the 4th East Asia Local and Regional Government Congress in 2013, based upon the group discussion, the representatives carried out group discussions about the last years' topic of "Social Security in the Era of Ageing with Fewer Children" and new topic of "Revitalization of Regional Economy and Employment". The representatives of Nara, Kagawa Prefecture and Baler Governments shared their measures in improving the tourism resources and attracting tourists.

In regard to the topic of "Revitalization of Regional Economy and Employment", the representative of Nara considered the industrial revitalization based on sightseeing was a topic. By preserving the traditional street, they set up "Nara-machi House Bank", rebuilt the vacant house as a tourism resource, and held Nara To-Kae to realize effective allocation of the tourism resources. In addition, Kagawa Prefecture relied on arts to drive the tourism to develop. Baler provided ecological tourism by forest rejuvenation and improving the construction of infrastructure such as hiking trails, as well as culturing mountaineering guides and diving guides, so that the number of tourists kept increasing.

VI. 5th East Asia Local and Regional Government Congress

The 5th East Asia Local and Regional Government Congress was held in Nara on October 27-29, 2014, when 40 local governments of 6 countries delegated their representatives to this conference. In the congress, Mr. Hanklim, President of Academic Consulting Conference of Economic Research Institute for ASEAN and East Asia (ERIA) and Ms. Jennifer Stanger, Director of Pacific Centre Career and Publicity Department of United Nations World Tourism Organization (UNWTO) delivered a keynote speech. All the representatives participating in the congress had an extensive and in-depth exchange relating to "Revitalizing the Tourism", "Urban and Rural Construction" and "Revitalizing Regional Economy".

The local governments include: 40 local governments

China (4): Anhui Province, Shandong Province, Weifang City and Dongying City

Indonesia (1): Special Region of Yogyakarta

Malaysia (1): Malacca State

South Korea (5): Gyeonggi Province, South Chungcheong Province, Gongju, Seosan, and North Gyeongsang Province

Vietnam (3): Phú Thọ Province, Thừa Thiên Thuận Province, Viet Tri

Japan(26): Aomori Prefecture, Fukushima Prefecture, Niigata Prefecture, Fukui Prefecture, Yamanashi Prefecture, Nagano Prefecture, Shizuoka Prefecture, Mie Prefecture, Kyoto Prefecture, Wakayama Prefecture, Tottori Prefecture, Shimane Prefecture, Tokushima Prefecture, Kagawa Prefecture, Kōchi Prefecture, Nara Prefecture, Tagajō, Niigata, Dazaifu, Tenri, Kashihara, Gose, Ikaruga, Asuka, Kōryō and Shimoichi

※Special guest: Myanmar (Magwe Government and Ministry of Foreign Affairs)

In the keynote speech, Ms. Jennifer Stanger, Director of Pacific Centre Career and Publicity Department of United Nations World Tourism Organization (UNWTO) introduced the major projects and partnership of UNWTO, pointing a direction for the local governments to develop the tourism.

In the 5th East Asia Local and Regional Government Congress in 2014, "tourism" was mentioned many times by the representatives of local governments. With respect to the application and role of culture and tourism resources in urban and rural construction and regional revitalization, the representatives gave all kinds of examples about their real situation and made discussion on how to let the citizens and local enterprises be the main players, or on how the county and city governments divided their work rationaly, or on how to raise the management level of tourist destinations, and introduced their own experience. Through discussion, all the attendees reached a consensus. Namely, on the one side, the tourism industry is not only a source of tourism revenue, but also a mechanism making the local society well-being and happy by improving the tourism quality. The representatives participating in the congress provided a great deal of useful information through specific examples, so this congress was of far-reaching significance.

VII. 6th East Asia Local and Regional Government Congress

The 6th East Asia Local and Regional Government Congress was held in Nara on October 25-27, 2015, when the representatives of 42 local governments of 6 countries participated in the conference. The congress made a special discussion by focusing on promoting the regional economy, urban and rural construction, and revitalizing agriculture and countryside.

The local governments include: 42 local governments

China (6): Henan Province, Shaanxi Province, Chengdu City, Huangshan City, Suzhou City and Dongying City

Indonesia (2): West Java, Special Region of Yogyakarta

Malaysia (1): Malacca State

South Korea (6): Gyeonggi Province, South Chungcheong Province, Gongju, Seosan, Buyeo County and North Gyeongsang Province

Vietnam (2): Phú Thọ Province, Viet Tri

Japan (25): Aomori Prefecture, Yamagata Prefecture, Fukushima Prefecture, Niigata Prefecture, Fukui Prefecture, Yamanashi Prefecture, Nagano Prefecture, Shizuoka Prefecture, Mie Prefecture, Kyoto Prefecture, Wakayama Prefecture, Tottori Prefecture, Shimane Prefecture, Tokushima Prefecture, Kagawa Prefecture, Nara Prefecture Arakawa, Niigata, Nara, Tenri, Kashihara, Gose, Ikaruga, Asuka and Shimoichi

※Special guest: Quezon City (Philippines)

In the general assembly, Mr. Shogo Arai made a general speech and declared participation of Chengdu City, Sichuan Province, Suzhou City, Anhui Province and

Arakawa, Tokyo Prefecture as the new members. The Admissions Office announced the matters about the 7th East Asia Local and Regional Government Congress.

In the regional branch report meeting, Mr. Kazuki Tahei, Assistant Director of International Strategy Section of Mie Prefecture Employment Economy Ministry delivered a speech on "Revitalize the Tourism Industry to 'Promote Inbound Tourism'". He introduced the examples of related measures and topics on promoting inbound tourism, for example, transforming from pass-type sightseeing to stay-type sightseeing, dispersing foreign tourists to other regions, strengthening the non-governmental force, cooperating with the neighboring counties and cities, and improving the tourism environment. In addition, he also discussed the subject of large area, perfecting the local tourism environment, information dissemination and handling the Muslim issues.

In the 6th East Asia Local and Regional Government Congress in 2015, the representatives from local governments probed into their tourism development measures in different perspectives such as rural tourism, sports tourism and cultural tourism. The three measures, i.e. transformation of pass-type sightseeing to stay-type sightseeing, development of tourist commodities and increasing tourism consumption in dull season, and making flexible use of natural resources and enhancement of local citizens' consciousness realize the objective of revitalizing the regional economy through tourism and sightseeing.

Appendix 3 A Review of East Asia International Tourism Cooperation

1. ASEAN Plus China, Japan and South Korea (ASEAN Plus Three, APT) Summit

1.1 Background

[Background] In 1995, the ASEAN Summit in Bangkok proposed the convening of APT Summit. Malaysia hosted the 2nd ASEAN Informal Summit as the Chair of ASEAN for 1997, and actively facilitated the convening of APT Informal Summit.

[Members] 10ASEAN member countries (Brunei Darussalam, Cambodia, Indonesia, Laos, Malaysia, Myanmar, Philippines, Singapore, Thailand and Vietnam) and China, Japan and South Korea.

[Mechanisms] 65 dialogues and cooperation mechanisms have been established in APT cooperation, and a cooperation system with Summit as the core has been formed, which is supported by Ministers' Meetings, Senior Officials' Meetings, the ASEAN Committee of Permanent Representatives (CPR) Plus Three Meeting (CPR + 3) and Working Group Meetings.

As the highest-level mechanism, Summit is held once a year to provide strategic planning and guidance for APT development. So far, it has been held 19 times. The 17 Ministers' Meetings are responsible for policy planning and coordination in relevant fields. Senior Officials' Meetings are responsible for policy coordination. CPR+3 is responsible for coordinating specific issues of cooperation. In addition, within the framework of APT, the East Asia Forum (EAF) with the joint participation of government, enterprises and universities and the two-track (i.e. academic/research institutes) Network of East Asian Think-tanks (NEAT) provide intellectual support for APT cooperation.

1.2 Achievements

The 17th APT Summit was held in Nay Pyi Taw, Myanmar in November 2014. China's Premier LI Keqiang attended the meeting. Mr. LI Keqiang said, "The ten ASEAN countries and China, Japan and the South Korea are geographically close, economically complementary and culturally connected." and "The APT cooperation has become a strong impetus in the East Asian integration process." Parties in the region should firmly safeguard peace and stability, and step up coordination, keep firm to the general direction of mutually beneficial cooperation, carry out practical cooperation in relevant fields, and move steadily toward the goal of building an East Asian Community on this basis. Mr. LI Keqiang made a six-pronged proposal on enhancing APT cooperation: first, advance East Asia economic integration; second, upgrade financial cooperation in the region; third, achieve closer connectivity; fourth, deepen cooperation to improve people's well-being; fifth, expand channels for people-to-people and cultural exchanges; sixth, enhance cooperation in public health.

At the 17th APT Summit, Mr. LI Keqiang made a six-pronged proposal on enhancing APT cooperation. He mentioned the establishment of a regular exchange mechanism between the three ASEAN Centers in China, Japan and the South Korea to further deepen APT cooperation in culture, education, tourism and other fields in the proposal to expand channels for people-to-people and cultural exchanges, and "hopes that all parties could sign the *APT MOU on Tourism Cooperation* as soon as possible."

The 18th APT Summit was held in Kuala Lumpur, Malaysia in November 2015. Mr. LI Keqiang attended the meeting. Mr. LI Keqiang said, "Economic development in East Asia has maintained its upward trajectory, making it one of the most dynamic and promising regions in the world." and "To further deepen APT cooperation, China proposes that this meeting issue the APT Joint Statement on Promoting Regional Economic Growth and Financial Stability, and that all parties jointly formulate the Blueprint of an East Asian Economic Community and establish an Asian Financial Cooperation Association." He made a six-pronged proposal on enhancing APT cooperation: first, accelerate East Asia economic integration; second, make concerted efforts to maintain regional financial stability; third, increase the level of connectivity; fourth, conduct international production capacity cooperation; fifth, deepen cooperation in poverty reduction of agriculture; sixth, expand people-to-people exchanges.

At the 18th APT Summit, Mr. LI Keqiang reiterated that China supported closer interactions between East Asia Cultural Cities and ASEAN Cultural Cities programs and supported the early signing of an *MOU on APT Tourism Cooperation*. In addition, he also mentioned the "One Belt and One Road" initiative and proposed to promote connectivity in the entire East Asia to provide strong support for regional cooperation.

The 19th APT Summit was held in Vientiane, Laos in September 2016. Mr. LI Keqiang attended the meeting. He said, "Next year will mark the 20th anniversary of APT cooperation. I suggest that we take this as a new starting point to cement the role of APT as the main channel for regional economic integration and write a new chapter in East Asia cooperation." Mr. LI made a six-pronged proposal on enhancing APT cooperation: first, step up financial security cooperation; second, deepen trade and investment cooperation; third, advance cooperation in agriculture and poverty alleviation; fourth, advance connectivity building; fifth, create new models for production capacity cooperation; sixth, promote cultural and people-to-people exchanges.

In early 2016, APT signed the *MOU on APT Tourism Cooperation*. At the 18th APT Summit, to promote cultural and people-to-people exchanges and enhance exchanges between East Asia Cultural Cities and ASEAN Cultural Cities programs, Mr. LI

Keqiang announced that China would host Learn More about China Program for APT and Eyes on China Program for Mainstream Media in Asia in 2016.

2. East Asia Summit (EAS)

The 9th East Asia Summit was held in Nay Pyi Taw, the capital of Myanmar, in November 2014. The leaders of 10 ASEAN countries and 8 dialogue partners discussed the strategic issues related to the East Asian integration process and regional and global issues of common concern. Mr. LI Keqiang attended the meeting. He said that "we should strive for progress in both the political and security field and economic field in APT cooperation; a fundamental reason of East Asia's rapid development was the existence of a peaceful and stable regional environment; we should step up cooperation in nontraditional security areas in East Asia; we would strive to conclude negotiations on the RCEP (Regional Comprehensive Economic Partnership) before the end of 2015; we would complete negotiations on an upgraded version of the China-ASEAN FTA as early as possible; China firmly supported ASEAN in establishing the ASEAN Community next year comprising the three pillars of Political-Security Community, Economic Community and Socio-Cultural Community; we should promote cooperation in six key areas so as to advance East Asian economic integration; China would adhere to the dual-track approach for dealing with the South China Sea issue; China stood for denuclearization of the Korean Peninsula and for the interest of long-term peace and stability of the Peninsula and Northeast Asia; China would send more medical staff and give more material assistance to regions hit by the Ebola epidemic; in the interactions of neighbors, we should treat each other with sincerity and seek common ground while reserving differences; China and ASEAN countries were discussing the possibility of concluding a treaty on good-neighborliness, friendship and cooperation to promote lasting peace in East Asia."

The 10th East Asia Summit was held in Kuala Lumpur Convention Center in November 2015. Mr. LI Keqiang attended the meeting, and made five proposals to jointly safeguard peace and stability in the South China Sea. First, all countries make the commitment to observing the purposes and principles of the *UN Charter*, defend the outcome of WWII and post-war order, cherish hard-won peace and jointly safeguard peace and stability in the world and the region, including in the South China Sea. Second, sovereign countries directly concerned undertake, in accordance with universally recognized principles of international law, including *1982 United Nations Convention on the Law* of *the Sea (1982 UNCLOS)*, to peacefully settle sovereign and jurisdictional disputes through friendly consultation and negotiation. Third, China and ASEAN countries commit themselves to full and effective implementation of th*e Declaration on the Conduct of Parties in the South China Sea (D*OC) in its entirety, accelerate consultations to strive for early conclusion of a Code of Conduct (COC) in the South China Sea on the basis of consensus, and take steps to improve regional mechanisms for mutual trust and cooperation. Fourth, countries from outside the region undertake to respect and support efforts by countries in the region to uphold peace and stability in the South China Sea, play a positive and constructive role and refrain from taking actions that may cause tension in the region. Fifth, all countries undertake to exercise and uphold the freedom of navigation and over flight in the South China Sea in accordance with international law.

The 11th East Asia Summit was held in Vientiane, Laos in September 2016. Mr. LI Keqiang attended the meeting, and pointed out that East Asia now faced huge opportunities for peace, stability and prosperity as well as many challenges. He hoped that parties would work together to convert challenges into opportunities to promote steady progress of East Asian cooperation and contribute to peace, stability and enduring prosperity of the region, and the benefit of people of all countries. He also elaborated on China's principled stand on the South China Sea issue.

3. ASEAN Plus Three Tourism Ministers' Meeting

Table 1 A Review of ASEAN Plus Three Tourism Ministers' Meetings

Year	Number	Venue	Meeting Content
2002	1st	Jakarta, Indonesia	Establish a Senior Officials' Meeting to establish a mechanism for rapid information exchange, promote tourism convenience, promote tourism with APT countries as destinations, strengthen cooperation between private sectors, cooperate in human resources research and information technology etc.
2003	2nd	Phnom Penh, Cambodia	Decided to establish APT + China/Japan/South Korea Tourism Exchange Working Groups to further promote accurate exchange of information about tourism safety.
2004	3rd	Vientiane, Laos	Continue to strengthen cooperation between APT tourism organizations to jointly develop tourism markets; increase tourism investment and expand human resources development; exchange information and establish early warning mechanisms to effectively address issues such as political unrest, terrorist activities, economic crimes, natural disasters and the spread of atypical pneumonia (SARS) and other epidemics so as to ensure regional tourism development.
2005	4th	Langkawi, Malaysia	Encourage travel inside and outside ASEAN and help affected ASEAN countries restore tourism as soon as possible.
2007	6th	Singapore	Supported that APT cooperation focused on tourism exchanges, personnel exchanges, human resources development, cooperation in tourism market and other fields.
2012	11th	Manado, Indonesia	Exchanged views on aviation convenience in APT tourism, cruise tourism, MOU on APT Tourism Cooperation, product development, personnel training etc.
2013	12th	Vientiane, Laos	Exchanged views on aviation convenience in APT tourism, cruise tourism, MOU on APT Tourism Cooperation, product development, personnel training and investment, emergency and crisis disposal and so on, and adopted the joint statement aimed at promoting tourism development in the region.

Appendix 3 A Review of East Asia International Tourism Cooperation

Continued

Year	Number	Venue	Meeting Content
2014	13th	Kuching, Malaysia	Exchanged views on issues such as regional connectivity, joint route development, responses to climate change and disasters, personnel training, *2013-2017 APT Tourism Cooperation Work Plan*, the conclusion of *MOU on APT Tourism Cooperation* etc, and adopted the *Joint Press Release*.
2015	14th	Nay Pyi Taw, Myanmar	Studied the draft *MOU on APT Tourism Cooperation*, discussed and adopted the minutes of the 25th and the 26th meetings of APT tourism organizations, and listened to the report of Philippines on the time, venue and other information of the next APT Tourism Ministers' Meeting.
2016	15th	Manila, Philippines	Discussed the implementation of the tourism-related fruits of the ASEAN + China, Japan and South Korea (10+3) and ASEAN + China/Japan/South Korea (10+1) summits, signed the *MOU on APT Tourism Cooperation*, adopted the *Joint Press Release* and the minutes of the 27th and the 28th meetings of APT tourism organizations, and listened to the report of Singapore on the time, venue and other information of the next APT Tourism Ministers' Meeting.

4. China-Japan-South Korea Trilateral Tourism Ministers' Meeting

China-Japan-South Korea Trilateral Tourism Ministers' Meeting is a mechanism for regular meeting of trilateral Tourism Ministers, which is established by the tourism organizations of the three countries within the framework of APT to implement the spirit of China-Japan-South Korea Summit. It is one of the most successful tourism cooperation mechanisms in the world. It has made positive and effective contributions to enhancing people-to-people understanding, expanding sectoral cooperation, strengthening industry exchanges, exchanging market information, training tourism personnel, protecting tourists' interests, promoting sustainable development, etc. It is also a great opportunity for the host city to display its fine qualities, build brands, increase international popularity and promote tourism development.

The 1st China-Japan-South Korea Trilateral Tourism Ministers' Meeting was held in Sapporo, Hokkaido, Japan in 2006 and *Hokkaido Statement* was signed.

The meeting also adopted the "China-Japan-South Korea Tourism Exchange" Program, aiming to increase the number of mutual tourists between the three countries from 12 million in 2005 to 17 million in 2010.

In 2005, China received 46.8 million inbound overnight tourists, including 3.54 million from South Korea and 3.39 million from Japan, which ranked the top two among the sources of China's inbound tourists. In 2005, China became the largest source market in Asia with 31 million outbound tourists, an increase of 8% compared with 2004.

With "tourism, cooperation, harmony, win-win" as the theme, the 2nd China-Japan-South Korea Trilateral Tourism Ministers' Meeting in 2007 was aimed at promoting tourism exchanges and cooperation between the three countries. The meeting was opened in Qingdao and closed in Dalian, and *Qingdao Statement* was signed.

The 3rd China-Japan- South Korea Trilateral Tourism Ministers' Meeting was grandly opened in Busan Exhibition & Convention Center in 2008, which discussed topics such as strengthening cooperation, jointly solving the obstacles to tourism development, achieving sustainable tourism development, jointly developing attractive tourism products and expanding tourism exchanges and cooperation between the three countries. The Tourism Ministers of the three countries also signed the *Busan Statement*. The meeting was opened in Busan and closed in Cheongju, South Korea.

The 4th China-Japan-South Korea Trilateral Tourism Ministers' Meeting was opened in Nagoya, Japan on October 17, 2009. This meeting discussed how the tourism industry of the three countries should deal with the current crisis, how to greet the arrival of the era of Asian tourism exchanges and other issues in depth. It was closed in Takayama.

The 5th China-Japan-South Korea Trilateral Tourism Ministers' Meeting was opened in Hangzhou on August 21, 2010 and closed in Huzhou on August 23. The theme of the meeting was "looking toward the future, all-round cooperation, common prosperity". *Hangzhou Joint Statement* and *China-Japan-South Korea Low-Carbon Tourism Initiative* were signed.

The 6th China-Japan-South Korea Trilateral Tourism Ministers' Meeting was held in Pyeongchang, Kangwon-do, South Korea from May 28 to May 31, 2011. The purpose of this meeting was to promote tourism exchanges between the three countries, jointly develop tourism promotion programs and consolidate the basis of tourism cooperation in Northeast Asia through concerted efforts of the three countries. The Tourism Ministers of the three countries jointly signed the *Joint Statement of the 6th China-Japan-South Korea Trilateral Tourism Ministers' Meeting* and the *China-Japan-South Korea Initiative for Integrity in Tourism* at the meeting. The meeting discussed issues such as jointly establishing a response system to tourism emergencies and crisis, establishing and advancing tourism outlook 2020 to expand tourism exchanges among China, Japan and South Korea, promoting the signing of China-Japan-South Korea Initiative for Integrity in Tourism and developing common projects to expand tourism exchanges among China, Japan and South Korea.

The 7th China-Japan-South Korea Trilateral Tourism Ministers' Meeting was held in Tokyo, Japan on April 12, 2015. The Tourism Ministers of the three countries met in Tokyo to discuss major tourism programs. They discussed in depth issues such as opening a new era of tourism exchanges between China, Japan and South Korea, promoting travel to the east, improving the quality of tourism exchanges between China, Japan and South Korea etc, and reached many consensuses. The *Joint Statement of the 7th China-Japan-South Korea Trilateral Tourism Ministers' Meeting* was signed.

Table 2 A Review of China-Japan-South Korea Trilateral Tourism Ministers' Meetings

Year	Venue	Meeting Content	Consensus
2006	Hokkaido, Japan	China, Japan and South Korea should make concerted efforts to expand tourism exchanges and cooperation between the three countries, explore the constraints on tourism exchanges, and strengthen personnel exchanges among the three countries to attract tourists outside the region to the three countries	*Hokkaido Statement*, China-Japan-South Korea Tourism Exchange Program
2007	Qingdao and Dalian, China	With "tourism, cooperation, harmony, win-win" as the theme and promoting tourism exchanges and cooperation between the three countries as the purpose	*Qingdao Statement*
2008	Busan and Cheongju, South Korea	Discussed topics such as strengthening cooperation, jointly solving the obstacles to tourism development, achieving sustainable tourism development, jointly developing attractive tourism products and expanding tourism exchanges and cooperation between the three countries	*Busan Statement*
2009	Nagoya and Takayama, Japan	How should the tourism industry of the three countries deal with the current international financial crisis, H1N1 flu and other difficulties to restore international tourism, how to greet the arrival of the era of East Asian tourism exchanges and address global warming etc	*Joint Statement of the 4th China-Japan-South Korea Trilateral Tourism Ministers' Meeting*
2010	Hangzhou and Huzhou, China	Looking toward the future, all-round cooperation, common prosperity	Hangzhou *Joint Statement*, *China-Japan-South Korea Low-Carbon Tourism Initiative*
2011	Pyeongchang, Kangwon-do, South Korea	To promote tourism exchanges between the three countries, jointly develop tourism promotion programs and consolidate the basis of tourism cooperation in Northeast Asia through concerted efforts of the three countries.	*Joint Statement of the 6th China-Japan-South Korea Trilateral Tourism Ministers' Meeting*, *China-Japan-South Korea Initiative for Integrity in Tourism*

Continued

Year	Venue	Meeting Content	Consensus
2015	Tokyo, Japan	Open a new era of tourism exchanges between China, Japan and South Korea, promote travel to the east, and improve the quality of tourism exchanges between China, Japan and South Korea	Joint Statement of the 7th China-Japan- South Korea Trilateral Tourism Ministers' Meeting

The 1st China-Japan-South Korea Trilateral Tourism Ministers' Meeting drew to a successful close in the Japanese tourist attraction Hokkaido on July 3, 2006. During the three-day meeting, around the expansion of tourism exchanges and cooperation between the three countries and the expansion of tourism cooperation with countries and regions outside the region, the Tourism Ministers of the three countries signed and issued the *Hokkaido Statement* and developed the "China-Japan-South Korea Tourism Exchange Program"; the tourism organizations and industry representatives of the three countries jointly issued the *Hokkaido Initiative* to promote tourism in the three countries at a folk tourism conference held in the same period. In addition, the tourism industries of the three countries also conducted fruitful business negotiations and tourism promotion, and held the "Sister Cities Tourism Seminar". This meeting was of far-reaching significance. In the history of tourism exchanges between the three countries, it is the first time that the Tourism Ministers of China, Japan and South Korea, three important countries in East Asia, gathered to discuss plans for strengthening tourism exchanges and cooperation between the three countries. "The success of the Trilateral Tourism Ministers' Meeting has opened a new page of tourism cooperation and development in China, Japan and South Korea," Mr. Shao Qiwei, the then head of China National Tourism Administration said.

The 2nd China-Japan-South Korea Trilateral Tourism Ministers' Meeting released the *Qingdao Statement* on promoting tourism exchanges and cooperation between the three countries in Qingdao on June 26, 2007, which stressed that multilateral international tourism affairs of the three countries were an important part of global tourism affairs and played a positive role in improving the Asian tourism image and building a new world pattern of tourism. The Tourism Ministers of the three countries reached consensuses on issues such as opposing terrorism in any form, the threat of global warming to tourism development, the role of tourism in eliminating poverty, narrowing regional disparities and other aspects etc., and stressed that they would well organize the "China-Japan Two-Way Tourism Exchanges on the 35th Anniversary of the Normalization of China-Japan Diplomatic Relations", "2007 Exchange Activities to Commemorate the 400th Anniversary of Joseon Tongsinsa", "The 15th Anniversary of the Establishment of Diplomatic Relations between China and South Korea and 'China-Korea Tourism Week' of China-Korea Exchange Year" and other exchange activities. *Qingdao Statement* stressed that the three countries would focus on increasing youth exchanges between the three countries, accelerating the improvement of tourism personnel mechanism, strengthening exchanges between non-governmental organizations, jointly improving tourism statistics etc in future tourism cooperation. The Tourism Ministers of the three countries said that the three countries would share the opportunities brought by major international events, encourage their citizens to travel to each other's countries and outside the region, and make concerted efforts to build the regional image and attract tourists outside the region to the three countries.

The 3rd China-Japan- South Korea Trilateral Tourism Ministers' Meeting was held in Busan and Cheongju, South Korea from June 22 to June 25, 2008. Trilateral Tourism Ministers' Meeting and China-Japan- South Korea Tourism Forum were held in Busan on June 23. The tourism organizations and industries of the three countries conducted in-depth discussion about the central issues of the meeting. The Tourism Ministers of the three countries said that the three countries would work closely to expand tourism exchanges between them, eliminate the unfavorable factors that restrict tourism development, especially protect the safety of tourists, and exchange tourism crisis management and emergency information in time. The three Ministers stressed that the three countries should cooperate in strengthening response to natural disasters and climate warming and other fields. Mr. Jung Woo-shik, Chairman of Korea Association of Travel Agents (KATA), spoke highly of the meeting. He believed that the issues discussed at the meeting were more pragmatic and results were more significant. In addition, the Tourism Ministers of Japan and South Korea expressed concern over the tourism industry in the earthquake-stricken area in Sichuan and provided strong support for tourism recovery in the area.

The 4th China-Japan-South Korea Trilateral Tourism Ministers' Meeting was held in Nagoya, Aichi-ken and Takayama, Gifu-ken, Japan from October 17 to October 18, 2009, and over 400 representatives from the tourism organizations and industries of China, Japan and South Korea attended the meeting. The Tourism Ministers of the three countries discussed issues such as overcoming the current international financial crisis, H1N1 flu and other difficulties to restore international tourism, greeting the arrival of the era of East Asian tourism exchanges, addressing global warming, the next meeting etc. They issued the *Joint Statement of the 4th China-Japan-South Korea Trilateral Tourism Ministers' Meeting*, and reached many consensuses at the meeting. The three countries said that they would overcome the current international financial crisis, H1N1 flu and other difficulties to restore international tourism exchanges; seize the opportunity of World Expo 2010, Shanghai, China to actively develop Expo-related tourism products and promote international tourism exchanges; deepen cooperation between tourism sectors to greet the arrival of East Asian tourism exchanges in the 21st century; and jointly promote the sustainable development of tourism products.

The 5th China-Japan-South Korea Trilateral Tourism Ministers' Meeting was opened in Hangzhou on August 22, 2010, and over 300 people consisting of representatives of tourism enterprises, representatives of the aviation industry and media organizations of the three countries attended the meeting. There was a heated discussion around the theme of this industry exchange, namely "exchanges and cooperation, quality improvement, win-win development". The guests from the three countries made speeches on six topics such as "Learning the Advanced Experience of Friendly Nations to Improve the Overall Level of China's Travel Agency Industry", "On Exchanges and Cooperation", "Proposals for China-Japan-South Korea Common Tourism-themed FI Meeting", "Measures for China-Japan-South Korea Tourism Exchanges-Beijing-Seoul-Tokyo Plan in the Case of Silk Road Tourism", "On Quality Improvement and Win-win Development" and "Establishment of A Tourism Cooperation Mechanism Based on Asian Values". A consensus was reached at the meeting that the further prosperity of trilateral tourism markets was actually the promotion of trilateral economic development, the promotion of trilateral folk cultural exchanges and the promotion of understanding and deeper friendship between the three peoples. The meeting proposed that trilateral tourism should advance towards more specific and deeper areas such as risk control, environmental protection, personnel training, special exchanges, development and promotion of regional tourism routes etc.

The 6th China-Japan-South Korea Trilateral Tourism Ministers' Meeting was opened in Pyeongchang, South Korea in May 2011. The Tourism Ministers of the three countries had an in-depth discussion about issues such as jointly establishing a response system to tourism emergencies and crisis, establishing and advancing tourism outlook 2020 to expand tourism exchanges among China, Japan and South Korea, promoting the signing of China-Japan-South Korea Initiative for Integrity in Tourism and developing common projects to expand tourism exchanges between China, Japan and South Korea etc. On the basis of many consensuses, the three parties signed and released the *Joint Statement of the 6th China-Japan-South Korea Trilateral*

Tourism Ministers' Meeting. Mr. SHAO Qiwei said that the tourism industries of the three countries had become an important model of regional tourism exchanges and cooperation in the world through concerted efforts and common development, and had explored a successful path of industrial cooperation between countries in the context of regional economic integration. Mr. Jung Byung Kook, an official of South Korea Ministry of Culture, Sports and Tourism, said in his speech that since the 1st China-Japan-South Korea Trilateral Tourism Ministers' Meeting, the number of mutual tourists to the three countries had increased from 12 million six years ago to 16.65 million, and tourism had become the development focus of the three countries in the 21st century. Mr. Akihiro Ohata said in his speech that tourism between the three countries had not only brought an increase in personnel exchanges, but also enhanced understanding and trust among the three peoples, which was of far-reaching significance for peace, prosperity and development in Northeast Asia.

The 7th China-Japan-South Korea Trilateral Tourism Ministers' Meeting was held in Tokyo, Japan in April 2015. The joint statement released at the meeting proposed that the three countries jointly promote "Travel to the East" program as a common tourist destination to attract tourists from outside the region with the opening of a new era of tourism exchanges between China, Japan and South Korea as an opportunity. At the meeting, the Tourism Ministers of the three countries discussed in depth issues such as opening a new era of tourism exchanges between China, Japan and South Korea, promoting "Travel to the East ", improving the quality of tourism exchanges between China, Japan and South Korea etc, and reached many consensuses. They jointly signed and issued the *Joint Statement*, proposing to effectively enhance tourism convenience in China, Japan and South Korea, and strive to achieve the goal of 30 million mutual tourists to the three countries by 2020. The Tourism Ministers of the three countries believed that tourism between China, Japan and South Korea entered a new era as the number of mutual tourists to the three countries reached 20 million. The three countries would deepen trilateral cooperation to provide tourists with a more convenient and friendly tourism environment; jointly launch sports tourism products, festival tourism products and products for "multi-destination" tourism such as world heritage tours, ancient capital tours, food tours, cruise tours etc; and jointly strengthen supervision to improve the quality of tourism exchanges.

5. East Asian Business Forum

5.1 Background

East Asian Business Forum is one of the projects supported by the Special Fund for Regional Cooperation in Asia and approved by the Ministry of Foreign Affairs and the Ministry of Finance. It is an important measure to promote economic and trade exchanges and cooperation between China, Japan and South Korea and the 10 ASEAN countries. The Ministry of Foreign Affairs attaches great importance to it. At the 16th APT Summit, Mr. LI Keqiang particularly stressed that China should continue to hold East Asia Business Forum and other activities. In this context, China Council for the Promotion of International Trade (CCPIT) took the lead in organizing East Asia Business Forum to provide a platform for communication and practical cooperation in issues of common concern among business people from ASEAN, China, Japan, South Korea, Australia, New Zealand and India.

5.2 A review of previous meetings

Both the size and the standards of the forum are gradually increasing. One Minister, three Vice Ministers and nearly 500 business representatives attended the 6th East Asia Business Forum, which had certain impact in East Asia. The forum mainly consists of the opening ceremony, plenary sessions, themed roundtables, business talks, product demonstrations, inspection tours etc. It is aimed at promoting Asian economic and trade cooperation in key areas and promoting the process of East Asian economic integration. Through East Asian Business Docking Net, East Asian Trade Dispute Settlement Mechanism and other programs, the forum makes use of CCPIT's professional advantages to provide pragmatic help for enterprises. So far, East Asia Business Forum has been held seven times.

The 6th East Asia Business Forum & the 28th East Asia Business Council Meeting were held in Haikou City, Hainan Province on May 13, 2014. Nearly 400 representatives of government officials, international organizations, diplomatic envoys in China, business associations, scholars and industrial and commercial enterprises from 16 countries, including China, South Korea, Japan and ASEAN countries, attended the forum. With "mutually beneficial cooperation leads the development of East Asia" as the theme, the forum was aimed at strengthening dialogues and exchanges between business circles of East Asian countries and promoting regional economic and trade cooperation. Mr. LI Guoliang, Vice Governor of Hainan Province, said in his speech that Hainan would comprehensively deepen cooperation with countries in East Asia, Southeast Asia, Australia etc, strengthen cooperation in tropical high-efficiency agriculture, tourism, clean energy, marine fishery and other fields, promote a multilateral win-win, and strive to make Hainan become the bridgehead and service base of the 21st-Century Maritime Silk Road. The government officials and people from business and academic circles discussed issues such as focusing on economic development and expanding mutually beneficial win-win, innovating development model and deepening industrial cooperation etc. During the meeting, Mr. yu Ping, Vice Chairman of CCPIT, met with government officials and businessmen from Cambodia, Myanmar, Philippines and other countries separately, and discussed with them issues such as strengthening economic and trade cooperation between China and Cambodia, Myanmar and Philippines, organizing the " One Belt and One Road"-

related activities, the first East Asia Investment Forum, China-Philippines Business Council Meeting etc.

The 7th East Asia Business Forum was opened in Hangzhou on May 13, 2015. Business organizations and business representatives from 16 countries in East Asia, Southeast Asia, South Asia and Oceania, including China, attended the meeting. With "expanding practical cooperation and achieving common prosperity" as the theme, the forum discussed financial cooperation, cooperation between small and medium-sized enterprises etc. Mr. yu Ping, Vice Chairman of CCPIT, said that Asia would need a total investment of 800 billion US dollars from now to 2020, which provided unlimited business opportunities for enterprises. Mr. ZHANG Hongming, Mayor of Hangzhou, believed that both China's strategic vision to build the "One Belt and One Road" and ASEAN's initiative for regional comprehensive economic partnership had brought new opportunities for economic and trade cooperation between Hangzhou and East Asian countries. East Asia Business Forum provided a platform for domestic enterprises to understand the East Asian market, and enterprises displayed their brands through the forum. Many Hangzhou-based enterprises had the intention to march into the international market.

East Asian Business Forum is a special business activity of China for regional cooperation in Asia. It is an important measure to promote economic and trade exchanges and cooperation between China, Japan and South Korea and ASEAN countries, and it provides a communication platform for businessmen from ASEAN countries, China, Japan and South Korea. By virtue of the East Asia Business Forum, dialogues and coordination among East Asian countries have become increasingly enhanced, and East Asian countries have become increasingly interdependent and achieved remarkable results in economic and trade cooperation. In addition, many enterprises bring their quality products to the forum for display and publicity. For enterprises, East Asian countries have great potential for future development as an important part of the "One Belt and One Road", and this forum provides an opportunity for them to understand and even take root in the East Asian market.

6. East Asian (Liaoning) International Travel Fair

6.1 Background

East Asian International Travel Fair (EAITF) is a professional international exhibition sponsored by China National Tourism Administration, the People's Government of Liaoning Province and Dalian Municipal People's Government and organized by Liaoning Provincial Tourism Administration and Dalian Municipal Tourism Administration. With great support from more than 20 official tourism organizations at home and abroad, it is authoritative and extensive. EAITF is committed to inbound and outbound tourism promotion and exchanges in East Asia, especially in Northeast China and the Circum-Bohai Sea region.

In the meticulous care of China National Tourism Administration and the People's Government of Liaoning Province and Dalian Municipal People's Governments, EAITF has been held 12 times since 2004. Over 1,000 tourism enterprises from nearly 30 countries and regions and over 20 domestic provinces, municipalities and autonomous regions have successively taken part in the exhibition, and nearly ten thousand overseas tourism elites have attended the fair, which shows a growing trend. Based in East Asia and following the situation in Europe and the United States, the fair is a regional professional exhibition and the largest international exhibition in Northeast China, which covers over 30 domestic provinces, municipalities and autonomous regions and over 20 foreign countries and regions.

In recent years, the tourism industry in Liaoning Province has made great strides and rapid development through the vigorous development of Spa tourism, rural tourism, valley tourism, ski tourism and other tourism projects with characteristics based on its unique local customs and natural environment, and has become one of the most dynamic and fastest growing industries in Liaoning Province. EAITF gives a strong impetus to strategies such as promoting tourism products with characteristics, improving services, elongating the industry chain, building tourism brands, etc.

6.2 Achievements

The 1st EAITF, which was held in Dalian Xinghai Convention & Exhibition Center from August 5 to August 7, 2004, was held in the context of Liaoning's revitalization of old industrial bases and further expansion of opening-up. It is also the first regional international tourism exhibition organized by Liaoning.

The 2nd EAITF was held in Dalian from August 26 to August 28, 2005.

The 3rd EAITF was held in Dalian from October 20 to October 22, 2006.

The 4th EAITF was held in Dalian from October 19 to October 21, 2007. This fair organized a series of high-level activities such as Professional Buyers Fair, Travel Agency Exchange Conference, Tourism Products (Projects) Promotion etc.

The 5th EAITF was held in Dalian from October 10 to October 12, 2008.

The 8th EAITF and Benxi International Maple Leaf Festival, which were jointly organized by Liaoning Provincial Tourism Administration and Benxi Municipal People's Government, were held in Benxi City, Liaoning Province on the World Tourism Day (September 27) of 2011. This fair gave more prominence to its trading function, and it also integrated high-end activities such as SPA Tourism Forum, Ice and Snow Tourism Forum, Border Tourism Summit etc, becoming an important carrier and support for tourism exchanges and cooperation between East Asian countries and regions. In addition, this fair was updated in form. Permanent EAITF establishments were gradually established in Shenyang, Dalian, Dandong, Jinzhou and Panjin to expand the function of an information center displaying tourism resources in Liaoning.

As a result, there were four centers, i.e. Liaoning Tourism Information Center, East Asia and International Tourism Information Center, Liaoning and International Tourism Products Sales Center and Liaoning Souvenirs and Tourism Products Sales and Exhibition Center, which expanded the function and influence of the fair.

The 9th EAITF: In order to achieve the sustainable development of EAITF, Liaoning Provincial Tourism Administration set up the "EAITF Panjin Consulting Center" on the first floor of Trade Hotel in Panjin. Composed of Tourism Information Center, Tourism Sales Center, Tourism Promotion Center and Tourism Performing Arts Center, the Consulting Center displays the tourism resources and products of participating countries or regions and domestic provinces throughout the year, and implements and organizes promotion of travel to the above-mentioned places and other activities. This fair provided 40 booths for domestic and foreign exhibitors. In the joint brand exhibition of EAITF, the public feasted their eyes on tourism products from all over the world and from the city and the distinctive tourism product "Panjin Gift". This event highlighted Panjin elements with distinctive characteristics such as wetland features, sea-oriented development etc, and manifested the fundamental purpose to pave the way for economic development with tourism activities. Contracts were signed for a large number of key projects with amount adding up to 9.418 million yuan.

The 10th EAITF was held in Shenyang from May 17 to May 19, 2013. This fair provided over 400 booths for tourist destinations, hotel supplies, tourism products etc, and organized activities such as tourism products promotion, tourism products exhibition, tourism mart etc. More than one thousand tourism businessmen and people in the circle and more than ten thousand spectators from over ten countries and regions such as South Korea, Russia and Thailand attended the fair. This fair attached greater importance to the change from the previous professional tourism display to tourism trade, further expanded the field of exhibitors, and organized travel agencies, scenic spots, hotels and other tourism enterprises to carry out public exhibitions and sales, making new contributions to the improvement of exhibition services and innovation and development. Meanwhile, the fair also established a business docking platform to strengthen tourism exchanges and cooperation between China, South Korea and Russia, and displayed the overall image and distinctive tourism products of the East Asian countries and regions.

The 11th East Asia (Liaoning) International Travel Fair was held in Liaoning Industrial Exhibition Hall from May 16 to May 18, 2014. At this fair, the exhibition areas were divided into areas for tourism image, intelligent tourism, tourism mart, hotel supplies and food. More than 200 travel agencies and enterprises from 12 countries and regions such as Japan, South Korea, North Korea, the United States etc, 8 domestic provinces and 16 cities and counties in Liaoning Province attended the fair. There was a special intelligent tourism experience zone, and exhibition form was changed from tourism image display to tourism trade to further strengthen exchanges and cooperation with domestic key tourist sources such as Guangdong and other areas in the Yangtze River Delta and the Pearl River Delta regions on the basis of emphasis on exchanges and cooperation with the countries and regions and ten provinces in northern China, which were major sources of tourists to Liaoning. In addition, new breakthrough was made in the form of media publicity.

The 12th East Asia (Liaoning) International Travel Fair and Dandong Yalu River International Tourism Festival (hereinafter referred to as "EAITF") with "ecological Dandong, lohas tour in Liaoning, east Asia flavor and co-win event" as the theme were held in Dandong City, a frontier between China and North Korea, from September 10 to September 12, 2015. This fair was an important fair in 2015 identified by China National Tourism Administration, an important measure of Liaoning to take the initiative to integrate with the development of the "One Belt and One Road", implement the comprehensive revitalization of old industrial bases in the northeastern region, and build Liaoning into a Northeast Asian tourist distribution center and Dandong into a national China-North Korea tourism cluster, and a platform for the display, sales and exchanges of tourism products in East Asia. 20 Northeast Asian countries and regions, including South Korea, Japan, Russia, Mongolia, North Korea, Singapore, Malaysia, Indonesia, Hong Kong, Macau and Taiwan etc, took part in the exhibition. 16 important events were held during the three-day fair, including International Travel Business Cooperation and Development Conference, information meeting on travel to North Korea, exhibition of works of Liaoning Tourism Products Creative Design Competition, information meeting on travel to participating countries and regions, the 3rd Yalu River International Swimming Festival and other important professional tourism activities. At the same time, Dandong also launched the "four routes in a river" tourism product. In addition to enjoying the ecological landscape characterized by green mountains and clear waters of the Yalu River, Dandong, tourists could also have a one-day travel to North Korea to take in the beautiful scenery and customs of both China and North Korea. In addition, this EAITF focused on launching tourism goods, tourism accommodation vehicles, car camping, outdoor products, tourism equipment manufacturing, cruise ships and yachts, aviation and railways, speciality foods and other emerging tourism industries besides traditional travel agencies, hotels, scenic spots and other tourism products. The tourism goods launched at the fair were diversified and distinctive.